INTERNATIONAL TRADE

International Trade

Regional and Global Issues

Edited by

Michael Landeck

Professor of Marketing
Graduate School of International Trade and
Business Administration
Texas A & M International University
Laredo, Texas

St. Martin's Press

First published in Great Britain 1994 by
THE MACMILLAN PRESS LTD
Houndmills, Basingstoke, Hampshire RG21 2XS
and London
Companies and representatives
throughout the world

A catalogue record for this book is available
from the British Library.

ISBN 0-333-59590-4

Printed in Great Britain by
Antony Rowe Ltd
Chippenham, Wiltshire

First published in the United States of America 1994 by
Scholarly and Reference Division,
ST. MARTIN'S PRESS, INC.,
175 Fifth Avenue,
New York, N.Y. 10010

ISBN 0-312-10257-7

Library of Congress Cataloging-in-Publication Data
International trade : regional and global issues / edited by Michael
Landeck.
p.   cm.
Includes bibliographical references and index.
ISBN 0-312-10257-7
1. International trade.   2. International economic relations.
3. Commercial policy.   I. Landeck, Michael.
HF1379.I5847   1994
382—dc20   93–14617
                                              CIP

To my loving mother, Tanya, my sister, Polly, and daughter, Edie, and in living memory of my father, Heinz Günther Landeck

In memory of George N. Yannopoulos

Dr George N. Yannopoulos died on 11 September, 1992. He was a Professor and the Chairman of the Graduate School of European and International Studies at the University of Reading in England.

Dr Yannopoulos is best known as a pioneer scholar of the economics of the enlargement of the European Community. His works include *The EEC and the Mediterranean Countries, The EEC and Eastern Europe, Greece and the EEC: Integration and Convergence, Shipping Policies for an Open World Economy,* and *Europe and America 1992: US–EEC Economic Relations and the Single European Market.*

Dr Yannopoulos supervised twelve successful MPhil and PhD theses and more than 80 MA dissertations and was frequently called upon by other universities as external examiner. He served on the editorial boards of the *Journal of Common Market Studies* and *Estudos de Economia.* Between 1989 and 1991 he advised the Greek government on the privatization of the state-owned enterprises of the Industrial Reconstruction Organization. During this period Dr Yannopoulos commuted each week between Reading and Athens.

Dr George N. Yannopoulos will be sadly missed by his many colleagues and friends. On a professional level, his scholarly reputation will be difficult to replace.

Contents

Preface

Michael Landeck

In the last three decades we have been witnessing a dazzling development in the magnitude of international trade among the nations of the world. The International Monetary Fund reports that the value of total world exports in 1962 was merely $129.7 billion. In 1972, this number increased to $390.1 and in 1982 total world exports reached $1.73 trillion. In 1991, a new record figure was set at $3.44 trillion. These figures are also indicators of a steadily growing global economic activity and obviously indicate a steadily increasing interdependency of national economic systems.

Among the most significant occurrences in international trade during this period was the emergence of economic trading powers such as Japan, the European countries, and the emerging Asian 'Tigers'. Indeed, the less developed countries are also beginning to emerge with increased trade activities coming from Asia, the Middle East, Africa, as well as South America.

The US economy has also followed the general trend presented above and increased its export activities from $20.973 billion in 1962 to $49.199 billion in 1972, up to $216.442 billion in 1982, and finally to $422.158 billion in 1991. Nevertheless, in the last two decades the merchandise trade balance in the US shows a deficit which is gradually decreasing from –$132.130 billion in 1985 to –$109.399 billion in 1989, to –$101.718 billion in 1990 and –$66.205 billion in 1991. The US trade balance deficit is one of the most significant economic topics on the current agenda of politicians, economists, business professionals, and the American public in general. It is therefore understandable that a large number of the papers presented at the International Trade and Finance Association (IT&FA) conference related in one way or another, directly and indirectly, to the trade deficit and related international–US trade topics by discussing either specific geographically or global managerial international trade issues.

The formation of trade blocs in Europe, North and Central America, and Asia, and the discussions that are already taking place regarding the formation of other trade blocs, are increasingly capturing the attention of practitioners and academicians who deal with the issues of international trade. As a result, this book is a reflection of that focus and includes a significant number of publications which concentrate on European issues, mainly because of the developments and integration following Europe 1992. Due to the large number of papers dealing with the various aspects of the possible creation of the North American Free Trade Agreement (NAFTA), it was necessary to have a separate publication on that matter alone which was edited by Dr Khosrow Fatemi.

The Asian issues at the conference revolved mainly around trade with Japan, which is of a serious concern to European researchers and of even greater concern to US researchers in view of the ongoing enormous trade balance deficit that the USA has with Japan, totalling $43.436 billion in 1991 alone.

ORGANIZATION OF THE BOOK

This book, *International Trade: Regional and Global Issues*, is divided into four parts. The first two parts are regional in nature, and concentrate on international trade issues, referring to Europe in Part I and Asian Issues in Part II. Both parts are preceded by Chapter 1, which is an introduction entitled 'New Realities of International Trade' by Dr Khosrow Fatemi.

Part I includes three chapters. Chapter 2 deals with the competition in the European automobile markets after 1992 and was written by Fahri M. Unsal from Ithaca College and Sandra Richard from Laredo State University. Chapter 3 was written by the late George N. Yannopoulos from the University of Reading in the UK. His paper deals with the 1991 accord between Japan and the EC and discusses a common commercial policy on automobiles. It is my privilege to be able to publish one of Dr Yannopoulos's last works in this book. Chapter 4 also deals with Europe, and was edited by two Professors from the Institute of International Business at the Stockholm School of Economics, Kjell A. Nordström and Jan-Erik Vahlne. This chapter deals with the psychic distance and establishment of Swedish sales subsidiaries during the last one hundred years.

Part II covers international trade issues which refer to Asia. In Chapter 5, Gene E. Burton from California State University, Fresno analyzes the US trade deficit and the impact of Asian trade on it. In Chapter 6, Jong H. Park, a Professor at Kennesaw State College in Marietta, Georgia, discusses the effects of trading blocs on US–Japan relations and with regard to Pacific trade and cooperation. In Chapter 7, Hiro Lee from the University of California at Berkeley and David Roland-Holst of Mills College in Oakland, California also refer to US–Japan trade relations, but their area of research concentrates on agricultural liberalization and its implications on the trade relations between the two countries.

In the second half of the book, Parts III and IV deal with global issues. Part III concentrates on a variety of topics pertaining to global management. In Chapter 8, Attila Yaprak from Wayne State University and David

K. Shaheen from Michigan State University explore the state of the art of international acquisition and the eclectic paradigm. In Chapter 9, Franklin R. Root from The Wharton School and Kanoknart Visudtibhan, Professor at George Washington University, analyze international trade policies as they relate to corporate strategies. In Chapter 10, H. Peter Gray, Professor Emeritus of Rutgers University and Rensselaer Polytechnic Institute, discusses global management issues as they refer to labour force efficiency and adjustment costs.

In Part IV, various subjects related to international trade issues are presented. In Chapter 11, Alfred E. Eckes, Professor at Ohio University, discusses the issue of the escape clause that should have protected American industries and workers from being severely hurt by surging imports in Epitaph for the Escape Clause. Professor E. Ray Canterbery of Florida State University presents a general theory of international trade and domestic employment adjustments in Chapter 12. Finally, in Chapter 13, Linda Longfellow Blodgett discusses the results of an empirical survey of recent shifts in global countertrade.

Laredo, Texas   MICHAEL LANDECK

Acknowledgements

The articles published in this book were presented at the Second International Conference of the International Trade and Finance Association (IT&FA) which took place on 22–25 April, 1992 in Laredo, Texas.

My special thanks go to Dr Khosrow Fatemi, the Executive Vice-President of the IT&FA and Dean of the Graduate School of International Trade and Business Administration at Texas A&M International University, Laredo, Texas, for encouraging me and being my mentor during the preparation of this book. I would also like to express my deepest gratitude to the authors of all the papers that were presented at the conference, and especially for their willingness to revise their excellent research and to allow me to include their work in this book.

I would like to commend Ms Sue Nichols for coordinating this project and for her considerable efforts which greatly contributed to the timely publication of this volume. Finally, I would like to acknowledge my daughter, Edie Landeck, for her administrative help.

Laredo, Texas   MICHAEL LANDECK

Notes on the Contributors

Michael Landeck is Professor of Marketing and International Business at Texas A&M International University (formerly Laredo State University). Prior to his present appointment in Laredo he taught at St Mary's University in San Antonio. He received his Diplom-Kaufmann from the University of Hamburg in Germany with a major in industrial management and a minor in operations research, and received his PhD in marketing from North Texas State University in Denton, Texas. Dr Landeck's major areas of expertise are in marketing research, international consumer behaviour, and North American Free Trade Agreement issues. He served as the Director of the Institute for International Trade, and editor of the *Border Business Indicators*. At present he is editor of the *Southwest Review of International Business Research*. Dr Landeck has over eighteen years of practical experience in a variety of international managerial positions working for multinational corporations in the Middle East, Africa, Europe and the US.

Linda Longfellow Blodgett is Assistant Professor of International Business at Indiana University South Bend, where she has taught since 1987. She received a PhD in international business from the University of Michigan and a PhD in East European History from Indiana University. She has taught in the History Department of the University of Pittsburgh. Dr Blodgett's main research interests are corporate strategy, international joint ventures, and the problems of privatization and marketization in the former Eastern Bloc. Her work on international joint ventures has appeared in *The Strategic Management Journal*, *The Journal of International Business Studies*, and *The Journal of Global Marketing*.

Gene E. Burton is a Professor of Management at California State University, Fresno (CSUF). He holds the BBA and MBA degrees from the University of Texas at Arlington and the PhD in Management from North Texas State University (now called University of North Texas). Prior to his current assignment, Dr Burton served on a special one-year third-world appointment to Somalia funded by the World Bank. Before that, he served for five years as Dean of the School of Business and Administrative Sciences at CSUF. Previously Dr Burton was Chair of the Department of Business Administration at Eastern Kentucky University. He has also taught at Appalachian State University, North Texas State University,

Laredo State University, and the University of Texas at Arlington. His background includes twenty-five years of management experience with Rockwell International and General Electric. Dr Burton is the author of over 250 publications, including ten books and numerous articles in leading business journals. He is an experienced consultant and seminar leader, who has been a programme speaker on business and education topics throughout North America as well as Europe, Africa and Asia.

E. Ray Canterbery is Professor of Economics at Florida State University. He received a PhD in Economics from Washington University in St Louis, MO. Dr Canterbery's areas of research are international trade and finance; the history of economic thought; microeconomic theory including the theory of income and wealth distribution, and technological change; macroeconomic theory including such theories as instability and economic growth. He has published more than forty-five articles in the *Journal of Political Economy, Southern Economics Journal, The Canadian Economic Journal, Challenge, Eastern Economic Journal*, and others. Dr Canterbery is the author of eight books including *Foreign Exchange, Capital Flows and Monetary Policy: Studies in International Finance; Aquaculture and the Developing Countries: A Feasibility Study*; and *The Making of Economics*. He has contributed to sixteen other books.

Alfred E. Eckes is Eminent Research Professor at Ohio University, Athens. He teaches contemporary history, business administration and journalism. From 1981 to 1990 he was a Commissioner and Chairman (1982–4) of the US International Trade Commission. Dr Eckes is writing a book-length study of US trade policy, tentatively entitled, *Opening America's Market*.

Khosrow Fatemi is Dean of the Graduate School of International Trade and Business Administration at Texas A&M International University. He holds a PhD in international relations from the University of Southern California. He has edited six books, six *Proceedings*, and has presented over twenty-five papers at national and international conferences. His areas of research are international trade, the North American Free Trade Agreement, US–Mexico issues and international education. Dr Fatemi is the founding editor of *The International Trade Journal* and editor-in-chief for the *Series on International Business and Trade* published by Taylor & Francis. He is a founding member and serves as Executive Vice-President for the International Trade and Finance Association.

H. Peter Gray is Professor Emeritus of Economics and Management at Rutgers University and Rensselaer Polytechnic Institute and is currently an adjunct professor of international business at the Rutgers University Graduate School of Management. He obtained a PhD from the University of California, Berkeley, in Economics. His current research focuses on the role of profits and technology policy on international competitiveness, the dangers for the stability of the financial system of the steady erosion of the international net worth of the United States, intrafirm trade by TNCs and the theory of economic depression. Dr Peter Gray is a past president of both the Eastern Economic Association and the International Trade and Finance Association. He has also served as a consultant to the International Monetary Fund, the World Bank, the International Labour Office, the US Office of Technology Assessment as well as numerous private corporations.

Hiro Lee is Assistant Professor at the University of California, Irvine. In 1992 he was awarded an Abe Fellowship to undertake a research project on 'Cooperative Trade Strategies for the United States and Japan'. Currently, he is organizing a collaborative research agenda with David Roland-Holst on 'Japan's Emerging Role in Cooperative Economic Development in the Pacific Basin'. Dr Lee's recent articles include 'The Effects of Japanese Industrial Policy on Trade Flows and International Competitiveness', in M.G. Dagenais and P.A. Muet, (eds), *International Trade Modelling* and 'A General Equilibrium Evaluation of Industrial Policy in Japan', in the Spring 1993 issue of *The Journal of Asian Economics*.

Kjell A. Nordström is a research assistant at the Institute of International Business at the Stockholm School of Economics. He received his PhD in international business from the Stockholm School of Economics. Dr Nordström's areas of research are the internationalization process of the firm, economics of the MNC and business policy. He contributed to *Strategies in Global Competition*. Dr Nordström has taught at the Swedish Institute of Management, the Lahore Business School and Beijing Institute of Economics Management and has worked as a consultant for several large Scandinavian MNCs.

Jong H. Park is on the faculty of Economics and Finance, School of Business Administration, Kennesaw State College, Marietta, GA. He received his PhD in economics from Oklahoma State University, Stillwater. His primary teaching and research interests are in the areas of international business, trade, finance and development. Dr Park previously taught at

Oklahoma State University, Stillwater, North Dakota State University, Fargo, and Georgia State University, Atlanta. He also served as a Senior Fellow in Seoul, Korea and was a member of Korea Trade Delegation to Southeast Asia, including Bangladesh, India, Pakistan and Sri Lanka.

Sandra Richard is Chair of the Division of Business Administration and Associate Professor of Business Administration at Texas A&M International University. She received her PhD from the University of Texas, Austin. Her areas of research are management and statistics, including operations research and international business. Dr Richard's articles have been published in *Industrial Management, Advanced Management Journal, Asian Survey,* and *The Notre Dame Business Review.* She has served on the Board of Directors and holds the office of Historian for the International Trade and Finance Association.

David Roland-Holst is Associate Professor of Economics at Mills College, Oakland, California. He has worked extensively in quantitative analysis of international trade and development and is currently pursuing three multicountry research agendas, one dealing with Japan and its major Pacific trading partners, one on a detailed evaluation of North American trade relations, and one on economic data development for the newly independent republics of the former Soviet Union. Dr Roland-Holst's recent publications include 'Modeling Industry Structure and Conduct in an Applied General Equilibrium Context', in J.F. Francois and K.A. Reinert (eds), *Applied Trade Policy Modeling,* 'Tariffs and Export Subsidies when Domestic Markets are Oligopolistic', with J. de Melo in J. Mercenier and T.N. Srinivasan (eds), *Applied General Equilibrium and Economic Development* and 'Relative Income Determination in the United States', with F. Sancho, in the July issue of the *Review of Income and Wealth.*

Franklin R. Root is Professor of International Management at the Wharton School, University of Pennsylvania. He received his PhD in Economics from the University of Pennsylvania. Dr Root's areas of research are international entry strategies, public policy and MNCs, and international strategic management. He has published over forty professional articles in such journals as *Quarterly Review of Economics and Business, Columbia Journal of World Business, International Trade Journal, Journal of International Business Studies* and others. Dr Root is the author of *International Trade and Investment (6th edn), Strategic Planning for Export Markets, Entry Strategies for International Markets,* and *International Strategic Management.* He has worked for the United Nations and has done consulting in international business. Dr Root is a past President of the International Trade and Finance Association and is a member of the Academy of Management and the Academy of International Business.

David K. Shaheen is a doctoral student in the Department of Finance and Insurance at Michigan State University. He holds an MSBA from Indiana University. His areas of research are international business, insurance and corporate finance. Mr Shaheen is a CPA and has worked as an accountant.

Fahri M. Unsal is Associate Professor of Marketing and International Business at Ithaca College. He received his PhD in Marketing and Food Distribution from Cornell University. Dr Unsal's areas of research are international trade and international marketing. His articles have been published in several conference *Proceedings* of such organisations as the Academy of International Business – SE Region, the Association for Global Business, the International Trade and Finance Association and the North American Economic and Finance Association. Dr Unsal has also published articles in *The Journal of Small Business Management* and *The Journal of Economics and Business*.

Jan-Erik Vahlne is Professor and Researcher at the Institute of International Business at the Stockholm School of Economics. He received his PhD in international business from Uppsala University. Dr Vahlne's area of research is the internationalization processes of Western companies in Eastern Europe. He has co-authored *Multinationals: The Swedish Case* and *Strategies in Global Competition* and his articles have been published in *The Journal of International Business Studies, International Marketing Review* and *Scandinavian International Business Review*. Dr Vahlne has been a consultant for governments and multinationals and has worked with the Swedish Institute of Management and the Lahore Graduate School of Business. He is on the Board of Directors of the International Trade and Finance Association.

Kanoknart Visudtibhan is Assistant Professor at George Washington University. She received her PhD in Organization and Strategy from the Wharton School, University of Pennsylvania. Dr Visudtibhan's areas of research are in international business strategy, information systems in MNCs and Asia–Pacific business and trade. She co-authored *International Business Strategy: Opportunities and Threats* and has had articles published in *The European Journal of Operation Research*. Dr Visudtibhan is a member of the Academy of International Business, the Academy of Management and the International Trade and Finance Association.

George N. Yannopoulos was Professor and the Chairman of the Graduate School of European and International Studies at the University of Reading.

Attila Yaprak is Associate Professor of Marketing and International Business at Wayne State University in Detroit, Michigan. He holds a PhD in International Business and Marketing from Georgia State University. Dr Yaprak's areas of research are international business education and research. He is also the Director for the Center for International Business Education and Research (CIBER). Dr Yaprak has published in numerous books and scholarly journals such as *The Journal of International Business Studies, The International Marketing Review, Management International Review* and *Journal of Advertizing*. Dr Yaprak has served as Associate Editor of *The Journal of Business Research*. He is the current Executive Secretary for the Academy of International Business.

1 New Realities in International Trade

Khosrow Fatemi

F/D

The pace of change in the international economic scene in recent years is unquestionably without precedent. These changes may not be as dramatic or as traumatic as the crumbling of the Berlin Wall, the disintegration of the Soviet Union, or the reunification of Germany; but they are as significant. And nowhere is the pace more visible than in the arena of international trade. The most fundamental development in this field relates to the movement away from – some would argue, the demise of – multilateralism and towards regional cooperation. For all practical purposes, this movement was initiated in a significant way by the Treaty of Rome and, for many years, remained limited in its scope to the European Community. As such, regionalism was the exception rather than the rule. In recent years, however, this relationship has reversed and now regionalism has become the dominant trend.

The rapidly changing environment of the international economic scene is low in drama but high in continence. In fact the volatility, yet temperate nature, of this changing environment has been dichotomous. Many of the 'certainties' of the recent past are no longer plausible, much less certain; yet there are no pressing crises on the horizon. And many of the important national and supranational actors of the old system are no longer dominant, yet the global system is functioning fairly well. Regardless of the cause, the fortunate fact is that the resiliency of the international economic system has absorbed the initial shock of all the changes without completely disintegrating.

The resiliency of the old international economic order notwithstanding, the fact also remains that many of the pillars of the old regime are no longer in place. The bipolarity of the political system – the environment in which the economic system functioned – all but vanished with the disintegration of the Soviet Union. Less dramatically, but as significant, the multilateralism of the international trading system – and therefore the foundation of the system – is now in serious jeopardy. Finally, the core of all the premises which shaped, and more relevantly functionalized, economic realities of the last fours decades is now in question. As is the overwhelming superiority and dominance of the American economy – and

1

therefore its ability to act as the shock absorber of the global economy.[1] The domestic side of the US economy is seriously hampered by structural and budgetary problems. Internationally, however, one major reason for the diminished significance of US economic power is the country's inability to maintain balance in its international trade. Years of accumulating large trade imbalances are now hampering the country's ability to function as an economic superpower, much less the global shock absorber.

An analysis of the recent evolution of the international economic order should have two integrated components. First, *an ex post facto* part to take aim at determining the causes of the accelerated pace of change. This study should not be limited to the economic arena and should include the political arena as well.[2] Second, there should be a visionary yet pragmatic part aimed at developing the parameters of a *new* international economic regime.[3]

The fundamental – and theoretical – premise of trade under a floating exchange rate system is that trade imbalances between countries will automatically be eliminated by changes in the parity rates between the currencies of the countries experiencing trade imbalances. Specifically, under a floating exchange-rate system, when a country is running a balance-of-trade deficit its currency depreciates, thus accomplishing the dual objectives of (i) reducing its imports but making them more expensive to potential domestic consumers; and (ii) increasing its exports by making its products less expensive to foreign buyers. In reality, this has not happened in recent years.

The correlation between changes in the value of the dollar and the American trade deficit has barely been higher than purely coincidental levels. The 1983–91 period illustrates this point. Between the first quarter of 1983 and the first quarter of 1985 the dollar appreciated by 10–45 per cent against different major currencies, and as expected, the American trade deficit increased by 196 per cent, from $10.6 billion to $31.4 billion. On the other hand, between the first quarter of 1985 and the fourth quarter of 1987, the American dollar depreciated by 27–50 per cent and yet, and in complete contradiction of the above theory, the American trade deficit actually increased by 37 per cent, from $31.4 billion to $43.0 billion.[4] The American trade deficit is one of many manifestations of the subsystematic problems which have created broader – and systemic – problems for the global trading system. Recent attempts at regionalism and bilateralism are other examples. A central part of the post World War II global trading system has been its increasing emphasis on multilateralism. The General Agreement of Tariffs and Trade (GATT), after a modest beginning, has become an effective force in shaping policy and policing implementation of agreed upon policies. The successive rounds of GATT-sponsored multi-lateral trade negotiations have been instrumental in reducing both tariffs and non-tariff barriers. The last round of such talks, the Uruguay Round, is in serious trouble primarily because of disagreements between the European Community and the United States. Ironically, the major problem is over subsidies, agricultural subsidies in this case, and the EC's Common Agricultural Policy (CAP).

Probably a more fundamental reason for the failure of the GATT is an inward philosophical shift among the major trading countries around the world. The European Community members started this process by adopting a series of more integrative steps – commonly referred to as Europe 1992. What they had not envisioned was winning the cold war, specifically, the collapse of COMECON and the fall of communist regimes in Eastern Europe and the Soviet Union. Europe's leading economic power, Germany, is preoccupied with modernizing – more realistically, absorbing – the antiquated East German industries and infrastructural base. In addition, German leaders, as well as those of other European countries feel that it is their moral responsibility – not to mention the political power of large Eastern European minorities in their countries – to assist these countries in rebuilding their economies. They have little time and resources left for the rest of the world.

Reacting to the creation of what they perceived as 'Fortress Europe', Canada and the United States signed a free trade agreement in 1987 and later expanded it into a North American Free Trade Agreement (NAFTA) to include Mexico. Few experts anticipate that Mexico will be the last member of the NAFTA. In fact, several countries from Central and South America, among them Chile, Venezuela, Colombia, and Argentina, have already expressed interest in joining this 'hemispheric' free trade agreement. And to accommodate this, the NAFTA agreement includes an 'accession clause' specifically designed to make any future expansion of NAFTA easier.[5]

Not to be caught unprepared, the countries of East Asia have also begun negotiations for an expanded ASEAN (Association of South East Asian Nations). A joint proposal by Singapore-Malaysia for the establishment of an East Asian common market failed, only because of Japan's reluctance openly to support the proposal.[6] Yet other attempts at regionalism include a curious common market proposal between Iran, Turkey, Pakistan and the six former republics of the Soviet Union which have Moslem majorities and border these countries; several integration attempts in Africa and South America; and a large number of bilateral and regional free trade agreements.[7] None of these bodes well for the GATT and for multilateralism which has been the underlying philosophy of all the attempts at developing and improving the global trade scene since the 1940s.

CONCLUSIONS

For better or for worse, the environment in which the old international economic regime functioned has changed, as have many of its components. The intellectual challenge posed by this transition is to develop a replacement for the old system which, despite many shortcomings, worked for over four decades. The way to meet this challenge is to develop a new international economic regime which is better – that is, more functional, more equitable, and more flexible – than the old one. If not, the uncertainties of the recent past would only have been a preview of a more volatile future.

NOTES AND REFERENCES

1. It is an ironic dichotomy, and an interesting manifestation of the 'new world order', that American economic power around the world is diminishing as the country's military dominance is becoming unchallenged.
2. In doing so, it is very important to distinguish between the operational problems of the system, on the one hand, and systemic changes, on the other. The debt crisis and the expanding trade imbalance in many countries are mere manifestations of the evolution of the system and are to be expected. The collapse of the Bretton Woods system and the demise of the multilateralism in international trade – although the latter is not complete yet – are examples of systemic changes.
3. Among the ingredients of the new system should be a multitiered economic base, a new 'international currency, and an emphasis on global economic development.' For an elaboration of these points, see Khosrow Fatemi, 'The Need for a New International Economic Regime', in his *Selected Readings in International Trade* (New York: Taylor & Francis, 1991) pp. 1–7. For a different interpretation of the events of recent years and a different set of proposals for dealing with these changes, see, Jack N. Behrman, 'Restructuring and Reordering the World Economy', *The International Trade Journal*, vol. III, no. 1, Fall, 1988 as published in Khosrow Fatemi, *International Trade: Existing Problems and Prospective Solutions* (New York: Taylor & Francis, 1989) pp. 11–23.
4. For an elaboration of this point, see Khosrow Fatemi, 'US Trade Imbalance and the Dollar: Is There a Correlation?' *The International Journal of Finance*, vol. I, no. 2, Spring 1989, pp. 32–51.
5. The question of geographical expansion is addressed in Section 'f' of Article 102 and more specifically in Article 2205 of the North American Free Trade

Agreement. Article 102 includes a reference to the establishment of 'a framework for further trilateral, regional and multilateral cooperation to expand and enhance the benefits of this Agreement'. The Accession Clause included in Article 2205 is much more unequivocal and specific. It states that '1. Any country or group of countries may accede to this Agreement subject to such terms and conditions as may be agreed between such country or countries and the Commission and following approval in accordance with the applicable approval procedures of each country. 2. This Agreement shall not apply as between any Party and any acceding country or group of countries if, at the time of accession, either does not consent to such application.'

6. Ironically, Japan's decision not to support the East Asian common market was in response to pressure by the United States, which in turn feared that such an arrangement would make the Japanese market less open to American exporters. Recent isolationist sentiments in the United States could easily revive the concept.

7. The stated reason given for the growing number of attempts at developing free trade agreements is that such agreements increase the members' international competitiveness and eventually the global productivity. This (trade-creation) argument is countered by those who maintain that most – if not all – of the benefits accrued to the members comes at the expense of non-members (trade diversion). A second contributing factor may be the simple fear of losing existing markets. This was best exemplified in the case of the Canada–US Free Trade Agreement when fear of losing the lucrative Western European market to 'Europe-92' convinced both countries, particularly Canada, to pursue a regional FTA with the other country.

Part I
European Issues

2 Introduction

In their chapter "Competition in the European Automobile Markets after 1992', Fahri Unsal and Sandra Richard discuss the issue of how the establishment of the EEC in 1992 could impact on the competitive environment in the European Market regarding automobiles. The establishment of a single market in Europe as of 1993 could very well reverse the leading position that the Japanese producers embrace after they have taken this position away from the European auto industry. The special topics covered include an analysis of the competitive environment in Europe, strategies of Japanese producers in Europe, strategic alliances, and an exploration of the expected competitive structure in the European automobile industry following the market unification at the end of 1992. The authors conclude that the European market is expected to be the sight of the main battles between the global auto manufacturers during the rest of the 1990s, and that perhaps several European producers may not survive as independent firms due to a lack of global capacities as compared to their competitors. The Japanese auto producers are expected to dominate the global markets, and a restructuring of the European auto market is expected to continue throughout the decade and into the twenty-first century.

The late George N. Yannopoulos discusses the same problem of automobile global competition as it refers to the new internal market of the European community, and raises some important questions regarding the EC's external commercial policy; Yannopoulos specifically evaluates the 1991 accord between Japan and the EC regarding the automobile market. Yannopoulos points out that despite the reference to a 'common market' we are actually looking at a market that is still highly fragmented. The member countries mainly differentiate from each other based upon their state quotas, initiated to control the free circulation of goods originating from third countries within the internal market of the EC. The chapter looks into the trade policy arrangements between Japan and the EC, an agreement that should regulate for a period of seven years the inflow of Japanese cars into the countries of five EC members.

The third chapter, by Nordström and Vahlne, discusses the issues regarding the assumption of increasing global homogeneity, which in effect (if correct) is being expressed in a global shrinking. This observation is based upon the argument that the psychic distances are diminishing and the world in that sense is getting smaller. The authors attempt to test this proposition by examining empirical material on the patterns of Swedish firms' internationalization processes during the last one hundred years, which they use as a proxy for psychic distance. The authors do not find support for the notion of a 'smaller' world in psychic-distance terms.

3 Competition in the European Automobile Markets after 1992

L62

Fahri M. Unsal and Sandra Richard

3.1 INTRODUCTION

Europe

The automobile industry in Europe is the leading industrial sector contributing significantly to the value added in EC manufacturing and employment. However, the European auto industry lost its position as the world's largest motor vehicle exporter to the Japanese producers (Glatz, 1991). At the beginning of the decade, the European Community (EC) manufacturers accounted for about 40 per cent of world passenger car output (Ward's, 1990, p. 262). However, this picture could change dramatically with the establishment of a single market at the end of 1992. A *Fortune* analyst declared that Western Europe would be the battleground for leadership of the global auto industry in the 1990s (Tully, 1990a, p. 96). The elimination of fiscal, physical and technical barriers could further open the market for Japanese manufacturers. The Chairman of Ford in Europe delineated the issue: 'The Japanese will challenge the traditional market leaders and national champions. We're headed for an era of fierce competition' (ibid.).

As the decade began, Europe's six full-range car manufacturers, including General Motors (GM) and Ford, were doing well and were well matched in terms of market shares. Their positions might change after the single market is established. The producers of luxury cars, such as BMW and Mercedes-Benz, would also be affected by competition from the Japanese entries into this market segment.

The main objective of this chapter is to investigate the strategies followed by the European and the Japanese auto producers to meet the challenges of 1992 and identify potential problem areas. The specific topics include:

(a) the competitive environment in Europe including market shares and impact on consumers;
(b) strategies of Japanese producers in Europe;
(c) strategic alliances as a response to global competition;

11

(d) an exploration of the expected changes in the competitive structure of
     the European automobile industry after the market unification at the
     end of 1992.

3.2   HISTORICAL COMPETITIVE STRUCTURE OF GLOBAL INDUSTRY

In the early years of the motor vehicle industry, the United States (US) was
the dominant producer. In 1950 it still produced about 80 per cent of the
world's motor vehicles. In later years the US faced competition first from
the Europeans and then the Japanese. By 1970 the US share of world production had fallen to 30 per cent, and by 1989 the US produced only 13.8
per cent of the global motor vehicle output. Meanwhile, the EC output
declined from 38.0 per cent of the world output in 1960 to 30.7 per cent in
1989. During this period Japanese motor vehicle output rose from 1.0 per
cent in 1960 to 18.2 per cent in 1989 (Ward's, 1990, p. 260). The Japanese
producers recorded major gains particularly in passenger cars with their
global market share rising from 1.3 per cent in 1960 to 25.5 per cent in
1989, while the US share declined from 52.4 to 19.2 per cent during the
same period (MVMA, 1991a, p. 14).

During the 1950s and 1960s Europe and the US constituted separate and
distinct car markets where different combinations of economic, social and
political factors encouraged the development of different types of cars. In
the US the early construction of an extensive highway system, the physical
size of the country, very high disposable income and very cheap and plenti-
ful supplies of oil encouraged the production of larger, more powerful and
expensive cars that guzzled fuel. In Europe a different environment
demanded smaller, cheaper and more fuel efficient cars. Thus economy cars
dominated their domestic markets. Some of these producers also established
themselves as exporters to other countries, and they established production
facilities outside Europe. For example, Volkswagen (VW) established its
first international transplant in the United States in Westmoreland, Pennsylvania, in 1978 (Ward's, 1979, p. 29); but this plant was closed in 1988 due to
declining sales (Ward's, 1988, p. 83). The European producers also produced some luxury cars aimed at wealthy consumers and the export markets.

By the 1970s, as the global economic prosperity began to falter, trade in
cars began to grow. Japan, whose production was rising rapidly, exported a
growing proportion of that production, from 30 per cent of its output in
1971 to about 55 per cent by the early 1980s. Most of these exports reached
the United States but part went to Western Europe.

By the late 1970s the energy crisis affected the sales of 'gas guzzlers' in the United States. Consumers switched to smaller, more economical cars. The market share of Japanese-made cars rose from 12 to 21 per cent between 1978 and 1980 (Ward's, 1979 and 1981 issues). A vicious circle of financial losses and declining market shares threatened the ability of the US 'Big Three' to make the huge investments needed to adjust to market changes. In May 1981, voluntary restraints on exports to North America were announced in Tokyo. Meanwhile, Japanese exports disturbed the status quo of the Western European market dominated by 'national champions' as well. Governments responded by negotiating 'voluntary' or 'formal' restrictions during the 1970s and early 1980s.

As a result of these restrictions in Europe, the Japanese could not achieve the same success as they have in the United States. The powerful automobile lobby in Europe fought very hard to hang on to its privileged conditions while the manufacturers from Japan tried very hard to penetrate this market further through exports, local production and strategic alliances.

3.3   CURRENT COMPETITIVE STRUCTURE IN EUROPE

3.3.1   Current Market Shares

Traditionally Europe has not had an open market for automobiles. This is partially because many European automotive firms are either government owned or government dominated. Although regulation of the European automotive market has undergone some liberalization, tariffs are still higher than the American and the Japanese levels; and five EC members still maintain import quotas on Japanese cars.

In 1989 the size of the West European automotive market was 13.4 million vehicles, and 87 per cent of these vehicles were assembled in European plants, including those owned by US and Japanese firms. Japanese firms dominated the import market (10.8 per cent) with only a small number of additional imports coming from the United States (0.2 per cent), Korea (0.2 per cent), and 1.8 per cent from Eastern Europe (Ward's, 1990).

Five EC countries – Italy, France, Spain, Portugal and the United Kingdom (UK) – currently restrict Japanese automotive imports in one way or another. In Italy there is a longstanding, formal, explicit limit on Japanese imported vehicles that was sanctioned by GATT many years ago: 2550 vehicles in 1989, or 0.7 per cent of the Italian market. In France the vehicle registration procedure is used to limit Japanese imports to 3 per cent of the French market. In Spain and Portugal there are 0.3 per cent and 7.2 per cent limits, respectively. In the United Kingdom, the situation is more ambiguous; an industry-level 'gentlemen's agreement' limits Japanese imports to between 10 and 11 per cent of the market with a clear policy of encouraging Honda and Nissan to substitute imports with automobiles built in the United Kingdom (Brewer, 1990, p. 44). It should be noted that in Denmark, Greece and Ireland, countries that have no restrictions because they do not have their own auto industries, Japanese cars have more than 30 per cent market share.

An examination of European market shares of individual producers indicates that Volkswagen and Fiat groups were in the lead with 15.4 and 14.2 per cent shares, respectively, in 1990. The followers were the Peugeot group, Ford, GM/Opel, Japanese manufacturers, and the Renault group, each with market shares of about 10 per cent or higher (Table 3.1). However, it should be noted that the national producers dominated their home markets. Thus Volkswagen had a 26.9 per cent market share in Germany, Peugeot and Renault had a combined 60.8 per cent market share in France, and the Fiat group had a 52.4 per cent share in Italy. As was mentioned earlier, the dominant position of national firms in France and Italy was mainly due to protectionism. Obviously manufacturers in these countries are very much opposed to an immediate market opening after 1992.

Table 3.1   Automobile market share by company in major European markets, 1990

Company	W. Europe	Germany	France	Italy	UK	Spain
VW Group	15.4	26.9	10.3	12.9	6.2	19.9
Fiat	14.2	5.0	7.1	52.4	3.1	7.5
PSA Group	13.0	4.3	33.1	7.6	9.2	17.7
Ford	11.6	9.8	7.0	7.7	25.8	13.9
GM/Opel	11.4	17.1	5.0	4.4	16.1	14.0
Japanese	11.7	15.4	3.4	2.2	10.9	1.2
Renault	9.9	3.3	27.7	6.5	3.4	19.0
Mercedes	3.3	8.6	—	—	—	—
Rover Grp	2.9	—	1.9	—	14.0	—
BMW	2.8	6.3	1.3	—	—	—
Volvo	1.8	—	—	—	3.3	—
Others	2.0	3.3	3.2	6.3	2.7	6.8
Units sold (mil.)	13.2	3.0	2.3	2.3	2.3	1.0

Source: Compiled from *Ward's Automotive Yearbook* (1991) p. 87, 90–8.

The European position was exemplified by Reuter, Mercedes Chairman (Taylor, 1991, p. 63): 'We hope the Japanese will be wise enough to avoid killing the European automakers the way they did the US automakers. If the Japanese try to destroy the traditional European auto industry, Europe cannot stay away from taking protectionist measures.'

In spite of these threats, however, many in the German auto industry insist that they would prefer that no protectionist measures be imposed because, like the Japanese industry, it exports more than half of its output and stands to lose more than any other country should a trade war break out. Nevertheless, they do not think it is fair that Japanese cars invade their market because of restrictions by other European countries and the United States.

3.3.2   Japanese Producers' Presence

Within the EC, except for the five countries mentioned above, the Japanese manufacturers' market share of imports in individual countries ranged from 20 to 40 per cent. For the Western European market as a whole (13 million vehicles in 1989), the Japanese import share was approximately 11 per cent. Among the European Free Trade Association Countries (EFTA), the Japanese import market share was higher, generally between 30 to 40 per cent (Table 3.2).

Table 3.2   Japanese automotive import market shares in selected countries, 1989*

EC countries	Percentage	EFTA countries	Percentage
Ireland	40.0	Finland	38.9
Greece	28.7	Norway	35.2
Denmark	31.7	Austria	30.6
Netherlands	26.2	Switzerland	29.2
Belgium	19.5	Sweden	24.8
FRG	15.0	Iceland	n/a
UK	10.9		
Portugal	6.6	*Others*	*Percentage*
France	2.3		
Italy	1.5	United States	19.4
Spain	1.2	Australia	44.5
Luxembourg	n/a	New Zealand	61.7

* Local production by Japanese firms not included.

Source: MVMA World Motor Vehicle Data (1991) p. 29.

The combined market shares of Japanese producers would be expected to increase quickly and significantly if there were no European restrictions on imports. Estimates of such increases to a combined share of 15–25 per cent within a few years are common. If such increases were to occur, it would mean as many as 2.5 million additional imported vehicles a year, a threat to as many as ten European assembly plants and perhaps 300000 European auto workers' jobs (Brewer, 1990, p. 45). Although such numbers are inevitably subject to a considerable margin of uncertainty, they nevertheless are indicative of the extent to which the European auto industry could be threatened.

A unified market would be expected to lead to more investments in Europe by Japanese manufacturers. Currently, Nissan's plant in the UK remains by far the biggest direct investment with an expected output of 220000 in 1992–3. Honda, Isuzu and Toyota also have interests in the UK while Mitsubishi participates in an assembly plant in the Netherlands. Nissan and Suzuki are in Spain, and Suzuki entered into an agreement in Hungary. Daihatsu is in Italy. Mazda was seeking a collaborative agreement to enter the European market (Done, 1991).

The potential addition of new, highly efficient factories in an industry already suffering from fierce competition and overcapacity has radical implications for European automobile manufacturers, European governments and the EC. It is expected that, if Japanese-owned plants in Europe add more capacity, suppliers in Japan would also establish themselves in Europe as they did in the US The establishment of Japanese suppliers in Europe might threaten the viability of the European auto parts industry and hence fuel further protectionism.

In an effort to provide time for European auto producers to adjust to a more competitive market, the EC and Japan agreed in July 1991 on an external trade policy for the motor industry until 1999. A free market would be in effect after 1999. The agreement provided that direct exports from Japan to the EC would be limited to the current annual level of 1.2 million cars. The quotas in the five EC countries – France, Italy, Portugal, Spain, and the UK – would continue. Japanese transplants in Europe would be covered by an unwritten 'understanding' with a ceiling of 1.2 million cars per year, a fivefold increase over 1991 production levels (ibid.).

3.3.3   Impact of Competitive Structure on Consumers

The European consumers are currently the big losers due to protected markets and the lack of sufficient competition even internally. The internal competition is limited because of a 'block exemption' law granted to the auto industry in 1985 for ten years. This exemption allows manufacturers to impose highly restrictive agreements on all their dealers. Under it Peugeot, Volkswagen or Ford of Europe can bar their dealers from taking on a second brand (Tully, 1990b, p. 136).

To secure agreement on the block exemption, the industry pledged to hold prices for the same cars selling anywhere in Europe within a band of 12 per cent. However, according to a 1989 survey by the European Consumers' Organization, the auto makers seemed to be violating those terms. The survey found that, before taxes were added, the prices for identical models often varied by 60 per cent across Europe. On average, cars in Denmark cost 45 per cent less than the same models in Spain or Italy. In 1989, a compact Citroen AX, made in France, cost 19 per cent more in France than in neighbouring Belgium (ibid.).

However, after taxes are added, price differentials might be less pronounced. At the present time, the cumulated tax burden on the acquisition and registration of new passenger cars (including VAT and all other taxes and fees), expressed as a percentage of the pre-tax price, differs in the EC from 12 per cent in Luxembourg to over 230 per cent in Denmark and Greece. France, Germany, Italy, Luxembourg and Spain apply no tax other than VAT; all other countries levy special acquisition and registration taxes. The EC Commission has proposed to harmonize the VAT system fully after 1992. However, the other taxes that will not be harmonized in the near future may continue to distort prices (Perrin-Pelletier, 1989, pp. 91–2).

Nevertheless, given the price differences, consumers and resellers might be expected to seek the best deals throughout Europe. However, additional restrictions constrain buyers. The block exemption prohibits dealers in one country from advertising in another. It also restricts companies in one country from buying large quantities (e.g. 1000 cars) in a different country and selling them at home. Although the consumers are allowed to shop around, the red tape and special taxes remove the cost advantages. For example, to import a Belgian car, a French buyer must first register the vehicle in Belgium and then import it as a used car into France. The final step is replacing the Belgian white headlights with the yellow lamps required in France. The whole process takes two weeks and can cost $830 in extra taxes and mechanics' fees (Tully, 1990b, p. 136). However, if product standardization is achieved after 1992, some of these problems should be eliminated and cross-border consumer shopping will be made easier.

An added burden on the European consumer is the market unavailability of Japanese cars in sufficient quantities. Since the Japanese manufacturers can produce cars more efficiently than their protected and overmanned European counterparts, they ought to be able to offer bargain prices, even after paying the 10 per cent import duty. That would force down prices of competing European models. However, since quotas prevent them from gaining market share in half the EC countries, the Japanese manufacturers have no incentives to offer deep discounts. Instead, they simply match the prices of similar European cars. This practice leads to enormous profit margins for the Japanese producers and much higher prices for the consumers (ibid, p. 134).

A recent study concluded that the Japanese could drop their prices for mid-size cars by $2300, or 25 per cent if the quotas disappeared. That would set off a cycle of price and cost cutting among European producers that would save consumers $33 billion a year (ibid.).

3.3.4   European Producers' Efficiency and Product Quality

It is generally agreed that car producers in Europe, especially in Italy and France, have flourished, and grown uncompetitive, in highly protected markets in the past and that they will have a very hard time in adjusting to a more open environment. According to a recent five-year MIT study of the global car industry (Womack *et al.*, 1990), the Europeans are the least efficient car producers in the world. They are far behind the Japanese producers in terms of 'average engineering and development time per new car,' 'die development and prototype lead time', and 'return to normal productivity and quality' (Table 3.3). This study also reported that in certain German plants about one-third of the labour hours were spent in repairing cars after they were built. The study concluded that some German plants spent more effort on fixing problems they had created than a Japanese plant required to make a nearly perfect car the first time (ibid., pp. 82–103).

The above problems were faced even by luxury car producers such as BMW and Mercedes-Benz. As a result, both companies recently started losing market shares in the world's large, most competitive market, the United States. Their combined US sales tumbled from 196 000 cars in 1986 to 142 000 in 1990 and then continued to fall in 1991. They were hit by the recession and the new luxury tax. Car buyers now pay 10 per cent on any amount they spend above $30 000 (Taylor, 1991, p. 56).

In addition, these two German producers were also hurt by the new Japanese luxury cars which did not exist six years ago. The combined sales of Honda's Acura, Toyota's Lexus and Nissan's Infiniti at $25 000 and up were 117 000 in the US in 1990. During the first half of 1991, their sales rose to 78 000, more than Mercedes and BMW combined. The planned entry of other Japanese luxury cars from Mitsubishi, Mazda and others

Table 3.3   Product development performance by regional auto industries, mid-1980

	Japanese producers	American producers	European volume producers	European specialist producers
Average engineering hours per new car (millions)	1.7	3.1	2.9	3.1
Average development time per new car (in months)	46.2	60.4	57.3	59.9
Number of body types per new car	2.3	1.7	2.7	1.3
Average ratio of shared parts	18%	38%	28%	30%
Die development time (months)	13.8	25.0	28.0	
Prototype lead time (months)	6.2	12.4	10.9	
Time from production start to first sale (months)	1	4	2	
Return to normal productivity after new model (months)	4	5	12	
Return to normal quality After new model (months)	1.4	11	12	

Source: Adapted from Womack *et al.* (1990) p. 118.

could result in a more dramatic effect on the European and American producers in this segment. The Japanese producers now sell almost no luxury cars in Europe, but they could be expected to try to change that during the coming years (ibid.).

In regard to quality, four European producers ranked among the bottom five in Power's US initial quality ratings of 1991 models; the ratings assess problems in the first ninety days of car ownership. The firms included Alfa Romeo, Jaguar, Porsche, and VW. Peugeot and Sterling pulled out of the

US market in 1991 because of the cars' reputations for poor reliability (Woodruff and Levine, 1991, p. 72)

The current competitive structure in Europe provided protection for European auto manufacturers which resulted in a wide variation of prices paid by consumers in the different EC countries. The constraints on Japanese producers until 1999 were aimed at providing European producers transition time to close the competitive gap.

3.4   JAPANESE PRODUCERS' MARKETING STRATEGIES IN EUROPE

The Japanese producers passed through several stages in designing production and marketing strategies in the US during the last fifteen years with a great deal of success. These strategies could be expected to be followed in Europe also, even though the competitive environment is quite different.

Stages of the strategies are summarized below (Flint, 1991):

1 – Build market share through export of low margin, fuel-efficient cars.

In Europe the Japanese producers captured market share in countries that do not produce autos as well as markets to which European producers exported.

2 – Produce the lower-priced autos in the foreign market.

With two exceptions, all Japanese producers have transplants or other forms of participation in the European market.

3 – Export stylish sedans.

4 – Export luxury sedans.

The European market could be described as in the second stage. The battleground in Europe is expected to be in the subcompact or small family car market (Templeman, 1991).

In the global luxury car market, US and European producers bought leading-name companies, such as Ford's purchase of Jaguar. Japanese manufacturers, on the other hand, followed a strategy of using their own names, such as Mazda, or inventing new names, such as Lexus and Infiniti (*Economist*, 4 January, 1992, p. 59).

Strategies of Japanese producers in Europe were facilitated by the fact that many countries actively seek foreign investors, including the Japanese, in the auto industry. Grants, subsidies and soft loans for the investments are available from several governments. Both domestic and foreign companies are learning the art of maximizing government support by playing one government against another.

An issue that could result in modification of strategies in the future is the local content of transplants. If the unwritten agreement reached in July 1991 between EC and Japanese producers were reconsidered, the debate in the US about the 'nationality of a particular make – such as Honda Accord or Dodge Colt – could extend to Europe; and *The Economist* indicated that the chances are remote that the agreement would remain unchanged until 1999 (*Economist*, 3 August, 1991, p. 65). An 80 per cent local content seems to be acceptable to many governments. However, the traditional calculation of local content generally includes assembly and all associated overheads as well as marketing and administrative costs. The debate on how to compute local content continues. This issue could become more complicated as other firms start sourcing their components from non-EC countries, such as Eastern European countries.

3.5 STRATEGIC ALLIANCES AS RESPONSE TO GLOBAL COMPETITION

During the 1980s the automobile industry became truly global with many joint ventures and strategic alliances. Most of these collaborations resulted from the new competitive environment and the emergence of Japanese firms as major players in the industry. Almost all of the world's car firms had established some type of linkage with another car producer (*Economist*, 4 January, 1992, p. 59).

In the 1980s, American producers supported quotas for Japanese cars while actively opposing any domestic content rules. This latter position was taken because the American producers themselves relied on imports of foreign cars and components for their domestic success. In 1984 US manufacturers imported some 3.6 million engines for use in their US assembled cars (Tucker, 1988, p. 33). GM imported cars produced by Suzuki and Isuzu of Japan and Daewoo of South Korea. Ford also imported cars from South Korea. Meanwhile, Chrysler sold cars produced by Mitsubishi of Japan.

Each of the Big Three of US auto producers had equity stakes in Japanese companies as well as joint ventures. Chrysler owned part of Mitsubishi, which in turn owned part of Hyundai of South Korea and China Motors of Taiwan. Ford had an equity stake in Mazda while General Motors had holdings in Suzuki and in Isuzu (ibid.). Joint ventures for production in the United States involved GM and Toyota, Ford and Mazda, and Chrysler and Mitsubishi.

Europe also had its share of global alliances during recent years, partially because of the developments related to Europe in 1992. For instance, Renault and Volvo arranged cross-shareholdings. Ford aquired 100 per cent of Jaguar, and General Motors acquired 50 per cent of the automotive portion of Saab. Japanese firms also developed ties with European firms: Toyota and VW to produce trucks; Mazda and Saab for assembly; Mitsubishi and Daimler-Benz in commercial vehicles. In addition, Honda supplied Rover with engines and transmissions while Rover provided Honda with assembled autos (Brewer, 1990, p. 40).

European automakers meanwhile reportedly had a near monopoly of the emerging car industry in the People's Republic of China (Ward's, 1990, p. 160) and they moved into Eastern Europe. The recent revolutionary changes in the political economies of Eastern Europe added another dimension to the global restructuring of the automotive industry. VW, for example, announced plans for joint assembly operations in East Germany. GM (Europe) signed agreements with Hungary and the former East Germany while Fiat had major agreements with the former Soviet Union and Poland (ibid., p. 261). These projects and similar future cooperative arrangements involving Eastern Europe could affect trade and investment patterns within the EC and between the EC and the rest of the world. Spain in particular might lose out to Eastern European countries as a site for new automotive production facilities.

VW was viewed as the most daring company in Europe. Its major expansion programme included acquisition of the Spanish car maker Seat in 1986 and Czechoslovakia's Skoda in 1990. VW was building or refitting new plants from the former East Germany to China and from Spain to Mexico. It seems to be moving towards a Pan-European company with autonomous divisions, a much wider variety of cars, and production in comparatively low-wage regions (Avishai, 1991, pp. 103–13).

The success of the various strategic alliances must yet meet the test of time. Problems could continue to be expected, such as Chrysler and Mitsubishi or Volvo and Renault. However, collaboration could result in more effective resource utilization and provide a degree of independence for auto makers before further consolidation which *The Economist* described as 'inevitable' (*Economist*, 6 July, 1991, p. 68).

3.6 FUTURE COMPETITIVE POSITION IN EUROPE

With the US 'Big Three' auto producers operating at a loss, European producers have models of firms that have not yet closed the competitive gap. With the exception of Germany, the European auto markets were in trouble in 1991. Rolls Royce was expected to post its first-ever loss in 1991 (*Economist*, 14 December, 1991, p. 79) while Volvo went into deficit in 1990 for the first time in sixty years (Done, 1991, p. 70).

The American and Japanese manufacturers are transnational in production and market. They respond to the changes that have taken place in the industry by committing vast resources to modernize, automate and develop a global strategy for car production. However, the same cannot be said for the European industry.

The majority of the Western European producers are smaller than their global competitors. Their financial positions are far more precarious given the overcapacity that existed in Europe over the past decade. Producers such as Renault, Peugeot-Citroen and Fiat are very dependent on their domestic markets in Western Europe. Even the West German producers that enjoy significant sales in the US market, such as the luxury car market, are largely dependent upon European markets. In regard to production, the European producers do not have the global links of their US and Japanese competitors. Several European firms retreated from global markets while the Japanese firms advance. Examples include VW's retreat from production in the US, Renault's move away from its venture with the former American Motors, and Fiat's abandoning its markets in North and South America. A strategy of withdrawal raises questions concerning the continued independence or survival of certain European producers unless the industry is further protected. The attitude of many Europeans was reflected in the following comment by a senior European Commission staff member (Brewer, 1990, p. 33):

Yes, we are for free trade. But I don't mind making some exceptions or contradicting myself a bit to say that Europe won't be ready for totally free trade in automobiles by 1993. I am not so loyal to the phrase 'free trade' that I will let thousands of European auto workers be thrown out of work or witness the destruction of the most politically important companies in Europe, like Fiat and Renault.

The fact that the EC agreement with Japanese producers concerning Japanese transplants in Europe is an unwritten 'understanding' raises questions concerning a return to protectionism. The agreement in July 1991 provided a cap of 1.2 million autos annually on production at transplants in the EC with an open market after 1999. Prior to the agreement several European producers argued for specified levels of EC content; however, recent cases involving Japanese transplants in the US and Canada illustrated the difficulty in applying content rules of origin (Magnusson *et al.*, 1991).

For a volume European producer to survive in an open market with Japanese producers as competitors, Eaton, president of GM (Europe), indicated that it would need 10 per cent of the market (Templeman, 1991, p. 55). The European auto makers best positioned to fight the Japanese are GM, Ford and Volkswagen. GM was the most profitable producer in Europe with a lean production system. Ford's network of 8000 dealers was the strongest in Europe. Both of these US-based firms treated Europe as one market as contrasted to their European competitors that emphasized their home markets. Thus, the US-based European producers should be better prepared for competition in the unified market of 1992. VW held the top position in the German market, Europe's largest, as well as in other markets. With its expanded activities in Spain and East Europe, this firm could lead the European mass producers during the 1990s. Fiat, Peugeot and Renault are more dependent on their home markets and might face difficulty in competing (Tully, 1990a).

Niche players, such as Rolls Royce or Porsche, could be taken over by another car maker (*Economist*, 14 December, 1991, p. 79), or the firms could diversify, such as BMW which entered an alliance with Rolls Royce Aerospace to produce jet engines (*Economist*, 4 January, 1992, p. 60). Niche players could face greater difficulty than volume producers over the next decade because of the loss of the quality edge and escalating cost of small scale production in the auto industry (*Economist*, 4 January, 1992).

One view of the future expressed by global auto industry observers was succinctly stated in a 1991 article in *Forbes*: 'If Japanese control the Asian markets and win a third of North American and Europe, they will win the battle of scale and bring down their unit costs to the point where the war will be over' (Flint, 1991). That view could lead to renewed protectionist policies in the EC and the US Or, the view could be supported by consumers who seek affordable, safe, trouble-free autos without regard to the national origin of the producing company or the location of the plant where production took place.

3.7 SUMMARY AND CONCLUSIONS

All auto producers are expected to face severe competitive pressures in the coming years. The European market is expected to be the site of the main battles between the global auto manufacturers during the 1990s. Several European producers, and perhaps Chrysler of the US, might not survive as independent firms because they lack the global capacities of their competitors. Successful firms could be expected to enter into additional strategic alliances to remain profitable.

The Japanese auto producers are expected to dominate the global markets because of their market orientation and efficient production operations. Their global strategy resulted in production facilities located in each of the three key markets, the US, Europe, and Japan. In contrast, US companies have production facilities in two key markets, the US and Europe, while European producers have production facilities in only one key market, Europe. Restructuring of the European auto market is expected to continue throughout the decade and into the twenty-first century.

4 Towards a Common Commercial Policy on Automobiles: An Evaluation of the 1991 Accord between Japan and the EC

George N. Yannopoulos

4.1 INTRODUCTION

The completion of the internal market of the European Community (EC) has raised important questions for its external commercial policy (O'Cleireacain, 1990). The measures of the internal market programme eliminate the use of certain policy instruments that have been employed so far to control the circulation of goods of third-country origin inside the European common market. This forces changes in the present trading arrangements – changes which reduce the capacity of individual member states to employ specially tailored protectionist measures to cushion their domestic industries from the competitive pressures of third-country suppliers. Despite the references to a 'common market' a number of product markets in the EC are highly fragmented by a variety of devices. One such instrument of protection and market fragmentation has been the use of member state quotas to control the free circulation in the internal market of the EC of goods originating from third countries. The maintenance and effective implementation of such member state quotas have been achieved through the use of both legal instruments provided by the Treaty of Rome or the other common policies of the EC and 'grey area' instruments of dubious legality.

One important question for the external commercial policy of the EC – an issue which has proven both time consuming and potentially explosive – has been the future of the quantitative restrictions applied by five member states of the EC on imports of Japanese cars. The attempt to formulate a policy on Japanese car imports in the EC after 1992 has demonstrated the limits to external trade liberalization that the internal market programme has been expected to stimulate. It can also be said that these attempts have produced interesting insights into the determinants of the demand for and supply of protection when decision making power is redistributed from the governments of member states to Community institutions.

In this chapter we look at the trade policy arrangements agreed between Japan and the EC to regulate for a seven year transition period the inflow of Japanese cars in the hitherto protected markets of five EC member states, and discuss how far they contribute towards an eventual liberalization of the EC motor car markets. In the first two sections after these introductory remarks the chapter looks at the competitive advantages of the Japanese car industry and the responses of the EC industry to fend off this challenge. This response has been defensive and protectionist by five of the twelve member states which have been using voluntary export restraints administered by means of member state quotas and control on 'parallel' imports of cars of Japanese origin.

The consequences of these trading arrangements are explored in the subsequent section. The following section looks at the attempts to reconcile the conflicting interests of member states by 'communitising' the trade policy on imports of Japanese cars. Finally, the provisions of the accord reached between Japan and the EC in July 1991 to provide a solution to these problems are evaluated.

4.2 THE COMPETITIVE CHALLENGE OF THE JAPANESE CAR INDUSTRY

Japan is the second largest world producer of cars after the EC. The EC producing countries accounted in 1989 for 32.1 per cent of world vehicle production compared to 26.1 per cent accounted by Japan and 21.6 per cent contributed by the US. Nearly one third of EC vehicle production originates in Germany whilst France accounts for approximately one quarter and Italy and Spain for about one-sixth each (EIU, 1991).

Japanese producers have expanded their sales fast and penetrated rapidly several markets where access has been regulated by GATT principles. Japanese import penetration of the European Community market increased from 5 per cent in 1976 to nearly 10 per cent in 1989 (Table 4.1), rising to over 11 per cent by the end of 1991 (*Financial Times*, 25 April 1992).

The Japanese vehicle producers have thus a clear competitive edge as indicated by their ability to double their rate of import penetration in the EC within a period of a decade. In the 'non-controlled' import markets of Denmark, Germany, Greece, Ireland and the Netherlands,

Table 4.1   Import penetration of Japanese passenger cars

	1976	1987	Change
Belgium	18.00	20.60	2.60
Denmark	16.50	32.60	16.10
France	2.70	3.00	0.30
Germany	1.90	15.10	13.20
Greece	15.10	32.80	17.70
Ireland	12.70	43.90	31.20
Italy	0.01	0.70	0.69
Netherlands	16.80	25.90	9.10
Portugal	16.10	7.20	−8.90
Spain	0.00	0.30	0.30
United Kingdom	9.40	11.20	1.80
EC total	5.07	9.52	4.45

Source: EIU (1991) p. 90.

import penetration rates increased by more than 10 percentage points. The strengthened competitive position of Japan's motor manufacturers does not rest any longer on their low wage costs. The rapid appreciation of the yen meant that Japanese total labour costs per hour are now in fourth place in the costs' league, despite the fact that as late as 1980 the Japanese vehicle producing industry had the second lowest labour costs with only Spain in a more advantageous position. Thus the remarkable expansion of the Japanese car industry is a consequence of its ability to attain higher standards of production efficiency, to focus on product quality, to finance investments from internal funding but above all to organize and motivate people to work at peak performance.

Mass production techniques have been changed to 'lean' production methods that make it easier to produce a variety of vehicles within a large total volume of output (Womack *et al.*, 1990). The competitive advantage of the Japanese car manufacturers has been strengthened by their strategy to increase the variety of the ranges they offer by developing models more rapidly and producing them more flexibly. Emphasis on customer demand rather than mere technical aptitude explains how the Japanese car manufacturers have managed to maintain their competitive edge despite the adverse developments in their labour costs. The overall result of this competitive strategy is a higher productivity level and a shorter model development time. Japanese companies take less than 17 hours to make a car, against

Table 4.2   Total labour costs and hours worked in the car industry

	Total Labour Costs 1980	(DM per hour) 1988	Hours worked 1987
Belgium	28.14	32.10	1517
France	19.66	24.85	1563
Germany	26.91	38.49	1543
Italy	17.15	27.77	1685
Netherlands	23.33	30.41	1608
Spain	12.63	21.95	1722
UK	14.95	22.52	1802
USA	24.83	37.59	1938
Japan	14.50	33.41	2189

Source: V.D.A. German Motor Industry Association, 1989.

more than 25 hours required by their US competitors and 36 hours by their EC rivals. The time taken to develop a new model is 46 months on average in the Japanese car industry but almost 60 months for the US and EC vehicle producers (Table 4.2).

4.3   EUROPEAN RESPONSES TO THE JAPANESE COMPETITIVE THREAT

European reaction to the growing competitive threat of Japanese vehicle producers has varied from determination to meet the challenge through appropriate restructuring and adjustment policies (e.g. the building of new automated plants by Volkswagen in Emden and Fiat in Cassino near Naples, and the subsequent moves of both to Czechoslovakia, Poland and Russia to obtain better sourcing facilities) to measures to shield the domestic market for the benefit of indigenous producers. There is a widespread belief that Japan is 'special' and this explains the tendency to resort to measures outside the GATT framework to restrict Japanese imports into Europe. Just what is regarded as 'special' about competition with Japan varies through time (Curzon, 1987). Motivated by these beliefs and responding to pressures of the more protectionist of its member states, the EC Commission has resorted over the years to an escalation of measures in order to contain competition in the sectors where the Japanese are demonstrably more efficient (electronics, vehicles, etc.). Anti-dumping policy measures have been followed by local content rules to cope with the issue of the so-called screwdriver plants and then by specific rules of origin as in the case of chips.

In terms of the conditions applicable to the import of Japanese vehicles into their national markets, member states of the EC are divided into two distinct groups. The first group consisting of seven member states, some of which have no production of their own (Germany, Belgium, Luxembourg, the Netherlands, Denmark, Ireland and Greece) has an import trade regime which is compatible with GATT, i.e. uses GATT negotiated tariffs rather than 'grey area' measures to affect the volume of imports of Japanese cars. The second group consists of the remaining five countries (France, Italy, the UK, Portugal and Spain) which control the imports of Japanese motor cars into their territory by means of quantitative restrictions through the use of Voluntary Export Restraints (VERs) bilaterally negotiated with Japan up to the time (1991) the special agreement was negotiated by the EC Commission. The lack of a joint Community policy on Japanese trade means that the internal market of the EC is fragmented into an unrestricted segment, where competition is open and third-country imports, e.g. from Japan, are regulated solely by GATT determined tariffs and a restricted segment where imports from third countries are regulated by quantitative restrictions of the VER type and parallel imports from the open, unrestricted, segment are restricted through a variety of measures, some of which are linked to the availability of border controls inside the EC.

The national quotas on Japanese imports can be maintained by preventing transhipment of Japanese cars from the open to the restricted EC submarkets. A variety of policy instruments are used to this end in order to control the extent of arbitrage across the internal borders of the EC. These methods include:

(a) Recourse to Article 115 of the Treaty of Rome according to which authorization can be given to member states to restrict the entry into their territory of goods of third country origin imported via another member state. The facility of Article 115 can be granted under certain conditions only to cases where the national quotas are based on government to government agreements. However, not all VERs of the five member states are of this type. The UK VER, for example, is an industry to industry agreement where Article 115 authorization is not available. Italy's bilateral agreement with Tokyo which limits to 2500 the number of cars imported into that country directly from Japan is a government to government agreement and Article 115 authorization has been used to restrict 'parallel' imports.

(b) The use of selective distribution systems has been extensively employed to frustrate 'parallel' importing. The Competition Director-ate General of the Commission of the EC has sanctioned the use of selective distribution systems by granting a block exemption in 1985. The block exemption arrangement will come up for review in 1995. But already the EC Commissioner responsible for Competition Policy has expressed his dissatisfaction with the effectiveness of the current arrangements to bring down price differentials within the Community. Under the block exemption on selective distribution systems, manu-facturers are required to supply cars to dealers in one country for sale to buyers living in another EC country, on the understanding that such 'parallel' imports are sold to individuals or through so-called *man-dataires*. The block exemption does not specify what a *mandataire* is, or how many cars he can ship across borders. Thus through a strict interpretation on 'parallel' imports the system of selective distribution is effectively used to control the flow of Japanese vehicles from unrestricted, open markets to restricted ones.

(c) Delays in the introduction of a single EC-wide type approval system for cars. A single set of EC technical requirements for cars was nearly agreed in the early 1970s. After the surge of Japanese imports – espe-cially since 1976 – further adoption of the remaining common stand-ards on windscreens, tyres and towing weight was put on hold. Technical barriers to trade are thus targeted towards imports of specific origin.

(d) Use of the car registration system. Car registration systems are oper-ated by member state governments which can use them to restrict the inflow of imports originating from third countries. Thus the effective control of the implementation of the national quota can shift from the customs authorities at the border points to the Ministry of Transport registration of vehicles office inside the country.

(e) Finally, a host of small scale measures are employed with a similar result. Import licensing is still practised by several member states. Insurance difficulties may be experienced by buyers of cars prior to arrival of these cars in their country of final registration. Customs for-malities may require the personal attendance by the buyer – a proce-dure that may strengthen the restrictive nature of the block exemption on selective distribution systems.

Some of the methods used by the five restrictionist EC member states (France, Italy, Portugal, Spain and the United Kingdom) to control indirect exports routed through other EC countries will be unworkable after 1992 as a result of the removal of frontier controls inside the EC. Such is the case of Article 115 authorisations or of the measures under (e) above. Other methods of controlling such indirect exports can still be used. Member states may delay the full harmonization of technical standards, may use selectively their car registration procedures whilst they can still resort to the block exemption on selective distribution systems to achieve the same result. However, in the last case, the Japanese manufacturers can set up their own selective distribution networks to overcome this difficulty. At the moment, this is not facilitated by the sparse distribution network that Japanese manufacturers have in countries like France and Italy.

In view of this, the Commission proposed to take measures to reduce the fragmentation of the European car industry. Before the reactions of the European producers to the Commission proposals are examined, it is important to look at the consequences of using bilateral VERs to control Japanese car imports in certain markets which are part of a broader customs union.

4.4   EFFECTS OF VERs ON TRADE PATTERNS

The VERs on Japanese imports of cars practised by five of the twelve member states of the EC have an influence both on the ability of Japanese exporters to reap economic rents and on the ability of the unrestricted suppliers, especially those from other EC member states, to expand their volume of trade. As was shown by Dinopoulos and Kreinin (1988), the non-restricted suppliers gain from the VER, as their terms of trade improve and their volume of trade expands. Hamilton (1985) has also shown that VERs practised against selected traders from outside the customs union produce strong trade diversion effects in favour of producers from within the customs union whose exports cannot be restricted.

Assuming a competitive framework and the existence of three groups of countries (restricted markets within the EC, open markets within the EC and Japan), the imposition of VERs in order to stimulate domestic production will affect not only the price at which the restricted exporter will sell in the controlled market, but will also produce a change in the structure of imports into the restricted market by diverting trade flows in favour of the manufacturers from partner countries inside the EC. In Figure 4.1 S_R is the supply curve of the restricted market, S_{R+U} is the joint supply inside the customs union including both restricted and unrestricted markets (i.e. the difference between S_R and S_{R+U} is the supply originating in the unrestricted markets of the customs union) and D_R the demand curve in the restricted market. A policy to raise domestic production in the restricted market from Q_1 to Q_2 through the use of VERs will raise the price in the restricted market from P_1 to P_2 and at the same time raise the exports from the unrestricted markets inside the customs union from AD to CE. The difference between CE and AD represents the amount of trade diverted from third countries to the partner countries in the customs union.

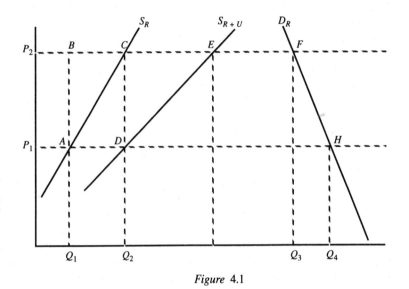

Figure 4.1

One can therefore hypothesise that (i) prices of imported items under VERs in the restricted markets will tend to be above the prices of the same imported items in the open, unrestricted markets unless the methods used to control 'parallel' imports are totally ineffective. Indeed, if these methods of controlling 'parallel' imports are progressively eroded, one would expect a reduction of the price differentials between restricted and unrestricted markets (ii) as suppliers of homogeneous products from the unrestricted markets (or, indeed, any other partner country) cannot be discriminated within a customs union, their share in the apparent consumption in the restricted markets will tend to increase. Thus the share of intra-area trade will tend to rise faster in the restricted markets compared to the non-restricted ones. Data from *Eurostat* have been utilised to examine how far the above hypotheses on the impact of VERs within the EC are borne out by the facts.

All studies that have attempted to assess the impact of VERs on the import prices of goods subject to these restraints use a common general approach. They compare price trends during the period the VERs were not in place with the actual price developments during the period the VERs have been in force. The details of the methodologies employed differ. Some authors (e.g. Crandall, 1986; Dinopoulos and Kreinin, 1988) develop a supply equation for the goods subject to VERs, where the import price of the products originating from the country subjected to VERs is related to input prices in the country of production and the bilateral exchange rate. Other authors adopt a more general equilibrium framework by building up a demand and supply model for the goods subject to VERs (Tarr and Morkre, 1984) or developing multiproduct cost functions for the manufacturing firms producing the goods under VERs (Winston *et al.*, 1987). In such exercises an important factor is to separate the impact of product quality change on prices especially because VERs are said to encourage foreign producers to introduce quality changes in the product subject to VERs. Feenstra (1984) suggested the use of hedonic regressions which have also been employed by Dinopoulos and Kreinin (1988).

However, in the context of the EC another yardstick of assessing the implications of VERs is to compare the price developments post-VER in the controlled submarkets of the customs union to similar developments during the same period in the non-controlled submarkets. In a customs union with free circulation of goods one would expect a convergence of prices if member states played by the rules. As we established in Section 4.3 this is not the case as far as trade in automobiles is concerned. Thus price differences between the restricted and the non-restricted submarkets must be due either to the impact of the VERs or to substantial differences in the demand for Japanese cars among member states. Our basic assumption here is that such differences in the demand for Japanese automobiles within the EC are not substantial and consequently a comparison of price developments in the two submarkets of the EC will enable us to assess the impact of VERs on the prices of Japanese automobiles.

Unit values of Japanese imported cars for three types of models differentiated according to engine capacity are compared between restricted and unrestricted markets during the period 1986 to 1990. The data on Table 4.3 show clearly that import unit values of the same type of Japanese vehicle have been persistently higher in the restricted markets both at the beginning and at the end of the period. Differences in unit values between restricted and unrestricted markets (Table 4.4) have however been falling over the years suggesting that the methods in use for the control of 'parallel' imports may have lost part of their effectiveness.

Table 4.3   Import unit values for Japanese cars: restricted markets compared to understricted (ECU)

Engine capacity of vehicles	Unrestricted markets		Restricted markets	
	1986	1990	1986	1990
Less than 1500 ccm	4.8651	5.8386	5.4533	6.0539
1500–3000 ccm	5.4360	6.5587	6.3494	7.1997
More than 3000 ccm	5.1555	7.1188	6.1647	7.2054

Source: Eurostat NIMEX statistics, 1991.

Table 4.4   Percentage differences in import unit values for Japanese cars between restricted and unrestricted markets

Engine capacity of vehicles	1986	1990
Less than 1500 ccm	12.09	3.68
1500–3000 ccm	16.80	9.77
More than 3000 ccm	19.58	1.22

Source: Eurostat NIMEX statistics, 1991

A comparison of the import unit values for Japanese cars between restricted and unrestricted markets within the EC reveals that VERs have enabled Japanese exporters to enjoy economic rents in the restricted markets, while penalizing consumers in those markets who have to pay a higher price for the same type of Japanese model than their fellow consumers in the unrestricted, open markets of the Community.

In order to study the trade diversion effects in favour of the unrestricted suppliers produced by the VERs practised by the five protectionist EC member states, we observed how total import shares in domestic demand and intra-EC import shares in domestic demand changed in both the restricted and the non-restricted markets (Table 4.5). Only EC countries with domestic production are included in the analysis. Spain and Portugal were omitted as latecomers to the EC.

In the countries practising VERs on Japanese car imports intra-area trade has accounted for a higher proportion of their increased share of imports in domestic demand. In the open economies, the proportion attributable to intra-area trade in the increasing share of imports has been either much smaller (as in Germany) or experienced an actual decline (as in Belgium

Table 4.5   Change in import shares in domestic demand 197–87 (percentages)

	Total import shares	Intra-EC import share	Increase in import share attributable to intra-EC trade
Belgium–Luxembourg	–9.7	–31.0	declined
Germany	18.7	3.2	17.1
France	23.9	19.6	82.0
Italy	18.9	12.0	63.5
Netherlands	5.4	–12.6	declined
UK	37.7	25.9	68.7

Source: Eurostat, production and trade statistics, various years.

and the Netherlands). In general, the imports of the five countries practising VERs account for 56.7 per cent of all imports of cars in the EC but for 64.4 per cent of intra-EC imports of cars. VERs have produced trade diversion effects and the beneficiaries from these changes in the structure of trade have been the EC member states whose exports cannot be restricted in the markets of the five countries practising VERs.

4.5   TOWARDS A SINGLE MARKET

The analysis in section 3 indicates that VERs could survive the opening up of borders in the EC (see also Pelkmans and Winters, 1988). However, the Commission put forward proposals in 1988 for the creation of a single market in cars involving the progressive elimination of all VERs currently in practice. The first draft of this proposal worked out by Commissioner Narjes in 1988 suggested an EC-wide import stabilization agreement with Japan with an end to the bilateral import restraint accords existing in France, UK, Italy, Spain and Portugal. The Commissioner that took over in 1989, Mr Bangemann, adopted a more liberal stance, proposing in April 1989 in the course of a meeting of EC industry ministers the wholesale removal of quotas on car imports to the EC. Bangemann's views were not accepted by the Commission unanimously. Divisions within the Commission forced several postponements in reaching an agreed proposal.

The dual decision making of the EC (Commission and Council of Ministers constantly interacting) has forced the Commission to modify its proposals on external trade policy issues many times, so that they can reflect the sum of the different national interests. The opposition here was led by the French and the Italian governments which were experiencing the impact of strong producers' coalitions to keep Japanese competition out of their market. On the other hand, the Commission's aim was to facilitate the implementation of the measures of the internal market – a goal with both economic and competence redistribution dimensions.

Eventually an agreement within the Commission enabled the competent Commissioner to start talks in the summer of 1989 with the Japanese government and the EC car producing countries on conditions for opening up the EC car market. The full plan for the internal market for cars prepared by the Commission and unveiled in January 1990, in the paper entitled 'A Single Market for the Automobile', included (i) the phasing out by the end of 1992 of all bilateral import quotas, (ii) the adoption of an EC-wide technical approval and the removal of differing national technical requirements in windscreens, tyres and towing weights, (iii) the prohibition of any specific local content rules to be observed by Japanese cars assembled in the EC, and (iv) the reduction in the national disparities in VAT rates and other car taxes.

The Commission proposals stimulated an intense lobbying activity by European car manufacturers including the setting up of a new European motor industry lobbying group, ACEA (Association des Constructeurs Européenes d'Automobiles). Their demand was to communitize member state quotas at the 1987 level of imports and to maintain them for a ten year period. In the meantime, Japanese response, by the setting up of production units especially in the UK by Nissan, Toyota and Honda, has complicated the issue further with ACEA asking for inclusion of cars from Japanese transplants in the EC in the EC-wide quota to be negotiated with the Japanese. The Commission was finally successful in the negotiations with the Japanese. In February 1990, Japan accepted the continuation of curbs on its car exports to the EC after 1992 but not after 2000.

The Commission has already agreed that a transition period was needed to give time to the shielded EC car manufacturers to adjust to a more open competitive regime. However, opposition from governments and industry in the restricted markets continued strongly with France and Italy refusing, for a short interval, to accept imports of Nissan Bluebird cars from the UK Sunderland factory of the company as qualifying for UK origin status. Eventually, the local content debate was resolved in favour of using the normal Kyoto convention rules to determine originating status rather than introducing specific origin rules. Such a move would have acted as a disincentive to Japanese investment in the EC which has accelerated considerably since 1986.

Another disagreement between the Commission and the industry lobbyists concerned the method of monitoring the proposed EC-wide restraints.

Bangemann wanted Japan to give an informal 'non-targeting' undertaking that its car makers would not flout the restraints simply by shipping cars from open EC markets to currently protected ones. Despite the fact that such an undertaking would invite Japanese collusion in cartelizing and segmenting the single market, industry representatives pressed for more effective monitoring rules. Industry lobbyists have also asked for a bilateral reciprocity clause to be inserted in the agreement with Japan – something which was rejected by the Commission. The talks with Japan revealed the disagreement within the EC on the role of industrial policy. At the end, the Commission initialled an accord with Japan, on 31 July 1991, which took into account some of the demands of the European car industry. This accord consists of a basic document entitled 'Elements of Consensus' together with the declarations and statements made by the EC Commissioner and the Japanese MITI.

The accord with Japan on automobile imports to the EC provides for the following measures. First, it sets Community-wide temporary quantitative limits on imports of Japanese cars to the EC. These quantitative restrictions are in the form of VERs due to be terminated by 31 December 1999. Secondly, the accord contains two types of 'safeguard' measures, namely a non-targeting clause restricting Japanese exporters from targeting the vulnerable shielded markets of the EC and provisions for a downwards adjustment of the VER quantitative limit if the Community car industry finds itself in 'crisis' during the period covered by the accord. Thirdly, the accord makes provisions for a joint monitoring procedure of the way it is to be implemented by both sides.

On the positive side of the accord, one should mention the separate treatment of transplants from direct exports from Japan and the rejection of any specific origin rules based on reinforced local content requirements. However, the provisions of the accord are characterized by a certain degree of vagueness. A few months after the accord was initialled, a dispute developed between the EC and the Japanese regarding the exact size of cuts agreed for 1992 for car and light commercial vehicle exports to the EC (*Financial Times*, 25 April 1992).

The July 1991 accord is based on a notional EC demand for cars and light trucks of 15.1 million by 1999. This notional market is then divided between European Community production, direct imports from Japan and Japanese production in their factories within the EC. Japan agreed to avoid 'causing disruption' in the emerging single market for cars by monitoring its car exports in accordance with a forecast of 1.23 million exports per year until 1999. Thus Japan will be allowed to increase its EC import penetration ratio to 16 per cent by 1999 from its current level of around 10 per cent. However, MITI has agreed that in the event of a slump in car sales in the EC they will lower their exports by 75 per cent of the difference between the expected sales by the accord and the actual demand in the Community.

Japan has agreed to monitor sales in protected EC markets such as France but would not do the same for open ones such as Germany. A joint review of the progress in keeping within the limits set by the quotas in the July 1991 agreement will be undertaken through a joint EC–Japan committee meeting twice a year.

The accord is expected to lead to an orderly market penetration by the Japanese whilst allowing time for adjustment to the EC industry. There are a number of issues that this agreement raises. First, the distribution between domestic EC production, direct imports from Japan and sales by Japanese transplants in the EC is precariously balanced. Between now and 1999 there are two full model cycles which are likely to render obsolete the projections upon which the original targets were worked out. Recent consultant reports predict a flat or declining car sales market in the EC during the 1990s (see, *The Economist*, vol. 1, no. 7, August 1992, p. 64). There is also the question of the treatment of Japanese exports to the EC from their plants outside the EC or Japan, for example from their US plants. Finally, there is a query over the accuracy of the forecast level of production by Japanese transplants in the EC. The implicit forecast in the accord with Japan was that Japanese car manufacturers will be producing about 1.2 million vehicles a year within the EC. Estimates by the British government suggest that this figure will be nearer to 2 million. Such a deviation will cause 'disruption' whose consequence about the future of this accord is difficult to predict.

The construction of new car factories by Japanese producers proceeded at a fast pace during the second half of the 1980s. Earlier expectations of a rapid growth of the European car market and fears of a 'Fortress Europe' led several Japanese producers to the construction of several new plants which, when they are in full operation, will add considerably to the production capacity of the industry in the EC. The following information about planned capacity and total investment (i.e. inclusive of projects involving R&D, engine construction, etc.) that is currently under construction or nearing completion has been assembled from various sources (see Table 4.6).

In addition to these plans for new capacity in passenger vehicles, there are several joint ventures for the production of trucks in several EC countries. Toyota already has a factory in Portugal for the production of light trucks, a truck venture in France and another joint venture with VW for pick-up trucks. Finally, Honda has a 20 per cent stake in Rover whilst

Table 4.6   New capacity and investment by Japanese producers in the EC

Company	Planned capacity	est. total investment (£m)
Nissan (UK)	300 000	271
Toyota (UK)	200 000	900
Honda (UK)	100 000	362
Mitsubishi (Holland)*	200 000	1300*

* Joint venture with Volvo through the sale of the share of the Dutch government in the existing plant; the level of indicated investment will be undertaken by all three parties.

Sources: Various.

Suzuki has a 49 per cent share in the Land Rover Santana company in Spain which in 1990 produced 6000 Land Rover Santana cars and 21 000 Suzuki cars. If the above estimates are close to the actual plans of the Japanese producers then the Commission projections are not far off the mark.

4.6   CONCLUDING REMARKS

Whether the accord with Japan will lead to the liberalization of the EC import car market depends a lot on whether one is prepared to accept it as truly transitional. To reinforce expectations that this is a transitory arrangement leading towards an open single market, the Commission has combined this agreement with proposals for assistance to the Community automobile makers to restructure particularly through aids for research and development projects. The Commission proposals have already been regarded as inadequate by car industry representatives.

However, the most important aspect of the July 1991 accord with Japan is that the EC-wide VER that it implies would stamp out the remaining free European car markets, allowing EC car makers to set prices in the knowledge that Japanese imports will be limited. At present in unrestricted markets car prices are influenced by an unrestricted level of Japanese imports. This influence spills over into the more protected markets. In addition, Japanese exporters will continue to enjoy the advantage of reaping economic rents through the cartelization induced by VERs. Finally, the accord projects an image of the EC conniving at discriminatory trading arrangements rather than championing world-wide free trade.

5 Is the Globe Shrinking? Psychic Distance and the Establishment of Swedish Sales Subsidiaries during the Last 100 Years

Kjell A. Nordström and Jan-Erik Vahlne

F23

5.1 INTRODUCTION

It has been argued that not only has the world become 'smaller' because of new technology for transportation and communication, but it has also become much more homogeneous, for example in terms of customer demand. However, even the most often cited proponent of this view, Theodor Levitt (1983), acknowledges that there exist cultural differences as well as differences in ways of doing business between regions and countries of the world, and indeed even between different parts of one country. The growth of research and education in the area of international business in recent years can be taken as an indication. To capitalize on the growing similarities in customer demand and to enjoy economies of scale, a company must develop skills for doing business in environments which it realizes are different from that of its home base. Still, the question remains: are countries generally getting 'closer' to each other over time? The aim of this chapter is first to justify and then to test a proposal that the world has shrunk, applying as an indicator of psychic distance the country pattern followed by Swedish companies in the establishment of foreign subsidiaries.

5.2 PSYCHIC DISTANCE

To the best of our knowledge, the concept of 'psychic distance' was first used by Beckerman (1956) in an attempt to explain the distribution of international trade. Other researchers also sensed that something beyond geographical distance was having an impact on the distribution of trade flows: Kindleberger (1969) refers to 'economic horizons' and Burenstam

Linder (1961) to 'limitations on businessmen's knowledge about sources and markets' in trying to identify factors which separate countries in ways other than mere physical distance.

Vahlne and Wiedersheim-Paul (1973) used the concept of psychic distance in an empirical study of the spatial distribution of Swedish exports. The model contained both trade-creating and trade-impeding variables. Impeding trade was 'economic distance', composed of 'physical distance' – that is factors preventing flows of goods and money – and 'psychic distance', defined as the *factors preventing or disturbing the flow of information between potential or actual suppliers and customers*. In an econometric analysis by Hörnell *et al.* (1973), psychic distance was shown to have considerable explanatory value for the country distribution of Swedish firms' foreign subsidiaries.

Almost twenty years later Nordström (1991) found that psychic distance still had a high explanatory value for the country pattern of the internationalization process. However, a much better explanation was provided if explicit attention was also paid to competitive considerations and country-specific characteristics.

The definition of psychic distance used in the 1973 study by Vahlne and Wiedersheim-Paul – factors preventing or disturbing flows of information – is too narrow as we now see it. A broader and more valid definition is *'factors preventing or disturbing firms' learning about and understanding a foreign environment'*. The reason why we prefer this definition is that not only does a firm interested in pursuing business projects in a foreign environment need to learn hard facts about laws, distribution systems, etc., but it must also understand enough of the culture to be able to relate to it and adjust its own behaviour, e.g. by marketing and cooperation with local partners. Furthermore, this definition underlines the fact that the *firm* – and at the aggregate level the business community – is the unit of analysis. Individuals have their own personal notion of the world in psychic distance terms. Here, we are interested in how the behaviour of business firms is affected by psychic distance.

The more different the culture of the foreign market from that of the home market, the more difficult it will be to learn about and understand the new environment. Hence, the tendency to start the internationalization process on markets close – in terms of psychic distance – to the home market (Johanson and Vahlne, 1977 and 1990) no doubt makes sense. The typical internationalization process tends to be a step-wise entry into gradually more distant markets.

It is, of course, difficult to separate more precisely actual cause and effect relationships in a discussion of the forces that are making psychic distance decrease. Political and technological, as well as psycho-social, forces are at work in complex interaction. However, disregarding the complex cause and effect relationships, we can still hypothesize that psychic distance has decreased.

There are two basic reasons for this implosion of the business community in psychic-distance terms. First, it is clear that the world in general and certain regions in particular are becoming more homogeneous. Administrative and legal structures – particularly for doing business – have been harmonized within large regions like the EC. English has more and more taken over as the universal second language of the world. It is the mother tongue for 400 million people, and by 1990 some 1 billion people could speak it (Naisbitt and Aburdene, 1990). The form, as well as the content, of the educational system in various countries is no longer as country specific as it used to be. More countries are approaching the stage of becoming 'industrialized countries'. These factors and many others make it probable that psychic distances have decreased.

Second, many firms – and international firms in particular – over time have learned how to handle and/or overcome the factors constituting psychic distance. There are more people than ever in the world with experience in doing business abroad and with knowledge of foreign environments. International trade and business have been continuously growing in importance – measured by share of the world economy – during the twentieth century. Regular markets for knowledge of various kinds – including country-specific knowledge – have been growing over time. The knowledge markets – i.e. first and foremost consultants – have made it easier to overcome at least some of the psychic distance factors. So, our hypothesis is: the world has shrunk in psychic distance terms.

5.3 MEASURING PSYCHIC DISTANCE

In their more narrow definition of psychic distance as 'factors preventing or disturbing information flows between potential or actual suppliers and customers', Vahlne and Wiedersheim-Paul (1973) used the following set of indicators:

(a) Level of economic development in the importing country.
(b) Difference in level of economic development between Sweden and the host country.
(c) Level of education in the importing country.

(d) Difference in level of education between Sweden and the respective host country.
(e) Difference in 'business language'.
(f) Difference in culture and local language.
(g) Existence of previous trading channels between Sweden and the respective host countries.

Data on many of these indicators were actually found in publicly available statistics. Others, such as difference in culture and local language, were estimated by knowledgeable officers of the Swedish Export Board. These data made it possible to create a ranking of countries according to psychic distance from Sweden. In a first draft of the ranking, the Anglo-Saxon countries of Canada, the US and Australia were all very close to Sweden. A panel of experts from the Swedish Export Board and some large exporting companies commented on, and suggested revisions of, this first draft of the ranking. In the final version of the fifteen most important Swedish export countries ranked in terms of psychic distance, the Nordic countries were closest to Sweden, followed by other Northern European countries. The US and Canada, though physically distant, were regarded as psychically closer to Sweden than the Latin European countries (see third column of Table 5.2).

The key difference in the estimation of psychic distance between Nordström's 1991 study and the 1973 study is the focus in the former on *perceived* psychic distance, while the earlier study tried to construct more 'objective' measures using statistics of various kinds, although these were modified according to perceptions. The 1991 study sought to establish a picture of how decision makers within firms actually perceive the world in psychic distance terms.

In three of the general management programmes offered by the Swedish Institute of Management (IFL) – Scandinavia's largest executive training institution – a questionnaire was distributed after a lecture on the concept of psychic distance (reference to earlier definition of that concept). The managers were asked to put an index value between 0 and 100 on twenty-two different countries, among them the most important Swedish export markets (Norway, Germany, the UK, the US, etc.). The lowest index value was to be put on the country perceived, in psychic distance terms, to be the closest to Sweden. Similarly, the highest index value was to be attributed to the country perceived as most distant from Sweden. Values in between were to be assigned to the remaining countries.

Of the 121 managers from various medium-sized and larger Swedish companies, most of them in the private sector but also a few public sector firms, 118 completed the questionnaire correctly. On the basis of their data, the average index of psychic distance was calculated for each of the twenty-two countries (see right-hand column of Table 5.1).

The average index figures had already converged towards a stable ranking after some fifty questionnaires had been reviewed. In effect, it can be concluded that a larger sample would have improved reliability only marginally.

The rankings produced in 1973 and 1991 are remarkably similar. Certainly, some countries have moved up or down one or two places. But the pattern is the same, with our Nordic neighbours being closest, followed by north-west European countries, Anglo-Saxon non-European countries and then Latin European countries. In the 1991 ranking Asian and Latin American countries follow thereafter. The small differences between the two rankings might be due as much to the different methods applied as to actual changes in psychic distance. The overall impression is that psychic distance is rather stable, at least to the extent that few changes in rankings were found. But it is difficult to draw any firm conclusions. First, there are only twenty years between the two studies. Second, we have no index – just the ranking – for the 1973 psychic distance. Clearly other indications of a 'shrinking globe' must be sought.

However, even if we had the relevant material for 1969 and earlier periods, some inherent problems with the concept of psychic distance would require a certain caution in the interpretation of any conclusions drawn. Psychic distance is here defined as created 'by factors which prevent and disturb learning about and understanding a foreign environment'. Obviously, cultural differences between countries constitute one such factor. However, the psychic distance concept and its operationalization capture not only the effect of a variety of factors – cultural differences being one of them – but also the effect of both the absolute psychic distance between two countries *and* the ability to overcome it. In a sense, all is in the eyes of the beholder. Thus, from the perspective of certain firms, psychic distance to a particular country might, in effect, be almost zero, in spite of obstacles in the form of significant cultural differences to 'learning about and understanding the foreign environment'. The firms (or business community within a particular country for that matter) might over time have developed ways and means to overcome these differences.

In order to highlight somewhat further this peculiarity of the psychic distance measures used by us, and at the same time to discuss the difference between the concept of 'psychic distance' and 'cultural distance', a comparison is made with an attempt to measure only the latter in absolute terms.

5.4   PSYCHIC DISTANCE AND HOFSTEDE'S CULTURAL
      DIFFERENCES

The best known quantitative study of cultural differences is Hofstede's (1980). To capture 'cultural differences' in general between Sweden and twenty-two other countries, Hofstede's four dimensions (power distance, uncertainty avoidance, individualism, and masculinity) are mathematically merged into one composite index.[1] This makes it possible to rank the countries on the basis of their average absolute cultural distance – in Hofstede's terms – from Sweden (Table 5.1).

At first glance we found a natural validity in the 1991 ranking, with the Nordic neighbours being closest, followed by other northern European countries, North America, southern European countries, Japan and South America. The countries tend to cluster in regions within which the psychic distance measure is of the same order of magnitude.

The Hofstede data provide a somewhat different clustering. The Netherlands have moved up into the Nordic group of countries, with a very low index value. Canada is found between the first and second cluster. And the second cluster (from the US to Italy) is a mixture of countries from various parts of the world. The similarity between the rankings of the two studies is still rather high. The Spearman rank correlation coefficient is 0.61 (significant at the 0.01 level).

Clearly the two measures are capturing different but overlapping phenomena. Hofstede's (1980) ambition was to 'show evidence of differences and similarities among the culture pattern of countries; differences and similarities that have very old historical roots (some for example going back as far as to the Roman Empire)'. It is emphasized in his study that the 'collective mental programming of the mind' (ibid., p. 13), which we usually refer to as culture, is a phenomenon that could be expected to be stable over time. It is argued that there are mechanisms in societies which permit the maintenance of stability in culture patterns across many generations.

Psychic distance was defined as 'factors preventing or disturbing firms' learning about and understanding of a foreign environment'. As we see it, there are three types of factors *creating* that distance: cultural (such as those defined by Hofstede), structural (such as legal and administrative systems) and language differences. On the other hand, the distance can be *bridged* by factors such as knowledge dissemination (consultants selling information on legal procedures and cultural habits, or language training courses) or trial and error processes (young people travelling abroad and companies entering foreign markets). Psychic distance is consequently the

Table 5.1   Ranking of twenty-two countries based on adjusted Hofstede (1980) data on cultural differences and Nordström's (1991) data on countries' psychic distance from Sweden

Adjusted Hofstede data		*The 1991 data*	
Rank country	*Index of cultural differences in relation to Sweden*	*Rank country*	*Index of psychic distance from Sweden to*
1 Norway	1.2	1 Norway	0.5
2 Denmark	1.9	2 Denmark	3.3
3 The Netherlands	3.4	3 Finland	8.5
4 Finland	7.1	4 Great Britain	14.8
5 Canada	17.7	5 West Germany	17.7
6 Australia	25.3	6 Switzerland	20.7
7 USA	25.9	7 Austria	22.4
8 Great Britain	27.6	8 The Netherlands	23.4
9 Spain	27.7	9 USA	25.3
10 France	30.3	10 Canada	27.1
11 Chile	30.7	11 Belgium	31.7
12 Germany	31.5	12 France	34.8
13 Switzerland	33.2	13 Spain	38.2
14 Brazil	34.0	14 Australia	39.2
15 Turkey	34.6	15 Italy	39.9
16 Argentina	35.4	16 Portugal	47.5
17 Belgium	39.9	17 Japan	59.5
18 Portugal	40.0	18 Turkey	71.6
19 Italy	40.2	19 Brazil	74.0
20 Austria	48.4	20 Mexico	74.2
21 Mexico	59.4	21 Argentina	78.2
22 Japan	78.1	22 Chile	79.2

Sources: Hofstede (1980) and Nordström (1991).

sum of the *distance-creating* factors minus the sum of the *distance-bridging* factors.

A distinction must be made between two different mechanisms affecting psychic distance over time. One is 'bridging'; for example by learning about a foreign legal system. Another is that the strength of a psychic distance creating factor can decrease over time. This is occurring, for example, as the EC is harmonizing certain legal systems. Furthermore, even culture changes over time, although at a very slow pace, as noted by Hofstede.

In this connection it is important to clarify *who* is experiencing psychic distance. A distinction can be made between three levels of aggregation: individual, company and country. When Pharmacia, the Swedish drug manufacturer, established its very first subsidiary in the US in 1947, this step was hard to explain, at least until it was learned that the president of Pharmacia had received his academic education in the US and that the person he picked to run the subsidiary was an old friend from the university. But companies have 'organizational memories', and many years of experience will no doubt facilitate business with companies from a different culture. At the national level it seems clear, for example, that trade has 'followed the flag'. British commercial interests have been strong in the former dominions.

In spite of these differences between the two measures, cultural differences and psychic distance, there is a considerable degree of correspondence between the two rankings in Table 5.1. It is tempting to attribute this to the fact that psychic distance to a large extent has its roots in basic cultural differences.

5.5 EXPLAINING COUNTRY PATTERNS IN THE ESTABLISHMENT OF FOREIGN SALES SUBSIDIARIES

The intention of this study is to see if we can find support for the notion of a shrinking globe – that is; of decreasing psychic distances. However, no data on psychic distance at different points in time during the last century are available. An indicator or proxy for psychic distance will have to be used. As we have access to data on the country pattern of Swedish firms' establishment of foreign sales subsidiaries, we will explore here the possibility of using that data as a proxy.

The data material on the establishment patterns of Swedish MNCs' foreign sales subsidiaries emanates from two studies. First, there is the 1973 survey (Hörnell *et al.*, 1973) which covered virtually *all* Swedish firms in the manufacturing industries; very few companies refused to participate. And for all practical purposes the data bank can be considered to include all Swedish-owned subsidiaries abroad (1044) established from the late 1800s up to 1969. The second source of data is the Nordström (1991) study. This study also had a very high response rate (93 per cent) and covers almost all Swedish sales subsidiaries abroad (348) established in the period 1969–1986 by Swedish manufacturers with no foreign manufacturing activities (that is companies rather inexperienced in international business). In effect, only data on sales subsidiaries from the 1973 study can be used for comparison.

The attractiveness of a certain country as a host for Swedish sales subsidiaries was measured as the Mean Establishment Rank (MR):

$$MR = \frac{\Sigma w_i R_i}{\Sigma w_i}$$

where

R_i = respective establishment rank, that is 1st, 2nd establishment, etc.,
W_i = number of establishments of a certain rank on a particular market.

The MR measure is a function of the number of establishments in a particular market and the rank of the respective establishment. As the measure is constructed, early establishments in terms of rank will by definition influence the measure more than later establishments. The number of first establishments will be larger than the number of second establishments, the number of second establishments will always be larger than the number of third establishments, and so on. This feature causes us no problem, since for reasons given elsewhere we prefer to focus on inexperienced investors. The rankings for the twenty most frequent host countries for Swedish manufacturing firms are presented in Table 5.2, together with countries ranked according to psychic distance from Sweden.

The rank correlation between the rankings (for the fifteen countries where both MR and psychic distance measures are available) is based on psychic distance and the MR measure is 0.89. Given that other factors *besides* psychic distance also affect the choice of market (size and growth of the economy, transport costs, tariffs, etc.), the explanatory value of psychic distance on this distribution of foreign sales subsidiaries seems to be fairly good. This observation is also quite consistent with what has been asserted in the FDI (foreign direct investment) literature:

> Casual evidence on other countries confirms the general impression that the bulk of their foreign investments go where the transactional and information-cost disadvantages are least: Japan to Southeast Asia (Yoshihara, 1978, Tsurumi, 1976), Australia to New Zealand (Deane, 1970), Sweden to neighbouring European countries and the United States (Swedenborg,1979), France to French-speaking areas and adjacent European countries (Michalet and Delapierre, 1976).
>
> (Caves, 1982, p. 64)[2]

Table 5.2   Mean Establishment Rank (MR) calculated for all establishments of
Swedish sales subsidiaries for twenty countries up to 1969, and ranking of countries
in terms of psychic distance from Sweden for fifteen countries in 1969

Country	MR	MR Rank	Psychic distance rank
Norway	2.2	1	2
Denmark	2.4	2	1
Finland	3.1	3	3
West Germany	3.1	4	4
Great Britain	3.3	5	5
USA	3.8	6	8
Switzerland	4.3	7	9
The Netherlands	5.1	8	6
France	5.2	9	12
Belgium	5.8	10	7
Austria	5.9	11	11
Italy	6.2	12	13
Spain	6.2	13	14
Brazil	7.6	14	N.A
Canada	7.7	15	10
Japan	8.7	16	N.A
Portugal	9.0	17	15
South Africa	9.2	18	N.A
Argentina	9.7	19	N.A
Australia	10.3	20	N.A

Source: Hörnell, Vahlne and Wiedersheim-Paul (1973).

The bulk of the flow of foreign direct investments is the financing of
manufacturing operations, which demand much heavier investments than
purely sales or service activities. In a 'rational' or neoclassical world, manufacturing investments would be directed to countries where advantages
complementary to those of the investor can be found (ibid., chapter 1).
However in reality – as the quotation above indicates – 'psychic distance'
also matters. The question is not 'whether' but 'how much'. Obviously,
one could expect that the country pattern of export activities would be
affected even more by 'psychic distance' than would foreign direct investment. Sales activities (and investment in sales organizations) on a particular foreign market are typically established before manufacturing
operations (Johanson and Vahlne, 1977). The incremental approach which
firms tend to follow when entering new markets – starting close to home
(in psychic distance terms) and then gradually moving further and further

away – not only makes sense theoretically but is firmly established empirically, thus underscoring the validity of country pattern of establishment of sales subsidiaries as a proxy for psychic distance.

Still, psychic distance is obviously not the only factor explaining patterns in firms' processes of internationalization. Nordström (1991) used a multiple regression model to test the influence of psychic distance as well as market potential on the establishment sequence of Swedish firms sales subsidiaries during the period 1960–86. Gross Domestic Product (GDP) 1986, and a weighted average of growth in GDP and population in 1986, served as a proxy for market potential. Psychic distance was measured with an index of psychic distance (see Table 4.1). About 55 per cent of the variation in MR was associated with or, explained by, the two variables[3] of psychic distance and population. The population variable explained as much as 33 per cent of the variation, while psychic distance explained only 22 per cent.

However, firms rarely do much desk research before establishing a sales subsidiary (Hörnell and Vahlne, 1973). Rather they tend to react to signals received from the market, perhaps from an agent or a customer. But such signals are certainly more probable between psychically close markets. Hence, the MR measure – in spite of these limitations – is probably a good proxy for psychic distance, especially when applied to a population of rather inexperienced companies.

The results of Nordström's (1991) study indicate that within a region encompassing certain Western industrialized countries, market potential has a somewhat greater explanatory power than psychic distance. Still, it is interesting to note that even within this fairly homogeneous group of industrialized Western European and North American countries, psychic distance still does matter substantially! This finding is somewhat surprising. It might imply that in a study of a less homogeneous group of countries, the explanatory power of psychic distance would have been considerably higher. The answer to the question 'how much' (does psychic distance affect the country pattern of establishing sales subsidiaries) is: 'quite a lot'.

A further indication of the explanatory power of psychic distance is the comparison of the ranking of countries in terms of psychic distance and MR values from the 1991 study (Nordström, 1991), using basically the same methodology as in the 1973 study (see Table 5.3).

Compared to the 1973 study, there are no great surprises in the 1991 study in the ranking of countries in terms of psychic distance. What is somewhat surprising, though, is that the index values increase rapidly as we go down the list, especially at the top of the ranking. Norway is not very 'far away' in psychic distance terms, but Denmark is already significantly

Table 5.3   Psychic distance (PD) and Mean Establishment Rank (MR) for ten
countries, 1989

Rank using the 1991 psychic distance measure	Country	Index of psychic distance	Rank using the MR measure	Country	MR
1	Norway	0.5	1	Norway	1.73
2	Denmark	3.3	2	Great Britain	1.82
3	Finland	8.5	3	West Germany	1.88
4	Great Britain	14.8	4	USA	1.89
5	West Germany	17.7	5	Denmark	2.04
6	Switzerland	20.7	6	Finland	2.12
7	Netherlands	23.4	7	Switzerland	2.40
8	USA	25.3	8	France	2.73
9	France	34.8	9	Italy	2.80
10	Italy	39.9	10	Netherlands	3.36

Source: Nordström (1991).

different. The MR index increases much more slowly. Still, the Spearman
rank correlation is as high as 0.67 (significant at the 0.05 level).

Our conclusion, therefore, is that the country pattern can be used as a
proxy for psychic distance in an attempt to answer our research question.

5.6   HAS PSYCHIC DISTANCE DECREASED?

Since we have no measure of psychic distance that would make it possible
to observe its development over time, we will use the MR values as
presented in the previous section.

Using the MR measure as a proxy for psychic distance provides some
preliminary indications (Table 5.4). It is clear that the ranking in the later
period is somewhat reshuffled. The group of Nordic countries is no longer
at the top; Great Britain, (West) Germany and the US have moved 'closer'
to Sweden than the Nordic countries of Denmark and Finland. The differences in the respective MR values, though, are very small. Brazil – a
somewhat odd country in this context – has (naturally) disappeared.[4] Switzerland, France and Italy have moved somewhat, but just marginally, while
Austria has taken a leap upwards. Overall there are no dramatic changes.
The data indicate that basically the same group of Western European and
North American countries were as close to Sweden in psychic distance

Table 5.4 Ranking of the twelve most frequent host countries for Swedish sales subsidiaries based on the Mean Establishment Rank, 1951–68 and 1969–86

1951–68		1969–86	
Denmark	1.80	Norway	1.73
Norway	1.90	Great Britain	1.87
Finland	2.10	West Germany	1.88
Germany	2.30	USA	1.89
USA	2.35	Denmark	2.04
Austria	2.55	Finland	2.12
Great Britain	2.65	Switzerland	2.40
Switzerland	2.75	France	2.73
Brazil	3.00	Italy	2.80
France	3.55	The Netherlands	3.36
Italy	3.65	Canada	3.40
The Netherlands	4.15	Austria	4.09

Source: Hörnell *et al.* (1973) and Nordström (1991).

terms in 1960–86 as in 1951–68, although the ranking of the various countries had changed somewhat. Hence, the results provide no support for a shrinking globe in this respect.

However, further scrutinizing the MR values, we find that every single ranking has a somewhat lower MR value in the second period. Given that the time periods studied are equally long, this might be a weak indication of a slight decrease in the general level of psychic distance. The whole period (1951–86) studied is, however, rather short.

To prolong the period under study and include all known establishments of sales subsidiaries, we dropped the MR measure as less reliable when the number of observations was low.

Table 5.5 presents the number of first, second and third establishments in four regions – Nordic countries, Europe, North America and rest of the world – for five seventeen-year[5] periods covering 1897–1986. From this table it is clear that the pattern in Swedish firms' establishment of their three first foreign operations is remarkably stable over a period of almost 100 years.

Although the distribution between the Nordic countries and Europe varies somewhat over time, it is within the area of those two regions that we find 85–95 per cent of the first three establishments. The Nordic region seems to be somewhat more frequent as a host region in the first periods. Conversely, this region seems to be somewhat less frequent in the last

Table 5.5 Number of first, second and third establishments of Swedish foreign
subsidiaries in four regions, 1897–1986[1]

	Nordic countries	Europe	North America	Rest of the world	Total no. of observations
1897–1914					
No. of 1st, 2nd and	11	5	1	0	17
3rd establishments	64%	29%	6%	0%	
1915–1932					
No. of 1st, 2nd and	15	11	1	1	28
3rd establishments	53%	39%	4%	4%	
1933–1950					
No. of 1st, 2nd and	15	17	3	1	36
3rd establishments	42%	47%	8%	3%	
1951–1968					
No. of 1st, 2nd and	137	152	18	5	312
3rd establishments	43%	49%	6%	2%	
1969–1986					
No. of 1st, 2nd and	116	148	40	11	315
3rd establishments	37%	47%	13%	3%	

Note:
[1] During the period 1880–97 there were two establishments of foreign sales
subsidiaries. Both of these were in the Nordic countries.

period than in any of the earlier ones. North America is the third most
frequent region – with a slight growth tendency over time – followed by
the residual category 'rest of the world', that seems to grow slightly in
importance, particularly during the last two periods.

Something of a change – although small – in the distribution of establishments could be discerned: there were a few establishments outside the region
of the Nordic countries and Europe during the first periods, but more in the last
two; the other side of the same coin is obviously the corresponding decrease in
the frequency of establishments in Europe and the Nordic countries.

The rather stable pattern in Table 5.5 is somewhat counter-intuitive. The
forces driving the world towards commonality (see Levitt, 1983) have
obviously not left any major imprints on the foreign establishment pattern
of Swedish firms. Neither has the often asserted 'geocentrism' (Perlmutter,
1969), or globalization of managers, firms and industries as well as the

business community at large, left any major traces on this pattern. The foreign establishment pattern of Swedish firms (Table 5.4 and 5.5), as an indicator of psychic distance, clearly points in the direction of rather stable psychic distances over a period of almost 100 years.

Clearly our findings are preliminary and should be interpreted with some caution. First, the theoretical definition as well as the operationalization of psychic distance capture both the absolute distance and the ability to overcome it. Although the latter is somewhat compensated for[6] in the construction of the MR measure[7] in Table 5.4 and the focus on only the first three establishments[8] in Table 5.5, it is probable that the measures still capture some of these learning effects at the firm level as well as at the societal level. Second, no matter how psychic distance is defined in the above terms, it is of course questionable whether the foreign establishment pattern of firms is a good proxy for psychic distance. Although the correlation historically has been rather high between the two measures, other factors also matter. Furthermore, it should be kept in mind that Swedish society in general – and the business community in particular – is rather small. The stable pattern in the establishment of foreign operations might to a certain extent reflect a 'bandwagon learning effect' over time between firms. Knowledge about certain countries or regions is accumulated in the business community at large – as in the case of Brazil – and might direct and reinforce the investment waves to certain regions over long periods of time given the measures used. It is obviously difficult to separate out the effect of this factor and other 'non-psychic distance' factors in our study.

In spite of using the concept of 'the globe' in the title of this article, we have only included a small number of countries from the developed part of the world, since these are the countries in which Swedish subsidiaries are located.

Finally, it should be mentioned that the number of observations in the first three periods is rather low. Although a clear pattern can be discerned, it should be remembered that the number of observations, as well as their age,[9] require a certain caution in the interpretation of the data.

With the methodological reservations in mind, we find no support for the notion of a 'smaller' world in psychic-distance terms. This finding might well be explained by the fact that psychic distance – in both definition and operationalization – mainly reflects absolute cultural differences in Hofstede's (1980) terms, i.e. 'a phenomenon that could be expected to be stable over time' (Hofstede, 1980, p. 13). The indications of a general decrease in psychic distance in the later periods of our material would then mainly be attributable to a recently improved ability to overcome psychic distances, rather than to any general decrease in psychic distance *per se*.

The overall conclusion would then be that we are slightly better at bridging absolute psychic distance gaps than in the past – in a world that is as large (or small ...) as it always has been in these terms.

NOTES AND REFERENCES

1. We based the composite index on the deviation along each of the four cultural dimensions of each country from the Swedish ranking. The deviations were then corrected for differences in the variance of each of the dimensions and then arithmetrically averaged. Algebraically, the index may be expressed as follows:

$$CD_j = \sum_{i=1}^{4} \left\{ (I_{ij} - I_{si})^2 / Vi \right\}^4$$

where

CD_j = cultural distance from Sweden to the j-th country
I_{ij} = the index for the i-th cultural dimension of the j-th country
V_i = the variance of the index of the i-th dimension
s = indicates Sweden

A similar methodology was applied by Kogut and Singh (1988).
2. See also Welch and Loustarinen (1988).
3. The other two proxies – GDP and weighted growth in GDP – had no significant explanatory value.
4. For a while during the 1950s and 1960s Brazil was a focal point for Swedish foreign investors. The word spread in the small Swedish business community, and something of a bandwagon effect reigned for a short period of time.
5. Periods of seventeen years were chosen because of limitations in the flexibility of the data material.
6. This finding is also confirmed to a certain extent by the previous comparison with Hofstede's data.
7. For a more thorough discussion, see page 00.
8. It could be expected that the 'learning effect' at the firm level is very limited at this very early stage of the establishment process.
9. The questionnaire was distributed in 1969. The respondents were asked to answer also for subsidiaries that had been established but later closed down. Data about establishments in the former Eastern Bloc countries are lacking, however.

Part II
Asian Issues

6 Introduction

The first chapter in this part, by Gene Burton, discusses the impact of trade with Asia on the US trade deficit. Burton discusses the many conditions that brought about the reversal in the role of the US, from world leader in trade surplus to a debtor nation since 1985, and that among the conditions that brought about the dramatic reversal in the trade balances of the US was the emergence of major developing nations in the Pacific basin dedicated to the creation of their own national trade surpluses, even if it meant that they referred to the use of trade barriers for the achievement of this goal. Burton is very sceptical as to whether there is any relief in sight for the US trade balance. Even if Japan and the Four Tigers open their doors to US product it seems that the US trade deficit will probably continue to exist. The author also mentions the increased momentum towards a new Asian economic body or an Asian trading zone.

Jong Park continues the thought of the emergence of trading blocs and relates those specifically to US–Japanese trade relations. The author seems to recognize that the world appears to be heading towards a tripolar economic order by the Big Three: the US, the European Community, and Japan. Park points out that one of the profound post-war developments has been a shift of both economic activities and international economic policy from the Atlantic to the Pacific basin Countries. The author expresses his fear that the ultimate impact of trading blocs will lead to an inevitable escalation in trade conflicts and trade wars among the completing blocs.

The chapter written by Lee and Roland-Holst refers to US–Japanese trade relations (as do the previous two chapters) but concentrates on agricultural trade issues. The authors point out that while Japan is the world's largest importer of agricultural products, it also maintains some of the highest rates of effective protection against agricultural imports, a fact that has become a serious liability in US–Japanese trade relations. The authors appraise a US–Japan CGE model to measure the prospects of the two countries agricultural trade liberalization. They believe that if such an agreement was negotiated then each country could realize substantial economic gains.

7 The US Trade Deficit and the Impact of Asian Trade

Gene E. Burton

F32 F14

7.1 INTRODUCTION

If the number one economic story of this quarter century has been the dramatic success of Japan Inc., the number two economic story has been the equally dramatic increase in the US trade deficit. The negative US trade imbalance first reached alarming levels in the late 1970s and early 1980s, when it varied between $20 and $40 billion. Then, in 1983, the deficit surged upwards by 60 per cent to $69 billion, followed by an 86 per cent jump to $128.5 billion the very next year. Americans will long remember 1985, when their trade deficit reached $139 billion and the US became a debtor nation for the first time in its history. Then, in 1987, the deficit reached its peak of $170 billion. The good news is that the deficit dropped in 1988 to $137 billion, followed by subsequent drops to $129 billion in 1989, $102 billion in 1990, and a predicted $90 billion in 1991 (US Department of Commerce, 1991). From 1980 to 1987, when the US deficit peaked, US exports increased by a significant 50 per cent, but the damage was caused by imports that almost tripled. In other words, despite an improving US export position, the US consumption of foreign goods rose at a frenzied rate. Since 1987, imports have come under better control, increasing by about 6 per cent, while exports rose by a whopping 53 per cent, reducing the deficit by almost half.

That is, the trade deficit's modest turnaround is due to vigorous increases in US exports. Of utmost importance to the US trade future is that those exports were the strongest in those industries in which the US must remain competitive to ensure future economic growth and development, with capital goods, manufactured goods, and high-technology products leading the way (*The Fresno Bee*, 13 May, 1991).

The deficit improvement could have been better except for exasperatingly consistent increases in US imports, although the recent lagging economy probably helped keep consumer purchases in check. For the past twenty years, US imports have soared upward by more than 171 per cent to a peak of $493 billion in 1989. Although US exports continued to be strong, 1991 imports was fuelled by the escalating costs of crude oil, and the US had another huge deficit for 1991 (US Department of Commerce, 1991).

7.2 US TRADE WITH ASIA

In 1989, the US imported $189.1 billion worth of products from the Pacific Rim, while it exported $106.7 billion to that region. Overall, the US had a $82.4 billion trade deficit with the Pacific Rim for 1989 (ibid.).

Most of that Pacific Rim trade is conducted with Japan and the Four Tigers – South Korea, Hong Kong, Singapore and Taiwan. Those five Asian nations accounted for $79.6 billion dollars or 62 per cent of the total US trade deficit for 1989. US exports to those five countries have grown from $33.4 billion in 1980 to $86.4 billion in 1989, an increase of more than two times. However, during this same time period, US imports from those five nations have increased from $44.2 billion to $166.1 billion, an increase of 400 per cent. Overall, in 1989, Japan and the Four Tigers accounted for 23.7 per cent of all US exports, 33.7 per cent of all US imports, and 62 per cent of the total US trade deficit. Such a significantly growing share of the US trade position demands further analysis.

7.2.1 US–Japan Trade

US exports to Japan have grown from $22.7 billion in 1980 to $46.4 billion in 1989, while US imports from Japan have grown from $32.4 billion in 1980 to $95.5 billion in 1989. That is, although US exports to Japan have almost doubled in the 1980s, US imports from Japan have tripled. The US trade deficit with Japan in 1980 was a manageable $9.8 billion, which has mushroomed into an unmanageable deficit of $49.1 billion at the end of the decade (ibid.).

7.2.2 US–South Korea Trade

US exports to South Korea rose from $4.8 billion in 1980 to $14.7 billion in 1989, for a threefold increase. However, US imports from South Korea rose from $4.5 billion in 1989 to $20.8 billion in 1989, for a fivefold increase. As a result, the US trade surplus with South Korea of $0.3 billion in 1980 became a deficit of $6.1 billion in 1989 (ibid.).

7.2.3   US–Hong Kong Trade

US exports to Hong Kong were $2.7 billion in 1980 and more than doubled to $6.1 billion in 1989. US imports from Hong Kong were 5.1 billion in 1980 and tripled to $14.4 billion in 1989. The resultant US trade deficit of $2.5 billion in 1980 rose threefold to $8.2 billion in 1989 (ibid.).

7.2.4   US–Singapore Trade

US exports to Singapore of $3.2 billion in 1980 almost doubled to $6.3 billion in 1989, while US imports from Singapore of $3.2 billion in 1980 rose more then fourfold to $9.8 billion in 1989. Consequently, the US trade surplus with Singapore of $1.0 billion in 1980 became a trade deficit of $1.9 billion by 1989 (ibid.).

7.2.5   US–Taiwan Trade

Usable US–Taiwan trade figures are not available for the early 1980s. But the 1983 US exports to Taiwan of $5.0 billion increased to $11.3 billion in 1989. US imports from Taiwan of $12.2 billion in 1983 rose to $25.6 billion in 1989. This caused the US trade deficit with Taiwan to double in just six years – from $7.5 billion in 1983 to $14.3 billion in 1989 (ibid.).

7.3   CAUSES OF THE US TRADE DEFICIT

Despite some very recent modestly successful reductions in the US trade deficits with Japan, South Korea, and Taiwan, the US just cannot seem to catch up. For example, gains made with Japan are offset by losses to Thailand and Malaysia. As world trade continues to increase, the US share of world exports has diminished by 20 per cent in the fifteen years between 1970 and 1985 (US Department of Commerce). There seem to be two major reasons for the decline in US exports: (i) declining US competitiveness; and (ii)trade barriers established by US trading partners.

7.4   DECLINING US COMPETITIVENESS

The dramatic decline in US competitiveness may be traced to five major problems: (i) government budget deficits; (ii) reduced productivity;

(iii) reduced national savings; (iv) an over-valued dollar; and (v) lack of strategic planning.

7.4.1 Government Budget Deficits

The developmental strength and staying power of the US economy is undermined by the continuing federal practice of spending more money than it takes in. The US budget deficit reached unbelievable levels – in excess of $200 billion a year – in the mid-1980s. However, the most optimistic projections from the US Congressional Budget Office show that the US budget should be reduced to *$140 billion by 1993*. It should also be noted that the budget deficit represents somewhere between 2 per cent and 3.5 per cent of the nation's GNP. As the dollar continues to fall, cutting this deficit will be even more difficult (US Treasury Department, 1988).

7.4.2 Reduced US Productivity

Since World War II, Japan's productivity has increased at a rate that is four times that of the US. From 1947 to 1967, US productivity climbed at an acceptable 3.2 annual per cent; but, from 1967 to 1978, the annual rate dropped to an average of only 1.6 per cent. US productivity for the 1980s actually declined, and the US, once the world's productivity leader, is now last among the world's twelve largest industrialized nations. According to the US Department of Labor, weak worker productivity was recorded through the first quarter of 1991, and the problem has not improved itself (LeBoeuf, 1982; *The Fresno Bee*, 6 June, 1991).

7.4.3 Reduced US savings

There is a powerful ethic in the Japanese culture to save, and that ethic is reinforced by low spending on the part of the Japanese government. The American saving ethic has been undermined by a lack of governmental control over spending. The American people are now living the way their government lives – buy now and pay later. US personal savings as a percentage of personal income has dropped by more than 50 per cent during the 1980s, and this reduction in the capital available for investment is partly responsible for the high cost of and the lack of capital investment in US industry (Dobrzynski *et al.*, 1986).

7.4.4   The Over-Valued Dollar

The Federal Reserve Board reports that one-third of the US–Japan trade imbalance is due to an overvalued dollar. In 1985, the Big Five – the US, Japan, West Germany, France and the United Kingdom – intervened in an attempt to deflate the value of the dollar. The effort has been somewhat successful in keeping the trade deficit from worsening. Unfortunately, many trading partners are not taking part in the devaluation, and so the dollar continues to contribute to the trade problem (Stevens, 1987).

7.4.5   Lack of Strategic Planning

Among US executives, there is an urgent need for less short-term plans and more long-term strategies to meet the challenges of the future. For instance, a *Business Week*/Harris executive survey found that almost 40 per cent of the respondents admitted that their firms had no long-term plan for competing with Asia in the future (Jackson, 1986).

7.5   FOREIGN TRADE BARRIERS

Without a doubt, the single greatest contributor to the US trade deficit results from the trade barriers established by US trading partners. Trade barriers are those nationalistic measures taken by a country to protect the interests of domestic agriculture and key domestic industries. The Director General of the General Agreement on Tariffs and Trade (GATT) estimates that there are more than 500 different kinds of protectionist measures that impact 40 per cent of world trade (Sommaruga, 1985).

Japan is probably the most expert nation at using trade barriers to support national interests, and the Japanese protectionist tactics are being emulated by the Four Tigers and other nations in the Pacific Rim. Because Japan and most Asian nations lack raw materials, they must import most of the inputs for their production processes. Therefore, they must resort to drastic measures to push exports and restrict imports in order to maintain a positive balance of trade. For example, in Japan, the Ministry of International Trade and Industry (MITI) assures 'hot-house' protective environments for critical 'targeted industries' by applying a myriad of tangible trade barriers and such intangible trade barriers as: (i) overly restrictive product standards; (ii) questionable standards and testing procedures; (iii) domestic purchase requirements in government procurement;

(iv) restrictive import licensing; and (v) debatable interpretations of what constitutes dumping and export subsidies (Tsurumi, 1982).

7.6 RESOLVING THE TRADE PROBLEMS

There seems to be little, if any, relief in sight for the US trade imbalance. Japan seems bent on incurring the wrath of the Japan-bashing members of the US Congress, and a strong anti-Japan trade bill may well be forthcoming. If the Four Tigers continue to follow the Japanese lead, they may get caught up in that legislation as well. In fact, that very sentiment is captured in headlines such as 'Asian Economics are Octopuses in Tigers' Clothing' (Schlachter, 1988).

Even if Japan and the Four Tigers opened their doors to US products, a report by the International Trade Commission states that the US trade deficit will probably continue for three primary reasons: (i) low economic growth in trading nations, such as Japan; (ii) less developed nations still cannot afford to buy US goods; (iii) the dollar value is still rising against the currencies of Mexico, Canada, Taiwan, Korea, Singapore and Hong Kong ('US Trade Outlook', *Business America*, 1986).

In the meantime, momentum is building for a new Asian economic body or an Asian trading zone. The Pacific Economic Cooperation Conference was started in 1980 by fifteen Pacific basin countries, and there is talk about an Asian Common Market supported by the ASEAN group. Some Asians do not want the US or Japan to be members, fearing their dominance. In light of Europe 1992, and recent North American economic cooperation, an Asian Common market would prove to be the biggest economic event of the twenty-first century. Certainly, the Pacific Rim is the single greatest trade opportunity facing US business today.

8 Trading Blocs and US–Japan Relations in Pacific Trade and Cooperation*

Jong H. Park

8.1 INTRODUCTION

Over the past three decades, the world economy has witnessed profound transformations of historical dimensions. Best known among them has been the shift of both economic activities and international economic policy from the Atlantic to the Pacific basin countries. This shift has started with the emergence of Japan as a Pacific as well as world economic power and the remarkable success of industrialization in East Asian countries such as Korea, Taiwan, Singapore and Hong Kong – the second generation of super exporters of manufactured goods after Japan. At the same time, the rise of a unified Europe (Europe 1992) has accentuated the 'splitting' of the Atlantic basin, resulting in the formation of a North American Free Trade Area (NAFTA). Thus, the world appears to be heading towards a tripolar economic order dominated by the Big Three – the US, the European Community and Japan. The tripolar management of the world economy by the Big Three, however, may not be a desirable substitute for the 'old' economic order, which was successfully maintained only because of the leadership provided by the US as a sole hegemon in both economic and military matters. The ultimate impact of such trading blocs will be the inevitable escalation in trade conflicts and ultimately trade wars among these blocs, only to bring about a decline in the standards of living for all.

This chapter examines the trend towards regional economic integration currently taking place in the world economy, and explores the need for establishing a new mechanism for economic cooperation among the Pacific Rim countries. Special emphasis is placed on the role of Japan and the United States in Pacific Asian trade and economic cooperation.

---

*This chapter was originally published in *World Competition*, vol. 15, no. 3, March 1992 and is reprinted with the kind permission of its publisher.

8.2   TRENDS TOWARDS REGIONAL ECONOMIC INTEGRATION

Although emphatically denied by the proponents of 'Europe 1992', there is no guarantee that Europe 1992 may not evolve into a 'Fortress Europe'. At present, it appears that European regionalism is clearly a reality. Along with Europe 1992, the recent trend towards regional economic integration has been further accentuated by several important developments. Among them has been, of course, the emergence of Japan and the East Asian NICs as major economic powers in the world economy and the continued decline in America's economic position *vis-à-vis* both Europe and Pacific Asia. Japan has now become a dominant economic superpower in Pacific Asia and beyond. Given the diversity of history, culture and tradition among the Asian countries, however, it would take a long time before Japan could be accepted as a 'trusted' leader representing the interests of the Pacific Asian countries. Accordingly, at least on the surface, it seems quite unlikely that an East Asian trading bloc centred upon Japan could materialize in the near future.

However, the continued decline in America's position *vis-à-vis* both Europe and Pacific Asia could produce further pressures for new trade controls and restrictions on foreign investment, thereby moving the world economy further away from the multilateral trading system. The end of the Cold War as evidenced by the collapse of communist regimes in the Soviet Union and Eastern Europe could only heighten the prospect of trade wars among the Big Three, simply because the security imperative in the East–West conflict is now virtually diminished. With the security issues no longer serving as a major determinant of post-war international relations, the US–Japanese economic problem could escalate into greater conflict. Moreover, if the European Community were to become more protectionist and turn aggressively inward, the US could face a two-front trade war.

A series of deadlocks in the Uruguay Round of GATT talks has left little hope for restoring confidence in the liberal, multilateral trading system, and only encouraged the bilateral approach in trade policy for both the US and the EC. The planned merger between the EC and the European Free Trade Association (EFTA) and the collapse of communist regimes in Eastern Europe, which is going to encourage other European countries to join the EC, can only help establish a huge European economic bloc or European Economic Area (EEA). At the same time, the recently negotiated North American Free Trade Agreement (NAFTA) could also include other Latin American countries to expand into an American economic bloc or American Economic Area (AEA). Given these developments, it is not surprising that there has been much discussion recently about the formation of a trading bloc in East Asia. Such a move, if it materialized, could ultimately divide the world economy into three giant and, in all probability, discriminatory trading blocs.

8.3 TRIADIZATION OF THE WORLD ECONOMY?

To what extent is the trend towards regional economic integration in recent years held up by the relevant economic data? How likely is it that the world economy will disintegrate into the often mentioned three giant, discriminatory trading blocs? This section examines intraregional as well as interregional trade data for the three would-be trading blocs – the EC, North America, and East Asia.[1]

8.3.1 The European Community

Trade data in Table 6.1 indicate that the growth in intra-EC trade has outpaced the growth in trade with third countries in the rest of the world. As of 1989, about 60 per cent of the EC's total exports and 57 per cent of total imports were accounted for by intra-EC trade, a complete reversal from the 1960s when intra-EC trade was less important than trade with the rest of the world. At the same time, the percentage shares of interregional trade going to East Asia and North America have either remained the same or declined slightly during 1980 and 1989.

Schott suggests at least four main characteristics for successful trading blocs: (i) similar levels of per capita income; (ii) geographic proximity; (iii) similar or compatible trading regimes; and (iv) political commitment to regional organization (Schott, 1991, p. 2). Unlike other would-be trading blocs, the EC best exhibits all of these main characteristics. Except Greece, Portugal, Spain and Ireland, all countries in the EC are at similar levels of economic development; their markets are all proximate to each other; all the EC's external trade policy issues are coordinated in Brussels since the passage of the Treaty of Rome, which established a common market in 1957; and all member countries share a political commitment to the Community.

The merger of the EC with the EFTA member countries into a free trade or customs pact will create the world's largest single market encompassing nineteen countries and a population of 380 million. Such integration will invariably increase the percentage share of intra-European trade further. There is little doubt that the evolution of a continent-wide European

Table 8.1   Intraregional and interregional trade (percentage share of total exports and imports)

	Year	Exports to:			
		EC-12	*N. America*	*E. Asia*	*World*
EC-12	1980	53	7	4	100
	1986	57	11	5	100
	1989	60	9	6	100
N. America	1980	22	30	17	100
	1986	18	40	18	100
	1989	20	40	23	100
E. Asia	1980	15	24	34	100
	1986	14	37	28	100
	1989	16	32	35	100
	Year	Imports from:			
		EC-12	*N. America*	*E. Asia*	*World*
EC-12	1980	48	10	6	100
	1986	57	8	8	100
	1989	57	9	9	100
N. America	1980	15	32	19	100
	1986	19	31	33	100
	1989	17	33	32	100
E. Asia	1980	10	20	32	100
	1986	13	23	38	100
	1989	14	22	40	100

Source: IMF, *Direction of Trade Statistics*; adapted from J.J. Schott (1991), tables 1A and 1B.

trading bloc will make the EC far less dependent upon GATT and encourage more 'inward looking' attitudes to international economic relations and policy. Even now, GATT regards all European countries as independent, and accordingly they have power as individual countries within GATT and, of course, within the EC itself. Thus GATT is too dominated by the EC to serve as an effective and honest mediator of trade disputes involving the EC. The GATT-based multilateral trading system would be simply incompatible with the presence of such a gigantic entity as the prospective European Economic Area (EEA). Accordingly, fears about the emergence of a 'Fortress Europe' are not at all totally unfounded.

8.3.2   North America

In January 1989, the US entered a free trade agreement with Canada, its largest trading partner. The trilateral negotiations to include Mexico within the pact to form a North American free trade area are now completed. The North American Free Trade Agreement (NAFTA) would thus represent a market similar in its aggregate GNP and population to those of the EC and EFTA combined. The divergent levels of per capita incomes between Mexico and its northern neighbours loom large as a major obstacle to speedy and successful integration of the North American markets. NAFTA, however, meets the other tests of a successful trading bloc – the geographic proximity and political commitment to the goal of regional economic integration. Also, Mexico's continued efforts towards privatization of key industries and market liberalization will certainly help reduce the differences in trade regimes and regulations among the three countries in North America.

It is unlikely, however, that the evolution of a North American trading bloc will diminish support in the region for the multilateral trading system. All three countries regard their bilateral and/or trilateral trade agreements as complementing but not supplanting their multilateral trade relations (Schott, 1991). Unlike the EC, intra-North American trade (combined exports and imports) accounted for only 36.5 per cent of North America's world trade in 1989 (compared to the EC's 58.5 per cent). At the same time, North America's interregional trade is much more diversified than the EC trade – about 19 per cent with the EC and 28 per cent with East Asia, whereas the EC's trade with East Asia and North America was limited to only 7.5 per cent and 9.0 per cent respectively. Aggregate trade data in Table 8.1 indicate that the non-North American markets (especially those of East Asia) are too important for these countries (the United States in particular) to turn aggressively inward in their trade policy in the near future. NAFTA is essentially a US-initiated defensive strategy against the ongoing process of Europe 1992 on the one hand, and the emergence of Japan as an economic superpower on the other. Few, however, speak of the prospect of NAFTA becoming a 'Fortress North America' or 'New North American Home'. The move towards NAFTA, if anything, is a second-best alternative to the multilateral trading system in the event that the Uruguay Round of the GATT falters.

8.3.3   East Asia/Pacific Basin

Recent developments towards regional economic integration in Europe and North America have directly contributed to much discussion about the formation of a trading bloc in the Pacific Asian region. Two forms of a potential East Asian trading bloc have been suggested and debated: one which is centred upon Japan and the other, a much broader one in scope, encompassing both Japan and the United States at the core and other countries in the Pacific basin.

The Japan-centred East Asian trading bloc is not a new concept. Its historical precedent goes back to the 'Greater East Asia Co-Prosperity Sphere' created by imperialist Japan during World War II. The argument for the current co-prosperity zone, however, while spearheaded by Japan, is purely economic in nature, and its rationale is based upon the ever increasing interdependence in trade and investment in the region. Some even suggest that economic factors would eventually override the sharp memory of the historical precedents and the deep-seated animosity towards Japan by her East Asian neighbours. In fact, a Japan-centred trading bloc may already have been developing on a *de facto* basis because of much closer economic ties now taking place between Japan and other East Asian countries. For instance, during the 1980s the growth in Japan's trade with other Asian countries has outpaced that of its trade with the US; there has been a rather dramatic increase in Japanese imports of manufactured goods from other Asian countries; and Japanese FDI in Asia has also increased substantially.

The Japanese trade and investment within East Asia has grown substantially during the latter part of the 1980s. As can be seen in Tables 8.2 and 8.3, however, trade and investment data also indicate that the growth in Japanese trade and investment has not been limited to East Asian countries alone. While Japan's combined export and import trade with North America has remained at about 33 per cent, her trade with the EC countries has also increased substantially from 9.5 per cent in 1985 to 17.3 per cent in 1990.

During the latter half of the 1980s, Japanese FDI has also exhibited a similar growth pattern. This is shown in Table 8.3: FDI in East Asia quadrupled from $2.0 billion to more than $8.0 billion from 1985 to 1988; so did FDI in North America and Europe for the same period. As of 1989, over 40 per cent of the cumulative Japanese FDI is accounted for by FDI in North America, followed by 22.3 per cent in East Asia and 16.2 per cent in Europe. Thus during the 1980s the growing internationalization of the Japanese economy has not been limited to East Asia alone.

While the growing regional economic integration now taking place in Europe has caused a doubling of the percentage share of its intra-EC trade from a little over 34 per cent in 1960 to 59 per cent in 1988, the growth in intra-Pacific basin trade has been equally dramatic, rising from 40 per cent in 1960 to 66 per cent in 1988. This is summed up in Table 6.4. The table

Table 8.2　Japanese Trade[a] with Regional Groups (percentage share of total trade)

Year	East Asia	North America	EC
1980	25.5	24.3	9.1
1981	24.0	25.4	9.3
1983	25.0	28.8	9.7
1985	23.5	34.4	9.5
1987	26.5	34.8	14.6
1988	28.0	33.3	15.7
1989	28.8	33.2	15.7
1990[b]	28.8	31.9	17.3

Notes:
[a]Combined exports and imports.
[b]Annualized data for January–September.
Source: IMF, OECD, and Bank of Japan data; adapted from J.J. Schott (1991) p. 11, table 2.

Table 8.3　Japanese foreign direct investment, 1985–89

Year	East Asia[a] Billion US $	%	North America[b] Billion US $	%	EC[c] Billion US $	%	Total Billion US $
1985	2.0	16.4	5.5	45.1	1.9	15.6	12.2
1986	3.0	14.8	10.4	46.6	3.5	15.7	22.3
1987	6.3	18.9	15.4	46.1	6.6	19.8	33.4
1988	8.2	17.4	22.3	47.4	9.1	19.4	47.0
Cumulative to 03/89	41.5	22.3	75.1	40.3	30.2	16.2	186.4

Notes:
[a]Includes People's Republic of China.
[b]U.S. and Canada, excluding Mexico.
[c]Includes Switzerland.
Source: Data from Ministry of Finance, Japan; adapted from J.J. Schott (1991) p. 12, table 3.

provides a bird's eye view of the shift of international economic activities from the Atlantic to the Pacific basin countries[2] that has taken place during the past three decades. The argument for the concept of a 'broadbased' trading bloc in the Pacific Asia region is essentially based upon this

Table 8.4   European Community and the Pacific basin in world trade, 1960–88
(percentages)

	1960[a]	1970[a]	1980[b]	1988[c]
European Community				
Share of world trade	22.2	39.6	35.1	39.1
Intra-EC trade	34.6	49.4	50.9	58.6
Growth of EC trade		24.2[d]	6.1[e]	6.0[f]
Pacific basin[g]				
Share of world trade	28.8	33.8	32.1	40.1
Intra-PB trade	40.3	56.7	54.3	65.7
Growth of PB trade		12.5[d]	6.7[e]	8.7[f]

Notes:
[a]EC had six member countries.
[b]EC had nine member countries.
[c]EC had twelve member countries.
[d]Average annual growth rate for 1960–70.
[e]Average annual growth rate for 1970–80.
[f]Average annual growth rate for 1980–88.
[g]Pacific basin includes fifteen countries of the Pacific Economic Cooperation Conference.
Source: World Bank data compiled by the East–West Center; adapted from L.B. Krause (1991) p. 2, table 1.

observed shift in international economic activities and economic policy from the Atlantic to the Pacific and the ever increasing importance of the Pacific Asian region in the world economy (Krause, 1990, 1991; Drysdale, 1988a,b). In addition, this broadbased trading bloc in the Pacific, which includes both Pacific economic powers, Japan and the United States, is clearly aimed at ameliorating the ongoing political and cultural concerns and fears in the East Asian countries about Japanese economic, if not military, domination in the region. In such an arrangement, the US would help shield the smaller Asian countries from Japanese hegemony.

Others, however, argue for such broadbased regional grouping in the Pacific for other reasons, contending that 'the United States is a Pacific country', and that 'in the case of actual or threatened disputes with Europe, a unified Pacific response will be the only effective way to mount countervailing pressure without starting a mutually destructive economic conflict' (Krause, 1991, pp. 9, 12).

Table 8.5   Size openness and income growth of Pacific Asian economies, 1965–88

Country	Population (million) 1988	Ratio of Exports to GDP (%)		Per Capita Income	
		1965	1988	US $ 1988	Annual growth rate 1965–88 (%)
Japan	123	11	13	21 000	4.3
Hong Kong	6	71	136	9 200	6.3
Korea	42	9	41	3 600	6.8
Taiwan	20	19	61	5 400	7.1
Singapore	3	123	138	9 100	7.2
Indonesia	175	5	25	440	4.3
Malaysia	17	42	67	1 940	4.0
Philippines	60	17	25	630	1.6
Thailand	55	16	34	1 000	4.0
China	1088	4	14	330	5.4
Australia	17	15	17	12 800	1.8
New Zealand	3	22	28	12 300	1.7
Canada	26	19	26	17 000	2.7
United States	246	6	11	19 800	1.6
World	4736	12	21	3 500	1.5

Sources: World Bank, *World Development Report 1990*; Council for Economic Planning and Development, *Taiwan Statistical Data Book, 1990*.

8.4   ROLE OF JAPAN AND THE US IN THE PACIFIC ASIAN REGION

Both of the two suggested forms of regional groupings in the Pacific Asia region (a Japan-centred East Asian bloc and a broadbased Pacific basin bloc) miserably fail to pass the basic characteristics tests of a successful trading bloc.[3] However, the fundamental problem is that neither form of regional trading bloc in the Pacific Asian region is desirable. Accordingly, the possibility for either of the forms of regional integration to materialize should be seriously considered and discouraged. Herein lies the most important role and responsibility that must be accepted and shared by the two Pacific economic powers, Japan and the United States, in preventing a regional trading bloc from taking place in the Pacific Asian region.

No region in the world has surpassed the remarkable economic performance achieved by the East Asian countries in the past three decades, first with the emergence of Japan as a Pacific economic power, followed by the four East Asian NICs, which, in turn, are now closely followed by the ASEAN countries, the second-tier Asian NICs. This remarkable success in industrialization and economic growth in the region during the period 1965–88 is shown in Table 8.5. Increased participation in international trade (as shown by increased openness measured by the percentage share of exports to GDP for many Asian countries) has been known to have contributed to successful export-led growth for these countries, especially for the four East Asian NICs. While the per capita income for the world has grown at only 1.5 per cent during 1965 to 1988, Japan's income growth was 4.3 per cent compared to 1.6 per cent for the United States; the income growth for the Asian NICs ranged from 6.3 per cent to 7.2 per cent, and for the ASEAN countries a little over 4 per cent except for the Philippines with a poor growth rate of 1.6 per cent. China's open door policy has also brought about a remarkable per capita income growth rate of 5.4 per cent.

During the 1980s at least two key developments have taken place, seriously affecting and complicating bilateral US–Japan relations and their role in the Pacific Asian region. One is that Japan has caught up with the other industrial countries in the West; Japan's per capita income now exceeds that of the US. The other is that a massive trade surplus for Japan and deficits for the US have turned Japan into a major creditor and the US into a net debtor. This reversal of the post-war economic positions of the two countries has, of course, marked the beginning of the so-called "US–Japan economic problem" and the ensuing trade conflicts. Unless the US–Japan economic problem is soon resolved, the continued expansion in trade and economic growth in the Pacific basin countries (and in the rest of the world for that matter) are very likely to be constrained by the future changes in US–Japan economic relations.

8.4.1 Dependence of Pacific Asian Trade on the US and Japan

As shown in Table 8.6, Japan and the US are major trading partners. For Japan the US is the largest trading partner; the US accounted for 37 per cent of Japan's exports and 20 per cent of her imports. For the US Japan is the second largest trading partner after Canada, accounting for 11 per cent of US exports and 20 per cent of US imports.

For the majority of Pacific Asian countries, both the US and Japan are their major trading partners. Accordingly, much of the intra-regional trade in the Pacific Asian region is accounted for by trade with the US and Japan.

Table 8.6   Dependence of Pacific Asian trade on the US and Japan, 1988

Country	Ratio of Exports To GDP	Export Share and Dependence			Import Share (%)	
	(%)	To US	Dep.[a]	To Japan	Dep.[a]	From US	From Japan
U.S.	11	—	—	11	1.2	—	20
Japan	13	37	4.8	—	—	20	—
Korea	41	36	14.8	15	6.2	21	25
Taiwan	61	48	29.3	11	6.7	24	28
Hong Kong	136	44	59.8	3	4.1	9	23
Singapore	128	21	29.0	9	12.4	15	17
Malaysia	67	13	8.7	25	16.8	15	23
Thailand	34	20	6.8	13	4.4	11	26
Indonesia	25	23	5.8	49	12.3	18	24
Philippines	25	36	9.0	19	4.8	25	14
China	14	9	1.3	22	3.1	12	36

Note:
[a]Trade dependency shows the percentage share of each country's output absorbed by the US and Japan, and is obtained by multiplying the ratio of exports to GDP by export share.
Sources: IMF, *International Financial Statistics and Direction of Trade*; *Taiwan Statistical Data Book*, 1990. World Bank, *World Development Report 1990*.

From the export side, the US is the largest export market for Asian countries except the primary product/raw material exporting countries – namely, Malaysia (tin), Indonesia (oil and gas), and Australia (coal and iron ore) for which Japan is the largest export market. For the East Asian NICs especially, the dependence of their exports on the US market is astoundingly high; the shares of their exports going to the US were 21 per cent for Singapore, 36 per cent for Korea, 44 per cent for Hong Kong and 48 per cent for Taiwan. Coupled with their high exports/GDP ratios, the impact of their export trade with the US on their economies is obvious as shown in column (3) of Table 8.6: about 15 per cent of Korea's total output was absorbed by the US, 29 per cent for Taiwan, 60 per cent for Hong Kong, and 29 per cent for Singapore. Thus, the economies of the East Asian NICs are very susceptible to fluctuations in US import demand.

Table 8.7   Foreign direct investment in Asia

Country	Total FDI (Billion $US)	FDI Shares From: (%)			Date
		Japan	U.S.	ROW	
Hong Kong	$1.5	22	54	24	9/84
Korea	2.0	48	30	22	6/84
Taiwan	3.3	30	42	29	12/84
Singapore	5.0	20	33	47	6/83
Thailand	7.0	23	9	68	12/83
Indonesia	14.4	35	8	58	12/83
Malaysia	3.4	18	7	75	12/83
Philippines	2.5	16	52	32	12/83

Note: ROW = Rest of the World
Source: E.J. Lincoln (1989a) p. 9, table 4.

From the import side, the roles of the US and Japan are reversed. Japan is the major source of imports for all Asian countries except the Philippines, whose largest share of imports is from the US mainly because of historical ties. Japan has been the major supplier of parts and components for manufactured goods to the Asian NICs, who in turn supplied the bulk of their manufactured goods to the US. This trade pattern among the three parties (the United States, Japan, and the East Asian NICs) has created the so-called 'triangular trade' problem unique to Pacific Asian trade.

In sum, both Japan and the US are major trading partners for all Asian countries in the Pacific. True, the ascendancy of Japan as a dominant economic power in recent years has increased its economic ties with other Asian neighbours. In no sense, however, has Japan replaced the US as a major economic player in the Pacific Asian region. In fact, both Japan and the US have come to dominate the trade pattern of these Pacific Asian countries more than before. This is largely due to the shift of economic activities and economic policy from the Atlantic to the Pacific and the 'splitting' of the Atlantic basin brought about by the move towards regional economic integration in Europe and North America.

8.4.2   US and Japanese Foreign Direct Investment in the Pacific

Special economic ties between the two Pacific economic powers and the Asian countries can also be observed in terms of their foreign direct investment (FDI) in the region. Table 8.7 shows that investment patterns are similar to those of trade; both Japan and the US are the largest investors in most cases. In the East Asian NICs, the US FDI dominates Japan's FDI except in Korea where Japanese FDI accounted for 48 per cent of the total FDI compared to the US's 30 per cent. In the ASEAN countries, Japan's FDI dominates that of the US except in the Philippines (again beacause of its historical ties with the US). Only in the case of Malaysia is neither Japan nor the US the single largest investor. Singapore is the largest investor in Malaysia.

As a resource-poor country, Japan's FDI in Asia has been primarily for resource development projects in the ASEAN countries, especially in Indonesia. Despite the lower wages available in the Asian LDCs, Japanese FDI in manufacturing has accounted for only a small portion of its FDI in Asia. This can be explained at least partly by the fact that, unlike the US firms, Japanese firms have sought to cut labour costs through automation rather than moving abroad to take advantage of the lower wage rates (Lincoln, 1989a, p. 10). Japanese FDI in manufacturing has been primarily motivated to supply products to local markets or to third markets, especially the US, by circumventing increased import protectionism in these countries.

One of the new perceptions that prevails in Japan these days is that other Asian countries, especially the four East Asian NICs, are quite capable of producing goods of sufficient quality for the Japanese market. Accordingly, they now see Asia as a base for producing goods for consumption in Japan rather than for local consumption or for export to third markets as in the past (ibid., pp. 14–15). Such a new perception, coupled with the stronger yen, is likely to provide strong incentives for Japanese FDI to increase in the Pacific Asian region.

8.4.3 Foreign aid and US–Japan Relations

Unlike the areas of trade and investment, Japan has replaced the US as the major donor of foreign aid for Asian LDCs. According to OECD data, Japan's official development assistance (ODA) has been growing at 5.7 per cent per year during the period 1982–1987 while the growth rate of US ODA has been limited to only 2.2 per cent (OECD, 1988, p. 172).

As shown in Table 8.8, Japanese ODA in Asia has been concentrated in the ASEAN countries. In 1987, half or more of the total net ODA received by each of the south-east Asian countries came from Japan. Bilateral aid from the US for these countries except for the Philippines has been virtually none. Even for the Philippines, the US was the second largest donor accounting for 30 per cent of the total net ODA inflows compared to Japan's 49 per cent. For all ASEAN countries as a whole, 55 per cent of

Table 8.8   Net official development assistance receipts in Asia, 1987

Country	Total net ODA receipts (Million $ US)	Japan		U.S.		Multilateral agencies	
Malaysia	$363	$276	(76%)	$0	(0%)	$11	(3%)
Indonesia	1245	709	(57)	36	(3%)	112	(9)
Philippines	775	379	(49)	230	(30)	69	(9)
Singapore	23	11	(48)	1	(4)	6	(26)
Thailand	506	302	(60)	23	(5)	75	(15)
ASEAN	2549	1399	(55)	290	(11)	262	(10)
China	1449	553	(39)	0	(0)	588	(40)

Source: OECD data; compiled from Lincoln (1989a) p. 12, table 5.

total net ODA came from Japan, 11 per cent from the US, and 10 per cent from other multilateral organizations. Recently, Japan has also become a major aid donor to China, providing almost 40 per cent of China's total ODA receipts in 1987.

It is evident that Japan's aid policy has clearly focused on Asia while the US has extended more assistance to strategically important areas in the world. Japan's ODA policy has been criticized, among other things, for a high ratio of tied aid (presumably intended to promote the interests of the Japanese manufacturers), for being excessively motivated by her commercial interests, and for disregarding questions of economic development as well as a charity and/or strategic rationale for aid in the ODA recipient countries. To discourage the commercial use of aid by Japan and to encourage Japan to increase its aid and contribute more to international peace and stability, some argue for creating a mechanism for US–Japan aid coordination (Orr, 1990). Regardless of whether Japan's aid is tied or not, and regardless of whether Japan's ODA is commercially biased or not, there is no doubt that 'the increasing presence of Japanese aid will gradually expand Japan's economic clout in other fields' (ibid., p. 488). This will be the case especially for the Pacific Asian region.

8.4.4   US Trade Deficits and US–Japan Trade Conflicts

As noted earlier, in the 1980s one of the key developments that has brought important changes in bilateral US–Japan economic relations has been massive trade surpluses for Japan and deficits for the US, transforming Japan into a major creditor and the US into a net debtor. This reversal of the post-war economic positions of the two countries has fuelled the US–Japan trade conflicts. As is widely known, the US's response to this crisis, unfortunately, has been the increased use of 'process protection'[4] and unilateral protectionism in its trade policy, thereby moving further away from the multilateral approach to trade issues.

Among the multitude of suggested causes of the US trade deficits, three major diagnoses stand out: (i) misguided macroeconomic policies in the early 1980s; (ii) gradual changes in the global competitive environment and the alleged decline in US competitiveness in the world markets; and (iii) unfair trading practices by foreign trading partners. It is unfortunate that out of these suggested causes, perhaps the least important cause of the trade deficit – unfair foreign trade practices – receives most attention in the current debate on the problems of US trade and the US–Japan economic problem.

Even if some serious cases of unfair trade practices exist in many countries, including Japan and the US, these practices, however unfair they may be, cannot be the major cause of today's US trade problems. The US trade deficits occurred *across* a wide range of its major trading partners, not just Japan. It is simply inconceivable to believe that unfair trading practices increased in these countries and regions at the same time, and no available evidence indicates that they did. Of course, the US bilateral trade deficits with Japan accounted for almost one third of the US global trade deficits in the latter part of the 1980s. That does not, however, provide us with any clear-cut evidence as to whether or not Japan has engaged in unfair trade practices more extensively than others, and whether or not Japanese markets have been more closed than others.

None the less, the belief that the trade deficit is due mainly to unfair trading practices from abroad, especially from Japan, has led to a Congressional consensus encouraging the greater application of trade laws in order to support 'fair trade' and ensure a 'level playing field' for US firms. As a result, US trade policy has moved increasingly towards process protection and unilateral protectionism, and there has been little indication that the US–Japan trade conflicts are waning.

The US must avoid the continued drift towards a protectionist and bilateral approach in its trade policy. Even though the case for the US–Canada Free Trade Agreement has been argued as harmless and at best complementing but not supplanting the multilateral trading system, it is doubtful whether the same argument can be made for the prospective NAFTA. With the security imperatives gone following the end of the Cold War, the US's continued move towards such a regional approach to international relations could only aggravate the US–Japan economic relations in the Pacific.

The bulk of the US trade deficit in the 1980s can be traced to internal macroeconomic imbalances, namely the net national dissavings primarily caused by huge budget deficits at home (J. Park, 1990, p. 42). Such being the case, the US must put its fiscal house in order. And Japan must provide a better response to the unprecedented rise in the value of the yen. This can be accomplished by allowing a rapid increase in imports in response to the high yen and by finding ways of reducing import barriers.

8.4.5 US–Japan Economic Cooperation in the Pacific Asian Region

The US–Japan relationship in the Pacific is certainly one of a special kind and may be viewed as a contentious marriage: 'The husband and wife have been together for some time, conflicts are frequent, divorce is often mentioned, but because of the mutual advantage of being together, neither wants to go it alone' (Krause, 1991, p. 14).

An examination of the major shifts in economic forces and US–Japan relations in the Pacific indicates that a regional grouping among the Pacific Asian countries no longer appears to be as unrealistic and undesirable as it did a few years back. In addition, the Brussels agreement of 22 October 1991 to merge the EC and EFTA to create the European Economic Area (*Wall Street Journal*, 24 October 1991, p. A 16), coupled with the recently completed NAFTA, could only heighten Japan's interests in any form of an Asian trading bloc.

More than anything, economic matters will continue to reign as the dominant determinant of post-Cold War international relations in the 1990s. The substantial role reversal in the Pacific Asian region between Japan and the US in key economic relations will no doubt boost Japan's image at the expense of the US Japan will become a growing market for Asian manufactured goods, gradually replacing the US market; Japan will become a major source of FDI; and Japan's ODA will continue to grow. Given these developments, the animosity and antagonism against Japan by her Asian neighbours will eventually diminish.[5]

The Japan-centred Asian trading bloc that excludes the US, however, is clearly undesirable; such a bloc could only escalate the US–Japan economic problem into greater conflict, and speed up the process of disintegration of the world economy into three giant, discriminatory trading blocs. Trade wars are simply too high a risk whatever the favourable effects of trade creation and other dynamic effects that regional economic integration might produce. One of the most important challenges for both Japan and the US in the 1990s and beyond is to find ways of refining and strengthening the process of 'collective leadership' in global economic management, especially in the Pacific Asian region. Efforts by both parties to establish a framework for broader Pacific economic cooperation is certainly a first step towards meeting such a challenge.

8.5   SUMMARY AND CONCLUSIONS

At present, the world economy appears to be in the process of disintegrating into three giant, discriminatory trading blocs. One of the profound postwar developments has been the shift of both economic activities and international economic policy from the Atlantic to the Pacific basin countries. This shift has started with the emergence of Japan as a Pacific as well as world economic power and the remarkable success of industrialization and rapid economic growth in other East Asian countries. At the same time, the rise of a unified Europe has accentuated the splitting of the Atlantic basin, creating a North American trading bloc. It is feared that the ultimate impact of such trading blocs will be inevitable escalation in trade conflicts and trade wars among the competing blocs.

This chapter has examined intra-regional as well as interregional trade and other economic data for the three would be trading blocs – the EC, North America and East Asia. Special emphasis was placed on the role of Japan and the United States in Pacific Asian trade and cooperation. The US–Japan relations in the Pacific are one of a special kind, akin to a 'contentious marriage' aptly summed up by Professor Krause. This special relationship between the two was examined in terms of (i) their Pacific Asian export and import trade; (ii) US and Japanese investments in the Pacific; (iii) official development assistance; and (iv) US–Japan trade conflicts.

Examination of these key economic relations between the US and Japan in the Pacific indicates that a regional grouping among the Pacific Asian countries no longer appears to be as unrealistic and undesirable as it did a few years ago. The most recent Brussels agreement to merge the EC and EFTA to create the EEA on the one hand, and the newly created NAFTA on the other, simply help to raise the voice for the need for an Asian trading bloc. With the end of the Cold War, economic matters are likely to determine international relations. Although Japan has not yet 'replaced' the US in all areas, there has been substantial role reversal in some key economic relations in the Pacific Asian region. This, coupled with the continued relative decline in the US's economic hegemony in the world, could only increase the possibility for a Japan-centred Asian trading bloc to materialize.

The Japan-centred Asian trading bloc which excludes the US and other non-Asian countries, however, should be discouraged. One of the most important challenges in the 1990s and beyond for both Japan and the United States as two Pacific economic powers is to search for ways of preventing such a trading bloc from taking place through collaboration and cooperation.

NOTES AND REFERENCES

1. The EC includes twelve member countries – Belgium, Britain, Denmark, France, Germany, Greece, Ireland, Italy, Luxembourg, Netherlands, Portugal, and Spain. North America includes the United States, Canada and Mexico. East Asia here includes Japan, four East Asian NICs (Korea, Taiwan, Hong Kong, and Singapore), four ASEAN member countries other than Singapore and Brunei (Indonesia, Thailand, the Phillipines and Malaysia), and two countries from Australasia (Australia and New Zealand). It should be noted that the definition of 'East Asia' varies according to individual writers.
2. Pacific basin countries here include five developed countries (the United States, Canada, Japan, Australia and New Zealand), four East Asian NICs (Korea, Taiwan, Hong Kong and Singapore), ASEAN countries (Brunei, Indonesia, Malaysia, the Phillipines and Thailand), and China.
3. A broad based Pacific basin trading bloc would even fail to meet the geographic proximity test, let alone the tests of similar stages of economic development, similar trading regimes, and political commitment to regional integration. Likewise, a Japan-centred trading bloc would also fail to meet all the tests except the geographic proximity test.
4. Protectionism has become embedded in the administrative 'process' of determining import relief and of retaliating against foreign trade practices that are deemed to have an 'unjustifiable, unreasonable, or discriminatory' effect on US trade. The major channels of process protection include: Section 201 and Section 301 of the Trade Act of 1974, antidumping and countervailing duty laws, voluntary export restraints (VERs), and Super 301 provisions in the Trade Act of 1988.
5. Some instances such as the death of the Showa emperor, a symbol of Asian distrust of Japan, and the willingness of all Asian countries to attend the funeral of the emperor in 1989, and the public apology by the Japanese prime minister to the people of Korea for its 36-year colonial rule, all tend to help speed up the process of healing.

9   Agricultural Liberalization and Its Implications for US–Japan Trade Relations[1]

Hiro Lee and David Roland-Holst

9.1   INTRODUCTION

Japanese agricultural protection has become a serious liability in multilateral negotiations and a source of chronic disequilibrium in the domestic economy. While Japan is the world's largest importer of agricultural products, it maintains some of the highest rates of effective protection against agricultural imports (Anderson and Tyers, 1987; Honma and Hayami, 1986). As its current surplus surged to $118 billion in 1992 and continues to a record level in 1993, external pressure for agricultural trade liberalization has increased sharply. Recently, the United States has intensified bilateral negotiations to liberalize the Japanese agricultural market. Although Japan has agreed to replace quantitative restrictions with *ad valorem* tariffs on some products (e.g. beef and fresh oranges), it has strongly resisted the removal of import quotas on many other commodities, rice in particular.

As the world's largest agricultural producer and exporter of agricultural commodities, the US has focused its policy on domestic and international marketing of its agricultural surplus. Although it maintains import restrictions on some products, including quotas on sugar and dairy products, effective US agricultural protection is below the average of its industrial trading partners.

In many industrialized countries, domestic political forces often prevail over efficiency considerations in trade policy. Domestic political origins of agricultural protection generally arise from the need to appease decisive rural voting blocs, defend cultural integrity, and secure a national subsistence base. The opportunity cost of protection, however, is not simply the sum of efficiency losses and the difference between changes in consumer and producer surpluses resulting from higher prices, but includes detrimental general equilibrium effects on the whole economy. Such effects include extensive indirect price distortions through upstream and downstream links to the protected sectors, factor market distortions which misdirect domestic employment and investment, and a wide variety of wasteful

84

rent seeking activities. In addition, import restrictions distort international prices from the perspective of domestic producers, limiting the economy's ability to exploit gains from trade and restraining full participation in a growing international marketplace.

Japanese agricultural protection appears also to have caused an economy-wide distortion in its capital markets. Japanese agricultural policy has contributed significantly to the meteoric rise in real estate values during the 1980s. This has happened in two ways. First, direct protection for agriculture apparently has been capitalized into land values. A second and more significant distortionary component is the scarcity premium on non-agricultural land induced by restrictive land use policies which favour agriculture.

Evaluating the allocative effects of sectoral policies like agricultural protection requires a detailed structural analysis. In this chapter, we use a computable general equilibrium (CGE) model to assess the effects of agricultural liberalization in bilateral trade between the United States and Japan. Japanese agricultural protection is large enough to exert significant influence domestically and in trade relations with the US. At the same time, the US–Japan trade relationship is a unique and complex one and a number of interesting aspects of it emerge in this study.

In section 9.2, we discuss the overall structure of the two economies and their trade relations with one another and with the rest of the world. We summarize the structure and functioning of the CGE model in Section 9.3, and assess the results of policy simulations in section 9.4. Finally, we offer some concluding remarks in section 9.5.

9.2 THE STRUCTURE OF PRODUCTION AND TRADE

Table 9.1 summarizes the main structural features of the US and Japan in 1985.[2] As the first column makes apparent, Japanese sectoral output is generally less diversified than in the US. Both economies have large service sectors, but the US is significantly more service oriented while Japan is more reliant on manufacturing. The composition of value added (column 2) differs substantially from that of total output and between the two countries. Most non-service sectors are more dependent on intermediate goods, and thus they generate less direct income to labour and non-labour factors than their total levels of activity would suggest. Service oriented sectors (sectors 10–12) generate a disproportionate share of direct national income in both countries.

The composition of exports and imports for Japan and the US are quite different, both in bilateral trade and in trade with the rest of the

Table 9.1   Sectoral composition of output, income and trade, 1985 (percentages)[a]

		(1)	(2)	(3)	(4)	(5)	(6)	(7)	(8)
Japan		X	VA	E	M	E/X	M/Q	E^b/E	M^b/M
1	Cereals	1.7	1.1	0.0	1.9	0.1	6.3	3.5	45.5
2	MeatPoult	0.9	0.3	0.1	2.1	0.7	12.7	5.4	21.7
3	Dairy	0.4	0.2	0.0	0.2	0.3	2.5	0.0	3.0
4	Sugar	0.1	0.0	0.0	0.4	0.1	17.8	0.0	1.3
5	AgForFsh	1.5	1.8	0.2	7.0	0.9	22.5	87.1	19.8
6	PetMining	2.7	0.6	0.8	41.8	2.4	49.3	4.9	2.1
7	FoodProc	4.1	2.1	0.5	3.0	0.9	4.3	28.8	25.0
8	NonDrMfg	10.3	7.1	8.4	11.1	6.4	6.5	21.1	23.5
9	DurMfg	20.3	15.4	71.6	15.7	27.6	6.1	38.5	33.8
10	TrComUt	8.7	9.8	8.3	5.6	7.5	4.1	2.8	15.0
11	Trade	10.2	13.2	6.2	3.9	4.8	2.4	38.0	49.0
12	Services	39.1	48.5	3.8	7.2	0.8	1.1	82.4	9.5
	Wgt Avg					7.8	6.2	35.4	15.7
United States		X	VA	E	M	E/X	M/Q	E^b/E	M^b/M
1	Cereals	1.1	0.6	3.1	0.1	11.9	0.4	15.0	0.8
2	MeatPoult	1.5	0.4	1.3	1.0	3.4	3.8	19.4	0.2
3	Dairy	0.8	0.3	0.2	0.1	1.0	1.0	1.4	0.0
4	Sugar	0.1	0.1	0.1	0.3	2.6	17.2	5.0	0.0
5	AgForFsh	1.0	0.9	2.8	3.1	11.0	17.0	26.8	2.3
6	PetMining	5.2	3.7	4.2	12.2	3.2	12.9	11.5	0.2
7	FoodProc	2.6	1.6	2.9	2.8	4.6	6.5	13.6	2.5
8	NonDrMfg	8.9	6.5	12.4	16.3	5.6	10.5	11.5	5.6
9	DurMfg	14.0	11.6	43.1	47.1	12.4	18.9	6.7	29.6
10	TrComUt	9.2	9.9	11.9	2.4	5.2	1.6	3.8	4.9
11	Trade	11.1	11.7	8.0	1.2	2.9	0.7	12.8	11.6
12	Services	44.6	52.7	10.1	13.5	0.9	0.8	3.6	11.6
	Wgt Avg					4.0	5.9	8.5	17.9

Notes:
[a] (1) Gross output shares, (2) total value-added shares, (3) export shares, (4) import shares, (5) ratios of exports to gross output, (6) ratios of imports to total demand, (7) ratios of bilateral exports to total exports, (8) ratios of bilateral imports to total imports.
[b] bilateral.

Source: MITI (1989).

world. Column (3) presents the sectoral shares of exports for each country, and these patterns of overall trade dependence are consistent with conventional wisdom. The lion's share of Japanese exports are durable manufactures, accounting for 71.6 per cent of total exports. Although US exports are also led by durables, their composition is considerably more diversified than Japan's. Exports of agricultural products (sectors 1–5) from the US dominate those of Japan both in relative (7.5 per cent versus 0.3 per cent combined) and absolute terms (the US is the world's largest agricultural exporter). In addition, the US export share for services is almost three times that of Japan's service sector.

Column (5) lists the ratios of exports to domestic output for each sector and country, giving a sectoral measure of trade dependence. In Japan, the most export dependent sector by far is durable manufactures, 27.6 per cent of which are shipped abroad. The pattern is more dispersed in the US, where both primary and secondary sectors have significant but moderate levels of export dependence. Durable manufacturing (12.4 per cent) leads cereals (11.9 per cent) and other agricultural products, forestry, and fisheries (AgForFsh: 11.0 per cent), yet no sector exports more than 15% of its output.

Columns (4) and (6) give the corresponding levels of national and sectoral dependence on imports. As predicted, Japan is very reliant on imported petroleum and mining products, which represent 41.8 per cent of their total import bill. This is followed by durable (15.7 per cent) and non-durable (11.1 per cent) manufactured imports, but the import shares of manufactures in Japan are considerably smaller than those in other industrialized countries. In contrast, the US imports are dominated by durable (47.1 per cent) and nondurable manufactures (16.3 per cent), which together account for almost two-thirds of all imports.[3]

The last two columns list the percentage of bilateral trade in total trade for the two countries. The patterns which emerge here are quite interesting and they imply that extensive gains from bilateral trade exist for the US and Japan. Japan relies on the US to purchase a large proportion of its secondary and tertiary sector exports, while the US sends a large share of its primary sector exports to Japan. Likewise, Japan imports a large portion of its primary products from the US and the latter depends on the former for almost a third of its imported durable manufactures. What emerges from this data is a highly elaborated trade relationship between the two countries.

9.3 A US–JAPAN CGE MODEL

The CGE model described here is typical of most comparative static, multi-sectoral, economywide models in use today.[4] The present model differs from the mainstream of CGE modelling in a variety of aspects. Most significantly, it is a two-country model, so both the US and Japan are fully endogenous at a twelve sector level of disaggregation. Trade between the two countries is thus endogenous, while their individual trade flows with respect to the rest of the world (ROW) are each governed by the small country assumption.[5] The resulting six sets of sectoral trade flows are then governed by two endogenous price equations (US–Japan imports and exports) and four exogenous price systems (US–ROW and Japan–ROW imports and exports).

The extent of price adjustments, as well as the volume and pattern of trade creation and trade diversion, are all important factors in determining the ultimate welfare effects of bilateral trade policy. In the present model, import demand and export supply are characterized by the so-called differentiated product specification. That is, domestic demand is constituted of goods differentiated by origin (domestic imports from the trading partner and imports from ROW) and domestic production is supplied to differentiated destinations (domestic market, exports to the trading partner, and exports to ROW). A number of similar devices occur in the CGE literature (e.g. de Melo and Tarr, 1992). This model uses a nested CES specification for demand and a nested CET for supply.

In this model, every sector is characterized by constant returns to scale and perfect competition. Although previous studies have shown that the existence of scale economies in manufacturing sectors could affect the costs and benefits of trade policy, the extent of scale economies in the highly aggregated non-durable and durable manufacturing sectors would be relatively small and unrealized plant-level economies are unlikely to play a major role in trade expansion between these two large economies.[6]

Our model is calibrated to a two-country social accounting matrix (SAM) for the US and Japan, estimated for the year 1985. This SAM provides detailed economywide transactions between firms, households, government, as well as bilateral and multilateral trade for the two countries.[7] Structural parameters of the model are determined by calibration, direct estimation, or imputation from other sources. The appendix contains the sectoral rates of nominal import protection and *ad valorem* equivalents of non-tariff barriers in Japan and the US.

9.4 SIMULATION RESULTS

What is the opportunity cost of agricultural protection to the US and Japan? We provide a partial answer to this question by first evaluating the gains from trade the two countries would enjoy if they liberalized bilateral relations, with particular reference to the removal of trade barriers in agricultural products. Second, we evaluate the effects of US and Japanese removal of trade barriers on all imports, regardless of source. While multilateral liberalization may yield more extensive efficiency gains than bilateral arrangements, enormous political barriers and powerful agricultural organizations in Japan are likely to prevent a realization of such an agreement in the near future. It none the less provides a convenient reference for the gains from trade which can be realized by bilateral liberalization alone. Aggregate economywide results are discussed in the next section, followed by more detailed assessments of sectoral adjustment of the two experiments.

9.4.1 Aggregate Results

The aggregate economywide results are summarized in Table 9.2. As classical trade theory dictates, removing trade distortions leads to expanded trade, intensified comparative advantage and greater economywide and global efficiency, all of which contribute to an increase in aggregate welfare. The first row of Table 9.2 indicates that both forms of liberalization are beneficial in terms of real output. Average wages (Japan), employment gains (US), and average rental rates all increase. Japan generally benefits more than the US in both experiments because of a greater overall increase in factor incomes. In the US, increased employment resulting from liberalization expands production possibilities and real output. As expected, larger aggregate gains accrue to larger liberalization, since more trade expansion and efficiency are realized. The patterns of aggregate trade adjustment indicate an expansion of both imports and exports (rows 7 and 8). Most significantly, however, bilateral liberalization leads to an increase in real total exports which is proportionally larger than the increase in real total imports for both countries. The yen depreciates against the dollar (row 5) because Japan began with the higher import barriers and a more overvalued exchange rate.[8]

Trade diversion is an important component of adjustment to any form of trade preferences, bilateral, regional, or otherwise. To better appraise this effect, an index of trade diversion is presented in rows 9 and 10.[9] Trade diversion in the bilateral cases is generally greater than that in the multi-

Table 9.2   Aggregate effects of US–Japan trade liberalization (percentage changes)

		Bilateral liberalization		Multilateral liberalization	
		Japan	US	Japan	US
1	Real GDP	0.19	0.13	0.88	0.57
2	Rental rate	0.41	0.22	1.18	0.67
3	Wage rate	0.48		1.58	
4	Employment		0.25		0.93
5	Bilateral exchange rate	1.53	−1.51	6.64	−6.22
6	ROW exchange rate	1.26	−0.27	7.85	1.14
7	Total imports	1.66	1.23	10.37	2.66
8	Total exports	2.40	1.53	9.61	3.08
9	Import diversion	3.46	1.35	0.55	1.86
10	Export diversion	2.33	2.21	0.27	1.56
11	Structural adjustment	0.53	0.28	2.04	0.28
12	Employment adjustment	0.60	0.16	2.55	0.17

Notes
[a] Closure assumptions:
(a) Both countries have a fixed aggregate stock of domestic capital which is mobile between sectors, while the economywide average rental rate adjusts to equate aggregate capital demand to the fixed total supply.
(b) Labour in both countries is mobile between sectors. In Japan, total employment is fixed while a variable average wage adjusts labour demand. In the US, the wage is fixed while aggregate employment varies to meet demand.
(c) In the product markets in each country, prices are normalized by a fixed numéraire chosen to be the GDP price deflator.
(d) Bilateral and ROW exchange rates are flexible while their corresponding trade balances are fixed.

lateral cases. Japan experiences more diversion in bilateral liberalization, largely because of its higher protection levels and more specialized trade patterns.

The last two rows in Table 9.2 are analogous to the trade diversion index, but apply to each country's vector of sectoral output and employment, respectively. Structural adjustment is an index of sectoral shifting in the pattern of domestic production, while the employment adjustment index measures the shift in employment across sectors. Structural and employment adjustments are generally greater for Japan, again because of its greater liberalization and specialization.

Table 9.3   Sectoral results for US–Japan bilateral liberalization (percentage changes)[a]

		(1)	*(2)*	*(3)*	*(4)*	*(5)*	*(6)*	*(7)*	*(8)*	*(9)*
Japan		X	VA	C	E	E^b	E^r	M	M^b	M^r
1	Cereals	−5.7	−5.3	2.7	−4.4	0.0	−4.5	72.5	180.8	0.0
2	MeatPoult	−3.9	−3.4	1.7	1.3	2.6	−1.6	23.7	176.7	−8.0
3	Dairy	0.0	0.4	0.5	0.9	0.0	0.9	0.7	165.6	−2.8
4	Sugar	0.2	0.7	0.0	0.7	0.0	0.7	0.4	125.6	−0.7
5	AgForFsh	0.0	0.4	0.0	4.7	5.4	−0.1	0.0	3.7	−0.9
6	PetMining	1.1	1.5	−0.8	1.5	3.1	1.4	0.0	1.2	−0.1
7	FoodProc	0.3	0.7	0.4	1.6	4.4	0.5	0.9	5.4	−0.6
8	NonDrMfg	0.4	0.9	0.0	1.4	6.9	0.0	−0.5	1.5	−1.0
9	DurMfg	1.3	1.8	0.6	2.6	6.1	0.4	−0.9	0.9	−1.8
10	TrComUt	0.3	0.7	−0.2	1.2	6.2	1.0	−0.3	2.3	−0.8
11	Trade	0.2	0.6	−0.1	3.2	5.5	1.7	0.2	2.3	−1.7
12	Services	0.1	0.6	−0.1	3.1	4.0	−1.3	−0.5	2.8	−0.9
United States										
1	Cereals	6.9	7.0	1.4	36.5	180.8	4.2	−1.5	0.0	−1.6
2	MeatPoult	3.5	3.6	0.9	43.4	176.7	2.4	−1.5	2.6	−1.5
3	Dairy	0.6	0.8	0.5	4.1	165.6	1.1	0.0	0.0	0.0
4	Sugar	1.1	1.2	0.0	7.4	125.6	−0.3	0.0	0.0	0.0
5	AgForFsh	0.5	0.6	0.1	0.9	3.7	−0.2	1.1	5.4	1.0
6	PetMining	0.1	0.3	0.1	−0.1	1.2	−0.2	0.4	3.1	0.4
7	FoodProc	0.4	0.5	0.3	0.5	5.4	−0.3	0.7	4.4	0.7
8	NonDrMfg	0.2	0.2	0.1	0.0	1.5	−0.2	0.7	6.9	0.3
9	DurMfg	−0.3	−0.2	0.3	−0.4	0.9	−0.5	1.8	6.1	0.0
10	TrComUt	0.1	0.2	0.1	−0.2	2.3	−0.3	0.8	6.2	0.5
11	Trade	0.1	0.2	0.1	−0.2	2.3	−0.5	5.5	5.5	0.0
12	Services	0.1	0.2	0.1	−0.1	2.8	−0.2	0.8	4.0	0.4

Notes
[a] (1) Real output, (2) nominal value-added, (3) real consumption, (4) total exports, (5) bilateral exports, (6) exports to ROW, (7) total imports, (8) bilateral imports, (9) imports from ROW.
[b] bilateral.
[r] world (ROW).

9.4.2   Sectoral Results

In a disaggregated neoclassical model, the most interesting results are at the sectoral level, where the real structural adjustments and reallocations occur in response to policy changes. Table 9.3 presents the sectoral results of bilateral liberalization. Perhaps the most arresting outcome is the moderate contraction of Japanese agricultural sectors, despite their previously high levels of protection. It is largely caused by positive Japanese income effects resulting from liberalization and the limited substitutability of rice varieties in the Japanese diet. The removal of protection leads to a depreciation of the yen, making Japanese products more competitive. Real income gains from the net trade expansion stimulate real Japanese consumption (column 3) and largely offset the decline in domestic agricultural output. Also, it is well documented that Japanese consumers view imported rice as a very imperfect substitute for their domestic varieties, which is recognized in our import demand specification. Thus, Japanese with rising incomes consume more of both goods, but substitution effects are limited. These results raise serious questions about the efficacy of Japanese agricultural protection. Such policies appear to encourage higher domestic output, but only moderately, and at a very high cost in terms of aggregate welfare, other sectoral development and the competitiveness of the Japanese economy.

Apart from a small reduction in real output of durable goods, all other US sectors gain from bilateral liberalization for two reasons: the first is a sharp increase in agricultural exports; the second is the domestic demand expansion induced by the real export surplus. Most new exports are channelled to Japan, generating new income for the exporter and leading to an increase in the rental rate, employment, factor incomes and consumption. A large expansion in agricultural output induces sizable increases in demand for intermediate goods and contributes to domestic demand growth. The result is a broadly based expansion in the US economy.

Table 9.4 presents the results of a multilateral liberalization experiment. While this case is more hypothetical than a bilateral agreement, the results do clarify the motives of the Japanese in protecting agriculture. As column (1) indicates, Japanese cereals would contract by 19 per cent in real terms, while the meat and poultry sector declines 30 per cent, dairy 5 per cent, and the small sugar sector 33 per cent. The US sugar sector is also hard hit, but its losses are dwarfed by gains elsewhere in the economy. Admittedly, we are unlikely to see these two countries removing all their trade barriers spontaneously, but if they did so they would both benefit substantially in real terms. Multilateral liberalization would extend the gains of bilateral liberalization, including real output gains and greater efficiency in sectors of each country's

Table 9.4   Sectoral results for US and Japanese removal of trade barriers on all imports (percentage changes)[a]

		(1)	(2)	(3)	(4)	(5)	(6)	(7)	(8)	(9)
Japan		X	VA	C	E	E^b	E^r	M	M^b	M^r
1	Cereals	−19.0	−18.0	9.1	−13.7	−6.8	−14.0	299.1	217.7	385.2
2	MeatPoult	−29.9	−29.0	12.6	−19.5	−8.4	−20.2	265.9	119.6	313.0
3	Dairy	−5.1	−3.8	5.2	0.8	0.0	0.8	337.9	142.7	345.3
4	Sugar	−32.7	−31.7	10.2	−24.6	0.0	−24.6	234.1	61.4	237.3
5	AgForFsh	0.3	1.5	0.0	9.4	9.1	11.4	−0.1	0.9	−0.3
6	PetMining	4.6	6.0	−2.2	8.7	4.5	8.9	0.5	−0.8	0.6
7	FoodProc	1.8	3.3	2.3	8.3	6.7	8.9	1.3	2.7	0.8
8	NonDrMfg	2.3	3.8	0.2	6.9	8.5	6.5	−4.9	−2.6	−5.6
9	DurMfg	5.6	7.0	2.3	10.0	9.4	10.3	−8.3	−5.0	−10.0
10	TrComUt	1.9	3.3	−0.1	8.4	8.4	8.4	−2.5	−0.2	−3.0
11	Trade	1.1	2.6	−0.2	12.9	9.6	14.8	−4.0	−0.1	−7.8
12	Services	0.7	2.1	0.1	7.5	7.3	8.0	−2.8	0.0	−3.1
United States										
1	Cereals	8.5	9.1	2.1	47.5	217.7	8.4	−2.4	−6.8	−2.3
2	MeatPoult	3.1	3.3	1.0	31.6	119.6	6.2	−1.5	−8.4	−1.5
3	Dairy	0.1	0.5	1.3	6.9	142.7	4.4	107.4	0.0	107.4
4	Sugar	−30.6	−30.3	4.8	−14.2	61.4	−18.9	155.3	0.0	155.3
5	AgForFsh	0.8	1.2	0.5	2.3	0.9	2.9	3.2	9.1	3.1
6	PetMining	0.6	1.1	0.4	1.2	−0.8	1.4	0.7	4.5	0.7
7	FoodProc	1.3	1.6	1.1	2.4	2.7	2.3	0.6	6.7	0.4
8	NonDrMfg	0.6	0.8	0.6	1.1	−2.6	1.6	1.8	8.5	1.4
9	DurMfg	0.2	0.4	0.8	0.8	−5.0	1.2	2.9	9.4	0.2
10	TrComUt	0.6	0.9	0.5	1.5	−0.2	1.6	1.3	8.4	1.0
11	Trade	0.6	0.8	0.6	2.3	−0.1	2.7	9.6	9.6	0.0
12	Services	0.6	0.8	0.6	1.6	0.0	1.6	0.9	7.3	0.1

Notes
[a] See Table 9.3.
[b] bilateral.
[r] world (ROW).

greatest comparative advantage, real consumption gains in almost all product categories and gains in income which significantly exceed real output gains. Most of the gains are driven directly and indirectly by trade expansion. The main differences from bilateral results are tied to sectors with high ROW trade shares. For example, the US meat and poultry sector benefits from bilateral liberalization, but less so from multilateral liberalization because of Japan's high dependence on ROW imports (82 per cent). In contrast, US cereal farmers benefit more from multilateral liberalization because of Japan's relatively high dependence on US imports (46 per cent), coupled with the greater expansion of the Japanese economy. A larger depreciation of the yen resulting from multilateral liberalization strengthens the competitive position of Japanese manufacturing sectors.

Limitations in data and assumptions underlying the model specification require careful interpretation of the above results. First of all, the import share of agricultural products would have been much higher in Japan if the existing trade barriers were absent. Thus, the low base-year agricultural imports imply a downward bias in estimating the sectoral effects of liberalization. In addition, the historical import barriers tend to cause elasticities of substitution between domestic and imported goods to be lower than under free trade. For example, because of the virtual import ban on rice, many Japanese consumers might not be well informed about the availability of high quality varieties grown elsewhere. The low values of trade substitution elasticities would also underestimate the magnitudes of changes in imports and output.[10]

The second limitation is that official publications (e.g. input–output tables) do not provide data on value added accruing to land. As a result, land is excluded from the factors of production and the effect of agricultural liberalization on land prices could not be estimated empirically. A standard trade model predicts, however, that a reduction in the relative price of land-intensive products would lead to lower land prices. Thus, given the recent volatility in the Japanese property and financial markets, the risk of a bursting property bubble may seriously limit the government's ability to liberalize agriculture. This may help to explain recent Japanese reluctance at the bargaining table.

To remove the agricultural distortions without destabilizing Japanese capital markets, two distinct policies are necessary. If, as in the US, the future value of continued protection has already been capitalized into agricultural land values, then the government must devise a compensation scheme of equal present value. The more important problem of liberalizing land use policy must be solved gradually and with continuity so the scarcity component of land values can adjust smoothly.

Finally, we could not quantify the effects of US and Japanese liberalization on economic welfare of the rest of the world (ROW). This is because, due to the lack of accurate world sectoral production data, we were unable to construct a social accounting matrix for the ROW.

Bilateral liberalization could make the ROW worse off if the previous imports from the ROW are diverted to the bilateral partner. Column (9) of Table 9.3 indicates that Japan would reduce the ROW imports across the board, while the US would increase non-agricultural imports from the ROW. This suggests that to guarantee a global welfare improvement, trade barriers on all imports would have to be lowered in conjunction with bilateral liberalization.

9.5 CONCLUDING REMARKS

Today's system protection in Japan and the US is a highly evolved product of piecemeal concessions. Individually, each may have been justified for the direct beneficiaries and negligible in its effect on aggregate welfare. Taken together and in the context of vastly expanded trading opportunities, it is a serious impediment to economic growth. The main opportunity cost of protection is not cheaper imports in a few sectors, but the trade driven expansion of domestic demand which would increase real output of a wide range of activities.

In this chapter, a US–Japan CGE model has been used to appraise the prospects for the two countries of agricultural trade liberalization. If such an agreement were negotiated, each country could realize substantial gains in real income, consumption, and an intensification of comparative advantage which improves international competitiveness. According to the results of this study, bilateral trade liberalization between them is incentive compatible, distinctly beneficial to both countries in terms of aggregate welfare and their future prospects for competitive economic expansion.

As the world's leading economic powers, however, the US and Japan need to assess the impact of bilateral agreement for the rest of the world. Despite enormous political obstacles which have to be surmounted, they should strive for multilateral liberalization in the long run. Although this would require considerable structural adjustment in the Japanese economy, as evidenced in the aggregate results, the benefits to Japan's consumers far outweigh the costs to its farmers. If the Japanese government carefully works out a compensation scheme for farmers, the agricultural transition could be facilitated considerably. Agricultural liberalization should be a primary objective in realizing the full potential of US and Japanese trading relationship.

9.6   APPENDIX

Bilateral and ROW import tariff rates and *ad valorem* tariff equivalents of non-tariff barriers (percentages)

		Japan			United States		
		t^b_M	t^r_M	ρ_M	t^b_M	t^r_M	ρ_M
1	Cereal	4.8	2.9	296.0	2.9	1.6	
2	Meat Poult	5.2	3.7	159.0	4.0	1.3	
3	Dairy	5.1	7.6	190.0	n.a.*	1.2	45.0
4	Sugar	4.8	53.7	200.0	n.a.*	1.1	102.0
5	AgForFish	3.8	3.3	3.0	4.4	1.5	1.0
6	PetMining	1.6	3.7		5.6	1.0	
7	FoodProc	5.7	2.8	5.0	4.3	1.1	
8	NonDrMfg	3.0	2.0		5.9	2.1	
9	DurMfg	3.4	0.9		5.4	1.5	
10	TrComUt	3.2	2.1		5.4	1.4	
11	Trade	3.6	0.2		5.4	0.0	
12	Services	3.9	2.4		4.3	0.8	
	Wgt Avg	3.5	3.0		5.3	1.4	

Notes
[a] Not applicable since the US does not import dairy products or sugar from Japan.
Sources:
(a)   Bilateral and ROW import tariff rates (t^b_M and t^r_M): MITI (1989).
(b)   *Ad valorem* tariff equivalents of non-tariff barriers (ρ_M)
    (a)   Japanese sectors 1–4: Anderson and Tyers (1987). Their estimates are for 1980–2.
    (b)   Japanese sectors 5, 7: Cline *et al.* (1978), table 5-2.
    (c)   US sectors 3–5: USITC (1990) and US Department of Agriculture.

NOTES AND REFERENCES

1.   We thank Thomas Hertel, James Luke, and Jean Mercenier for helpful comments and Li Gan for research assistance. Financial support from the University of California's Pacific Rim Research Program and the Matsushita International Foundation is gratefully acknowledged.
2.   Twelve producing sectors are classified for the two countries as follows: (1) cereal, (2) meat and poultry, (3) dairy products, (4) sugar, (5) other agricultural products, forestry, and fishery, (6) petroleum and mining, (7) food processing, (8) non-durable manufacturing, (9) durable manufacturing, (10)

transport, communication, and utilities, (11) wholesale and retail trade, and (12) services.

3. The high and similar values of export and import shares for durable manufacturing in the US indicate significant levels of intra-industry trade.

4. Equations of the US – Japan two-country CGE model used in this study are provided in Lee and Roland-Holst (1991).

5. For moderate trade flow adjustments, empirical evidence appears to support this assumption. Estimates for export demand and import supply elasticities for the United States by Reinert and Roland-Holst (1990) are uniformly greater than ten at the two-digit SIC level.

6. The assumption of competitive market conduct is probably less innocuous, and will be evaluated in a separate study.

7. Complete documentation of the SAM estimation procedure is available from the authors. The estimated base table consists of 162 sectors, aggregated to 12 in the present study.

8. The bilateral and ROW exchange rates are quoted as domestic/foreign currency, so a positive change implies depreciation.

9. Formally, the diversion measure is given by the normalized deviation $\delta = 100 \| x_1 (|x_0|/|x_1|) - x_0 \| / \| x_0 \|$, where x denotes a 2-tuple of bilateral and ROW aggregate imports or exports in the base (x_0) and after the experiment (x_1), and $\| \cdot \|$ and $| \cdot |$ denote euclidian and simplex norms, respectively.

10. We have carried out bilateral and multilateral liberalization experiments using the values of trade substitution elasticities which are double the values used in the base model. Although this would increase the magnitudes of changes in virtually all variables as expected, the basic conclusion on welfare gains and sectoral adjustments still holds.

Part III

Global Management Issues

10   Introduction

Yaprak and Shaheen explore the state of the art regarding cross-national mergers and acquisitions that have become a frequent form of foreign direct investment in emerging international business activities. Only a handful of explanations have been offered for this phenomenon, and the authors feel that gaps still remain in the understanding of when and why mergers and acquisitions continue to be the form of choice of foreign direct investment. The authors offer propositions derived from the electic theory of international production, and hope that by doing so they will inspire deeper research in this area. They offer an overview of merger and acquisition theory, a discussion of the eclectic paradigm, and the propositions derived from that paradigm as well as suggestions for future research in this area.

In their chapter 'International Trade Policy and Corporate Strategy', Root and Visudtibhan offer a conceptual framework that relates strategic management theory to 'new' international trade theory and policy, which is based on the assumption of imperfect competition. The authors feel that is very timely due to the chronic US trade deficit, the decline in US international competitiveness, and the ongoing international trade disputes between the US and its trade partners. All these issues require that the US government develop a strategic international trade policy.

Peter Gray discusses the issue of labour force efficiency and adjustment cost and the effects of a possible mismatch between the skill requirement of a nation's capital stock and the skill available in its workforce. The author refers particularly to the adjustments that are caused by the establishment of free trade areas with a country that has lower labour force efficiency than that existing in the focus country. This issue is of utmost significance in the expansion of trade blocs in North America, Europe, Asia, and perhaps on other continents, in which countries with at times extremely differentiated workforce quality and efficiency attempt to open their markets to each other. The author suggests that the problems of labour force inefficiency are substantial, growing, and neglected both in analysis and in US social policy.

11 International Acquisitions and the Eclectic Paradigm: Exploring the State of the Art

$F21$

Attila Yaprak and David K. Shaheen

11.1 INTRODUCTION

With the explosive growth in international business activity within the last two decades, cross-national mergers and acquisitions have become a frequent form of foreign direct investment (FDI). While their popularity as an FDI form has grown, research on when and why they are preferred, especially when compared to greenfield investments, appears to have lagged behind.

Only a handful of explanations has been offered for this phenomenon. Rugman (1982), for example, has tied firms' preference for mergers and acquisitions over greenfield investments to their inherent desire for internalization advantages such as ease of market entry and managerial control. Calvert (1981, 1982) has correlated that preference to the exploitation of information asymmetries between the buyer and seller of an asset, a form of market imperfection; that is, to the different sets of expectations about the value of the asset held by the investors of the acquiring company and the current shareholders of the acquired company. Kogut (1985), Casson (1985), and Hennart (1988) have implied the accrual of transactions costs advantages to the firm through mergers and acquisitions, a byproduct of synergy.

Yet gaps still remain in our understanding of when and why mergers and acquisitions continue to be a popular form of FDI. The purpose of this chapter is to inspire deeper research in this area by offering propositions derived from the eclectic theory of international production. As debate on these propositions should lead to new perspectives on international investment, this chapter should be considered a modest contribution to the literature. To approach this purpose, we offer in the following pages an overview of merger and acquisition theory, a discussion of the eclectic paradigm as an extension of that theory base, propositions derived from that paradigm, and a critique of how our propositions enrich the literature. Our suggestions for future research conclude the chapter.

11.2 RELEVANT LITERATURE

Several explanations have been offered in the literature to explain the acquisition behaviour of firms. Improved efficiency through synergy is one such explanation. At the heart of this theory is the notion that overall managerial efficiency can be raised through a merger or an acquisition through the exploitation of a newly acquired differential advantage in efficiency (Calvert, 1981, 1982). A major weakness of this notion, however, is the fact that it views efficiency improvements as a linear phenomenon; it does not appreciate the idea that as a firm size grows beyond some optimal point, managerial efficiency will decline regardless of additional investments into efficiency improvements.

The pursuit of advantages sourced in economies of scale has been a second explanation (Anderson and Gatignon, 1986; Calvert, 1981). The reduction of risk, and consequently a lower cost of capital obtained from the mergers of two imperfectly correlated cash flow streams, provides an example of this. Economies of scale advantages obtained from the merging of marketing competencies with R&D skills, or from vertical integration of different stages of production, provide other examples. Perception of a gap between a firm's strategic objectives and strategic capabilities can also lead a firm to a merger or acquisition, presumably to help close that gap by acquiring newer skills or improving on current capabilities. That is, the potential to make additional investments in the combined firms that will yield positive net present values will lead the firm to pursue a merger or acquisition.

Information asymmetry and undervaluation of assets are other explanations (Casson, 1985; Kogut, 1985). Merger negotiations or the tender offer process may generate new information that may lead to a revaluation of the firm. Alternatively, the firm's assets may be undervalued (its q-ratio may be lower than it should be), to such a degree that an acquiring firm can pay a premium over the market price of the shares and still acquire the firm's assets at a cost that is below replacement cost.

Pursuit of increased market power, particularly through horizontal acquisitions in oligopolistic industries, is yet another explanation (Porter and Fuller, 1986). When a firm enters an industry through acquisition, it eliminates one of its competitors, thereby increasing its share of market power.

A final explanation centres around diversification or spreading of risk. Casson (1982) has shown that in the global financial arena, MNCs are superior vehicles for affecting international diversification since they can diversify at a lower costs than portfolio investors. The firm may, for example, pursue product/market diversification through acquisitions. Other studies have indicated, however, that multinationals are not necessarily efficient vehicles for investor diversification.

These explanations appear to be weak determinants as to why international mergers and acquisitions take place, particularly when compared to the formation of new subsidiaries. For example, efficiency pursuit theories do not provide satisfactory explanations as to why these advantages cannot be gained through greenfield investments. Economies of scale arguments do not explain why vertical integration should be accomplished via acquisition. Diversification explanations do not satisfactorily answer why a firm cannot just as easily diversify its product/market portfolio without acquisitions. In the next section, we make the case that the eclectic paradigm of international production provides a better explanation for international merger and acquisition activity than the above explanations. We derive propositions from theory to demonstrate the relevance and value of that paradigm in this context.

11.3   THE ECLECTIC PARADIGM

The eclectic paradigm of international production (Dunning, 1988) holds that the foreign involvement of firms, whether through export, contractual or investment modes, is determined by location-specific, ownership-specific and internalization advantages. FDI, and therefore acquisitions, require the presence of all three types of advantages.

The locational aspect of this paradigm is a departure from other FDI theories in that it allows for different modes of entry into different countries under different sets of circumstances. In this context, a distinction is made between structural and transactional market failures in that structural imperfections such as entry barriers, government intervention and spatial matters can collectively or independently encourage (or discourage) investment. In contrast, transaction gains can be derived from common governance of activities in different locations. These may include enhanced arbitrage and leverage opportunities, reduction of exchange risks, better coordination of financial decision making, protection through hedged marketing or multiple sourcing strategy, and possible gains through transfer price manipulation (ibid.). Both structural and transactional imperfections are country specific and will therefore influence the location of the investment, hence the type and nature of the acquisitions.

The eclectic theory also adds three sets of structural variables. In this context, country variables include developed versus developing country, large versus small market, and degree of industrialization as the major categories. Industry variables include high versus low technology, innovation versus mature stage of development, processing versus assembly, and competitive versus monopolistic market structure. The primary firm variables are size, age, firm strategy, leader versus follower role, and innovator versus imitator. All three types of structural variables can influence the decision to acquire a firm in a foreign market.

11.4 PROPOSITIONS

The eclectic paradigm would hold that a firm whose strategy involves extensive diversification is more likely to have ownership-specific advantages to exploit than less diversified firms. Diversified firms will have access to knowledge of varied production processes by virtue of their producing a wider array of products. A deliberate diversification strategy would also imply that firms venture into new lines where they will face uncertainty due to unfamiliarity with particular product areas. In addition, if a firm is diversifying, it is probably willing to accept a lower rate of return in exchange for the reduced risk, an important consideration given that acquisitions can be expensive both with respect to purchase price and the difficulty of coordinating the merged hierarchies. Thus diversification as part of a company strategy should lead to a greater propensity to acquire other firms. There may be limits on how far a firm is able to, or willing to diversify, however. The more new arenas the firm enters, the less likely it will want to diversity further, since the marginal benefits of further diversification will have been reduced. This logic would suggest the following proposition:

P1: Firms that follow a diversification strategy will be more acquisitive than those of the same size who do not. There will, however, be some optimal point beyond which diversifying firms will reduce their tendency to pursue acquisitions.

That is, beyond some point, a firm will choose to expand within its established lines once the benefits of further diversification are offset by the costs of such diversification.

Firms that engage in extensive R&D have an ownership-specific asset advantage in the form of technology or information. Implementation of information or technology-specific advantages is difficult. Such implementation is a lengthy process requiring detailed long-term appraisals and careful short-term synchronization. Knowledge is hard to safeguard once it has been traded, thus externalization increases the risks of dissipation of that advantage. It is also difficult to negotiate the sale of the asset as the buyer is not properly informed about the appropriate price of the asset. The owner of the advantage faces the difficulty of having to disclose sufficient information to reduce buyer uncertainty without disclosing so much information that the knowledge or technology is completely given away. This leads to the following proposition.

P2: Firms that are technology intensive will tend to engage in greater proportions of acquisition activity than those which are less technology intensive.

That is, acquisitions are more attractive as an FDI form due to the large valuation gap between the buyer and the seller about the value of the asset; a gap caused by the market's failure to avoid information asymmetries (Calvert, 1981; Rugman, 1982). Another factor that emerges here is the speed of an acquisition in comparison with a new venture; the diffusion of technology has become more rapid in recent years making immediate exploitation of that asset both possible and desirable.

The developed versus developing country dimension of the eclectic paradigm leads to another proposition. A developed country will have a wider array of markets, as well as a greater number of firms, and thus will provide more opportunities for a firm with ownership-specific advantages to exploit those advantages. LDCs are more likely than developed countries to restrict foreign ownership of home country firms. In addition, their markets will probably overvalue such inputs as raw materials, leaving little room for acquisitions of firms in those industries. Further, LDCs are likely to be plagued with wide and rapid currency fluctuations. Such financial instability discourages acquisitions since there is high risk of loss to the acquirer from the time that the acquisition is negotiated to the time that it is executed. Finally, the proximity hypothesis suggests that firms will be more likely to invest in countries that are geographically close. This is consistant with the eclectic theory which would suggest that firms would attempt to minimize psychic distance and buyer uncertainty factors which would lead to investments in countries. This would lead to the following proposition:

P3: Multinational enterprises (MNEs) will be more likely to pursue acquisitions in developed countries than in LDCs.

An interesting question arises here about the acquisition behaviour of US versus non-US multinationals. Although studies of the value of MNEs as diversification vehicles have been inconclusive, there is another rationale for US investors possessing greater enthusiasms for foreign acquisitions than investors of other nations. It has been shown that the US has the most sophisticated and efficient capital markets and investors. Thus the US market acquisitions would necessarily be more competitive than foreign markets with fewer bargains available. The result is that US firms would be more likely to seek foreign acquisitions than would firms headquartered elsewhere. Thus:

P4: US-based firms are more likely to pursue acquisitions as a form of FDI than non-US firms.

Of course, a second aspect of diversification is whether firms are more likely to acquire firms in related or in unrelated industries. Firms that have little experience abroad and choose to diversify through acquisitions will face more uncertainty in foreign markets than will more experienced firms. The more experienced producers are likely to be more diversified, and hence less in need of diversifying acquisitions. Additionally, less experienced firms may be seeking knowledge more fervently than their more experienced counterparts. Therefore:

P5: Firms with more international experience will be more likely than less experienced firms to pursue acquisitions in related industries.

The degree of internationalization experienced by a firm can influence its propensity to acquire other firms. The determination of the presence or absence of an internalization advantage requires that the cost of transacting in the market be compared with the cost of operating a hierarchy. The lower the cost of the hierarchy relative to the cost of the market, the more profitable it will be to engage in FDI. Hierarchical costs are related to the knowledge of how to operate a business abroad; that is, the more uncertainty, the higher the coordination costs associated with international operations. Firms with less experience will face more uncertainty, ergo, they will be more likely to use acquisitions to obtain the information needed to operate rather than obtaining it through market transactions. They will get a lower but more certain rate of return through an acquisition than through other alternatives. Therefore:

P6: A firm's degree of internationalization will be negatively correlated with its propensity to use acquisitions as a mode of entry.

Market failure is more prevalent in oligopolistic industries than in competitive industries. Since market failure makes internalization potentially more profitable, and since internalization advantages are a prerequisite to FDI in general, and therefore to acquisitions, the following proposition is derived:

P7: Acquisitions should be more prevalent in oligopolistic industries than in competitive industries.

The final phenomenon of interest in this chapter concerns the increased merger activity in Europe in recent years. Undoubtedly, the integration of the twelve EC nations into one common economic market in 1993 will subject producers to increased competition from more as well as larger firms. In addition, it is possible that the unified market will see greater restrictions placed on internal mergers after the advent of that integration. The removal of between-country restrictions can be seen as a change in the locational aspect of the eclectic paradigm, favouring an increase in all forms of inter-country involvement. The uncertainty over future regulations makes it more profitable for firms to internalize any ownership-specific advantages they possess. The speed with which an acquisition can be carried out makes that activity more desirable than it would be if Europe 1992 were not in the offing. In addition, technology appears to be one of the main factors behind the surge. Thus the increase in merger and acquisition activity in Europe is consistent with the eclectic paradigm.

11.5   DISCUSSION

There have been few studies of cross-border acquisitions both in the international business literature and the finance literature. Three are worthy of note: a study of acquisitions of Swedish firms (Forsgren, 1989), a study of US, UK, West German and Japanese acquisitions (Wilson 1980), and a study of US acquisitions (Hisey and Caves, 1985). Both Forsgren (1989) and Wilson (1980) found that the more diversified the acquirer was in its product line, the greater the propensity to engage in acquisitions. This represents at least some confirmation of our proposition 1 which suggests such a relationship. Both studies also found a negative relationship between the extent of R&D conducted by a firm and its tendency to acquire. As this finding is opposite to the logic which led to our proposition 2, we would propose further thinking and hypothesis formulation in this dimension. Wilson (1980) also found that investment was more likely to be carried out by acquisition in developed countries than in less developed countries, a confirmation of our proposition 3. In addition, in Wilson's study (1980), the nationality of the parent firm had an influence on the location of acquisitions as Japanese firms were more likely to invest in LDCs than were firms based in the US, UK or West Germany. US firms were found to have a higher level of diversification in their subsidiaries than MNC's based elsewhere, thus lending possible support to our proposition 4. Hisey and Caves (1985) examined related versus unrelated acquisitions and found that firms with considerable experience abroad were more likely to acquire related firms, while less experienced firms were more likely to acquire unrelated firms, confirming our proposition 5. There is one area of conflict between the findings of Forsgren and Wilson, however, in that Forsgren found a positive relationship between the degree of internationalization of the firm and its volume of acquisitions, while Wilson found a negative relationship. Hence, we cannot draw any conclusions about the validity of our proposition 6. Finally, we are unaware of any studies that would support or refute our proposition 7.

11.6   CONCLUSION

In this chapter, we explored the state-of-the-art in international acquisition behaviour of firms when viewed through the eclectic paradigm. Our review has shown that the eclectic paradigm is not as transparent a conveyor of information about cross-border acquisitions as we would like. On the other hand, it appears to communicate reasonably well some aspects of acquisition behaviour, such as differences in acquiring in developed versus developing countries, US-based versus non-US-based acquisitions, and more experienced versus less experienced investors. On balance, it seems safe to observe that while the evidence is inconclusive, the eclectic paradigm is an adequate communicator of international merger and acquisition behaviour. It is very clear that this domain of international finance is a fertile area for exploratory and experimental research.

12 International Trade Policy and Corporate Strategy

Franklin R. Root and Kanoknart Visudtibhan

12.1 INTRODUCTION

This chapter offers a conceptual framework that relates strategic management theory to 'new' international trade theory and policy based on the assumption of imperfect competition. The need for research on this relationship is evidenced by the many issues associated with the decline in US international competitiveness, the chronic US trade deficit, and trade disputes with Japan and other countries. These issues have prompted calls for the US government to behave *strategically* when setting its trade policy.

In this chapter we postulate that a government can formulate an effective trade policy only when it takes into account the likely strategic responses of corporations to trade policy actions, including corporations indirectly affected as well as those targeted by the policy. National trade policy depends most heavily on the responses of *multinational* firms that dominate international trade and direct foreign investment. To predict trade policy outcomes reasonably and their effectiveness in promoting the national interest, policy makers need to understand how corporate managers are likely to translate trade policy initiatives into actual business performance.

Corporate strategic responses to trade policies are not limited to changes in trade flows. Multinational firms have the capacity to shift from one country to another any of their value-added activities, ranging from R&D to marketing. The emergence of the 'global-web corporation' and the proliferation of strategic alliances among multinational firms have enhanced geographical mobility and 'leverage' within enterprise systems. Corporate boundaries have become more difficult to define as they broaden and shift over time, and national origin (or headquarters location) loses much of its traditional significance. The wide range of options open to corporate decision makers of multinational firms in responding to external threats and opportunities weakens the ability of policy makers to anticipate the effects of any specific trade policy action.

110

We begin our exploration of international trade policy and corporate strategy with a review of *strategic* trade policy. Next, we examine corporate roles in strategic trade policy and possible linkages between corporate strategy and trade policy, and offer a conceptual model. Finally, we suggest several avenues for future research.

12.2 STRATEGIC TRADE THEORY AND POLICY

Strategic trade theory maintains that government actions can alter the strategic game played by foreign and domestic firms in oligopolistic industries. Specifically, government can assist domestic firms in high-rent, high-technology industries in acquiring monopoly rents that would otherwise accrue to foreign firms, thereby increasing national welfare. It is argued that the government has access to 'tools' unavailable to firms – tariffs, subsidies and other forms of protection – that can constrain foreign rival firms both at home and abroad (Yoffie, 1989).

Strategic trade theory provides a rationale for strategic trade *policy* that aims to shift excess returns from foreign to domestic firms in high-technology oligopolistic industries. The support for strategic trade policy in the United States can best be understood by examining three related topics: (i) the evolution of US trade policy, (ii) the changing international economic position of the US; and (iii) new thinking in trade theory.

12.2.1 The Evolution of US Trade Policy

Contemporary US trade policy may be traced to the Reciprocal Trade Agreements (RTA) Act of 1934. The Act marked a shift in US trade policy from a highly protectionist (symbolized by the Smoot–Hawley Act of 1930) to a more liberal policy. Recognizing the relationship between imports and exports, the RTA Act authorized the President to lower tariff rates up to 50 per cent through the negotiation of bilateral trade agreements with foreign countries. Under the Act, US tariff rates fell consistently from an average of 51.4 per cent for dutiable imports in 1934 to 11.1 per cent in 1962 (Root, 1990). Starting in 1947, bilateral bargaining was superseded by more effective multilateral bargaining under the regime of a new organization, the General Agreement on Tariffs and Trade (GATT). After World War II, the United States became the leader in a global movement towards freer trade within the GATT framework.

To provide the President with more authority to bargain with the European Community, Congress passed the Trade Expansion Act of 1962 which replaced the RTA. Despite the fact that the 1962 Act was 'the largest tariff-cutting authority ever granted a President' (Congressional Quarterly Almanac, 1962, p. 262), it proved to be inadequate to deal with non-tariff barriers. The Trade Act of 1974 remedied this defect by allowing the President to negotiate non-tariff agreements in the Tokyo Round of GATT (1973–9).

Despite multilateral negotiations under several GATT Rounds, the 1980s witnessed a major revival of protectionism in response to short-run cyclical developments, long-run structural shifts in the US economy, the strong dollar of 1980–5, the rise in economic interdependence of the industrial nations, the decline in US competitiveness, and the persistent trade deficit. This revival is known as the *new protectionism* because it (i) relies heavily on new forms of non-tariff trade barriers, notably voluntary export restraints and anti-dumping/countervailing-duty actions, (ii) focuses on a comparatively small number of sectors, (iii) is bilaterally applied, and (iv) lacks transparency, allowing for a great deal of administrative discretion.

In 1988, Congress passed the Omnibus Trade and Competitiveness Act that instructs the President to identify foreign countries with unfair trade practices for subsequent negotiations and possible retaliation, and to provide relief for industries injured by import competition in return for their commitment to make 'positive adjustments' to restore competitiveness. It also grants authority to the President to continue the GATT negotiations in the current Uruguay Round that focuses on the removal of non-tariff barriers on trade in agriculture and services.

The evolution of US trade policy from 1934 reflects the growing importance of international trade and its changing nature. The United States economy is becoming more dependent on export sales and is facing more foreign competition in its domestic market. Competition in world markets is tied to the capability of the United States to keep pace with technological changes and to enjoy technological spillovers. Global competition coupled with a chronic trade deficit has fuelled trade disputes with US trading partners. The United States has accused the Japanese government of creating arbitrary competitive advantages for its high-technology firms through subsidies and non-tariff import barriers.

Summing up, US trade policy has evolved from the leadership of a movement to create a non-discriminatory, liberal world trading system to a defensive posture focused on 'fair trade' and a drift toward strategic trade.

12.2.2   US International Economic Position

Evidence of the decline in US international competitiveness commonly cited by observers (the Competitiveness Policy Council, 1992) includes:

- A persistent trade deficit that has totalled more than $1 trillion over the last decade.
- A deterioration of the net foreign investment position to a $400 billion liability.
- A national saving rate that is the lowest among the industrial countries.
- A slow-growing per capita income compared to that of Japan and Germany.
- A domestic investment rate that is below the rates of other industrial countries.
- A level of non-defence research as a percentage of gross domestic product that is lower than that of Japan and Germany.
- A low-quality educational system: US elementary and high school students rank at the bottom on standardized international tests.

The decline in the US relative economic performance has generated much debate as to its underlying causes and possible remedies. It has also forced the US to study its trading partners in virtually all aspects of their political, economic and social systems, including history, cultural characteristics, management styles and government policies. A common view in the United States sees other countries as having coherent and coordinated trade and industrial programmes whereby governments take active roles to create *artificial* competitive advantages through managing international trade. It is alleged that some foreign governments enhance their national welfare at the expense of the US by targeting 'rent-yielding' industries for support via subsidies and import restrictions that keep US as well as other foreign companies out of their domestic markets.

The establishment of strategic trade policy is supported by some US firms because they believe it would enable them to compete more strongly against foreign firms at home and possibly abroad. Some spokesmen in high-technology industries argue that government subsidies for basic research and an assured market (through government procurement and/or barriers to import) are necessary to stimulate innovation, particularly in emergent industries such as biotechnology. Some high-technology companies (such as those manufacturing semiconductors) ask for 'extra protection' on the grounds that their industries are critical to national welfare because they can generate spillovers to the rest of the economy.

12.2.3   New Thinking about Trade Theory

Traditional trade theory rests on the assumption of perfect competition: trade flows are determined by comparative advantage based on open markets. In a world of perfectly competitive markets, government would follow a policy of *laissez-faire* in trade policy. Such a world is a long way from the actual world we all must live in, and international economists are now developing trade models based on imperfectly competitive market structures. In particular, models coming out of industrial organization and game theory demonstrate that firms in oligopolistic industries can behave in ways that enable them to capture markets and anticipate rival reactions (Yoffie, 1989). More importantly, the strategic choices of these firms can help determine the structure of their industries (Caves, 1980; Krugman, 1990).

Economists have also paid more attention to the role of technological innovation in shaping national ventures and alliances among companies.

12.3   CORPORATE ROLES IN STRATEGIC TRADE POLICY

What international trade strategy should the US government pursue, granted that doing nothing is one alternative? What should be the specific content of that strategy? Which sectors of the economy, if any, should the government support as strategic? How can the government identify industries and firms in such sectors?

Strategic trade theory assumes sophisticated government behaviour but naive firm behaviour. It argues that a government can significantly influence international trade, but the effectiveness of government intervention depends critically on the reaction of domestic and foreign firms in a particular industry.

In modelling oligopolistic behaviour, economists have normally assumed one of three forms of *duopolistic* behaviour in a two-firm industry: Cournot, Stackelberg, and Bertrand. The Cournot firm treats the output of the other firm as fixed in deciding its own output level; the Stackelberg firm sets its output first, then the other firm makes its own output decision after considering the first firm's output; the Bertrand firm takes the price of its rival as fixed in setting its own price and the firm with the lower price captures all the sales. But it is impossible to know *a priori* which of these three competitiveness. Innovation creates new products and sometimes entire industries that are critical to the future growth of the national economies. Innovation also provides new, more economical production functions for existing products. Consequently, it is argued that effects of innovation should be factored into a trade policy. Specifically, certain business sectors characterized by intense technological innovation should be considered of *strategic* importance and deserve 'special' attention from the government.

There is not yet a consensus among economists and policy makers as to which factors define strategic industries. In her attempt to identify strategic industries, Spencer (1986 in Krugman, 1990) offered seven broad characteristics of industries to be targeted by strategic trade policy (12.6 Appendix). Nevertheless, she stopped short of naming such industries. In the context of the US–Canada Free Trade Agreement, Rugman and Verbeke (1990) mentioned several strategic industries. In its biennial report to the President (1991), the Office of Science and Technology Policy identified twenty-three critical *technologies* (12.7 Appendix). Although this list is the most exhaustive, policy makers still face a challenge of matching technologies with specific industries and firms. This may prove to be a difficult task given an increasing trend of cross-industry mergers, acquisitions, joint behaviors a given firm in an oligopolistic industry will follow.

These duopolistic behaviour models assume *product homogeneity*, whereas *product differentiation* actually dominates in reality. When the duopolistic assumptions are relaxed, multiple patterns of firm behaviour become possible in which price is only one of several forms of competition. Furthermore, the strategic responses of multinational firms (which dominate most strategic industries) to government intervention may involve shifts in the country location of their production or other activities, as well as alterations in trade flows.

Root (1974) conducted a study on how multinational corporations would respond to a global restrictive world and a global supportive world. He found that the objectives of US policy makers to increase production, employment, and R&D in the United States would be *counter-effective* in the restrictive world, as multinational firms shifted production and research facilities from the United States to other countries.

Porter (1990), in his recent work on why a nation's firms succeed in international competition offers another model for the oligopolistic behaviour. The model, shown in Figure 12.1, emphasizes that domestic demand conditions (which can influence the sophistication of products and timing of their introduction) and strong home-based suppliers and related industries can be sources of competitive advantage in addition to factor conditions. Most importantly for a discussion of strategic trade policy is *firm strategy, structure and rivalry* as sources of international competitive advantage. In effect, Porter maintains that strategic trade policy can be effective only in industries where the underlying determinants of national advantage are already present. If these underlying determinants are absent, governments *do not* have the power to create advantages. According to Porter, strategic trade policy should create an environment that fosters continuing innovation, but avoids direct interventions.

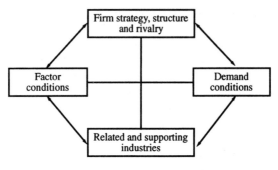

Source: M. Porter (1990) p. 72.

Figure 12.1   Determinants of national competitive advantage

The ability of a government to create a *national* competitive advantage becomes more questionable when one looks at recent developments in multinational enterprises. Increasingly, these corporations are losing their national identities (except for legal purposes). Instead, one observes *global corporate webs* (Reich, 1991) which locate their activities along value-added chains globally, raise financial resources globally, produce wherever the best technology is available, and actively engage in the formation of international alliances. In effect, strategic industries now consist of several global corporate webs with no singular connection to any one country. Hence competition takes place not among countries but among global webs of multinational firms.

The foregoing discussion points towards these conclusions: (i) Corporate competitiveness depends on both country-specific and firm(web)-specific advantages. An effective strategic trade policy, then, should be one that complements the firm-specific advantages of a company with country-specific advantages. (ii) Corporate strategies can neutralize national trade policies or even render them counter-effective. Multinational corporations with their 'webs' have a great deal of power to influence and exploit their environment, including government policies.

12.3.1   Corporate Strategy and Strategic Trade Policy

Strategy is a 'deliberate search for a plan of action that will develop a business's competitive advantage and compound it'. In searching for this plan, companies normally go through several processes – establishment of objectives, goal formulation, self-assessment and environmental analysis,

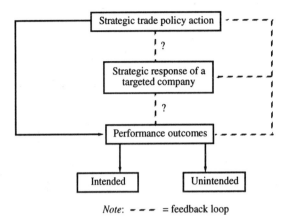

Note: – – – = feedback loop

Figure 12.2   Conventional approach of strategic trade policy

strategy formulation, strategy implementation, and feedback and control (Lorange and Vancil, 1977; Schendel and Hofer, 1979). Companies also try to balance the economic imperatives of global integration with the political imperatives of their stakeholders, including home and host governments (Chakravarthy and Perlmutter, 1985; Doz, 1980).

To a company, a national trade policy action in either home or host countries is a change in its environment with which it must cope. The change can be a source of opportunity as well as risk. When possible, the company will try to anticipate the change, incorporate it into its strategy and take proactive actions to exploit or minimize its effects. Lobbying is one example. Other actions that the corporation can take, depending on the nature of change, are coopting, negotiating with, or reacting to the change.

Conventional arguments for strategic trade policy focus on the social costs and benefits of specific government interventions to influence the performance of a targeted industry or company. However, the internal decisions and strategic behaviour of firms are largely ignored by policy makers. As depicted in Figure 12.2, the major emphasis of strategic trade policy is on effects of a policy on corporate performance (which, in turn, affects national welfare). The solid arrow linking policy to performance bypasses corporate strategic behaviour. But, in fact, a strategic trade policy action may or may not provoke a strategic response by the targeted company (dotted arrow), and a response, if it occurs, may or may not promote policy objectives. Subsequently, performance outcomes can feed back to stimulate a change in trade policy or company strategy. Also missing from

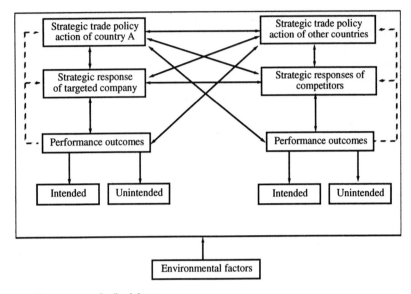

Note: – – –= feedback loop

Figure 12.3   A dynamic interactive model of strategic trade policy and corporate strategy

this conventional approach is an *explicit* recognition of potential responses from foreign competitors and possible retaliation from other countries.

These missing variables are incorporated in a dynamic interactive model of strategic trade policy and corporate strategy (Figure 12.3). The model is derived from the high degree of interdependency among nations, the existence of global corporate webs and strategic alliances, and country-specific and firm-specific competitive advantages. Because strategic trade policy is aimed at transferring economic rent from foreign to domestic firms, a country's strategic trade policy affects not only the targeted firm but also its foreign competitors. Depending on their strategic orientations and competitive strengths, these competitors may decide to respond defensively or offensively. In any event, their responses will affect the performance outcomes of the targeted company.

Moreover, strategic trade policy action in one country can invoke retaliation from other countries, forcing a change in the original policy and in corporate strategies. In sum, the performance outcome of the targeted company is contingent on the actions of other national governments, its competitors and its own adopted strategy. That outcome may be far different from that originally anticipated by policy makers.

The dynamic interactive model should also be viewed in the context of other environmental factors that may influence trade policies and corporate strategies (Scott, 1987). This is indicated by a one-way arrow linking environmental factors to the box containing all strategic trade policy and corporate strategy variables.

12.4   SOME DIRECTIONS FOR FUTURE RESEARCH

A single research study is unlikely to cover all the relationships shown in the interactive model. One relationship that urgently needs investigation is that between strategic trade policy and corporate strategy. Several questions need to be asked by researchers, including:

1. How do companies gather information about trade policies or changes in trade policy?
2. How do companies pursuing identical or different strategies respond to a trade policy action?
3. What factors influence corporate perception of a trade policy? How does this perception affect the company' strategic choices and strategic responses?
4. What are corporate response options? Which circumstance favours each of these options?
5. What are the effects of corporate strategic responses to trade policy action on corporate performance?
6. When are national interests and corporate interests congruent? Conflictual?

In answering these questions, researchers can draw on an inventory of past research in the fields of organization theory and strategic management. For example, researchers investigating responses to a change in the trade policy by corporations pursuing different strategies can use the Miles and Snow (1978) strategic typology. Miles and Snow differentiate corporate strategy into four types: defenders, prospectors, analyzers and reactors. The first two types are the most dominant and useful. The latter two are more difficult to identify and study. Reactors tend to be unstable and analyzers exhibit characteristics of both the defenders and prospectors. The following two-by-two matrix (Figure 12.4) captures the essence of a research framework.

Defenders have narrow product market domains. The top managers are expert in their firm's limited area of operation but do not tend to search outside its domain for new opportunities. Defenders seldom make adjustments

| | | Strategic trade policy | |
		Protect	Promote
Corporate strategy	Defender		
	Prospector		

Figure 12.4   A research framework

in their technology, attending primarily to improving the efficiency of existing operations. Examples of defenders are firms in the automobile and the
cigarette industries. *Prospectors* continually search markets for opportunities. They regularly experiment with potential responses to emerging
environmental trends. They are not fully efficient, but often confound their
competitors with change and uncertainty. Examples of prospector are firms
in the airline and the semiconductor industries. A specific trade policy action
can be designated as *protecting* or *promoting*. For each cell in Figure 12.4,
the researcher can identify an industry or a group of companies based on a
strategic group (McGee and McGee, 1986) or other classification scheme.

Research on the linkages between strategic trade policy and corporate
strategy is best done comparatively and longitudinally, including foreign as
well as domestic firms. Also, both retrospective and prospective studies can
help to clarify such linkages.

12.5   CONCLUSION

Strategic trade policy has become a prominent and controversial issue in
the United States. By abandoning the unrealistic assumption of perfect
competition, international economists, knowingly or unknowingly, have
opened avenues for a further development trade theory from the perspective of strategic management. This coming together of two fields, heretofore
insulated from each other, promises to enrich our understanding of trade
policy in general and strategic trade policy in particular.

12.6 APPENDIX: BROAD CHARACTERISTICS OF A TARGETED INDUSTRY

1. Must expect to earn additional returns sufficient to exceed the total cost of subsidy.
2. Must be subjected to serious foreign competition or potential competition.
3. Are more concentrated or equally concentrated as the rival foreign industry.
4. Does not have strong union, worker incomes are at least partly based on profit sharing, no key input is in fixed supply.
5. Have a fundamental cost advantage relative to the foreign competition.
6. There is a minimum of spillover of new domestic technology to rival foreign firms; government intervention aids the transfer of technology to domestic firms.
7. R&D and capital costs form a significant proportion of industry costs; its likely winning product is at an early stage of development, or production and R&D, and capital subsidies will raise its entry barriers to foreign firms.

12.7 APPENDIX: CRITICAL TECHNOLOGIES IDENTIFIED BY THE OFFICE OF SCIENCE AND TECHNOLOGY POLICY

Aeronautics
Applied molecular biology
Ceramics
Composites
Computer simulation and modelling
Data storage and peripherals
Electronics and photonics
Energy
Flexible computer integrated manufacturing
High definition imaging displays
High performance metals and alloys
Material synthesis and processing
Medical technology
Micro and non-fabrication
Microelectronics and optoelectronics
Photonic materials
Pollution minimization, remediation and waste management
Sensors and signal processing
Software
Surface transportation technologies
System management technologies

13 Labour Force Efficiency and Adjustment Costs

H. Peter Gray[*]

13.1 INTRODUCTION 033 $J21$

An economy is 'labour force efficient' when the quantity and skill mix of its population of working age match the requirements of the stock of physical capital sufficiently well so that the labour market clears at a better than subsistence wage. Labour force efficiency (the concept could also be called demographic efficiency) is assumed implicitly in most economic analyses. This chapter defines labour force efficiency and briefly explores the implications of *in*efficiency for the costs of adjustment following a change in the international trade environment (due either to an unforseen disturbance or to a change in commercial policies). The exposition is keyed to current conditions in the United States but the abstract concepts are quite general. Section 13.2 defines labour force efficiency and identifies its main determinants.[1] Section 13.3 identifies different categories of disturbance in terms of their impact on labour force efficiency and the consequent severity of adjustment costs. It is possible that policy action could reduce the adjustment costs relative to the costs of passive reliance on the workings of national and global markets: the question of whether and how to intervene constitutes 'adjustment policy'.[2]

13.2 LABOUR FORCE EFFICIENCY

Define a closed economy (country) as having a stock of physical capital and a labour force with a given distribution of skills. Given the extant stock of capital and its embodied technology, it is possible to conceive of a full-capacity-utilization, general equilibrium solution in which each individual person's income for services rendered (wages and salaries) can be determined. These individual incomes are the sum of the returns on each individual's stock of human capital as valued by the market and his/her value as an unskilled labourer. The mix of goods produced is determined

---

[*]The author is indebted to E. Ray Canterbery and Wolfgang Michalski for giving him major insights into this whole area of concern.

122

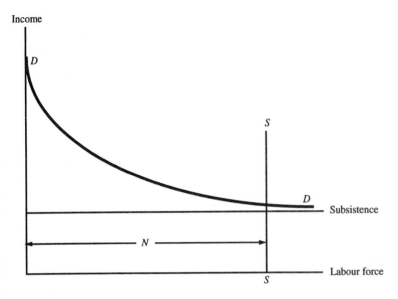

Figure 13.1   Labour force efficiency

by individual tastes and income distribution. From this construct, it would be possible to derive a schedule showing the distribution of marginal value product (i.e. income). Rank all people of working age (however defined)[3] by income without any transfer payments through welfare or unemployment compensation, beginning with the richest on the left and the poorest on the right. The poorest should include people who are physically and mentally handicapped so they can generate no income but, because their condition is unaffected by conditions in labour markets, they are not considered further here.[4] The 'incomes curve' will slope downwards throughout and will have a positive second derivative on the presumption that once people with particular and greatly demanded individual gifts have been identified, differences between consecutive individuals will get smaller as the level of skills decreases. Such a curve (assuming that all those with rentier income are not near the lower end of the income range) is drawn in Figure 13.1. Figure 13.1 also shows the total supply of non-handicapped labour (*N*) which is drawn as a vertical line (*SS*) and the subsistence income. If the intersection of *DD* and *SS* is higher than the subsistence wage (as in Figure 13.1), then all workers earn more than subsistence and, while there may be problems of social efficiency measured in terms of some judgementally determined desired distribution of income, there is no

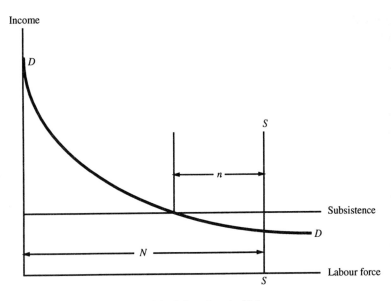

Figure 13.2   Labour force inefficiency

problem of surplus labour. The Reverend Thomas Malthus may rest in peace. This is the state of affairs assumed in analyses focusing on allocative efficiency and assuming full employment, i.e. nearly all welfare economics including the argument for free trade and similar Smithian (*laissez-faire*) proposals where the objective criterion is that of maximizing output.[5] Such an economy is *labour force efficient*. Now consider the possibility that subsistence income exceeds that at which *DD* and *SS* intersect: then, as shown in Figure 13.2, there are n people of working age destined to be unemployed or to earn less than subsistence with all that that may imply for human values, inadequate development of children and for socio-political stability.[6] The degree of labour force inefficiency may be measured as *n/N*.

Neglecting depressions, there is an obvious overlap between the concept of labour force inefficiency and structural unemployment. Note that labour force inefficiency is not caused by wage rigidities or by quasi-rents: it is caused by conditions affecting the marginal worker who will not have the bargaining power needed to generate quasi-rents or to resist downward pressure on wages. The inefficiency exists when the labour market fails to clear at a wage consonant with a subsistence income, i.e. because of an excess supply of inadequately skilled labour given the amount and technology of the capital stock.[7] Short-run labour force inefficiency could exist if firms have not had time to 'slide along their isoquant' and to change the capital/labour intensity of their capital stock, but this could presuppose the existence of more labour/capital substitutability than many economists would accept.

Taking N and subsistence income as being exogenously determined, the question of labour force efficiency depends upon the position and the shape of the incomes curve, DD. Position and shape can be affected by several forces, some secular and some cyclical. The position of the incomes curve is determined by the volume and mix of goods produced, the array of technologies embodied in the relevant stocks of physical capital, and the quantity and distribution of human capital among the workforce. Labour force efficiency will be reduced when new production technologies use highly skilled workers more and low-skilled workers less intensively, and when the mix of goods produced changes to include more skill-intensive and fewer low-skill-intensive goods: such events twist the incomes curve clockwise so that low-skilled jobs are eliminated or have lower marginal value products and n increases. Labour force efficiency will decrease (the curve will shift downward over the crucial range – say N to $N-2n$) when the stock of skills of the lower skilled segments of the work force diminishes, i.e. the skills possessed become outdated because of new technologies or a change in the mix of goods (as above), and when there is a net loss of skills over time as the skill profile of the workforce changes with entrances and retirements. Labour force efficiency will be increased when output increases over the cycle or when secular growth of output exceeds growth in the labour force.[8] However, cycles may have a ratchet effect which allows firms not to replace some (low-skilled) workers in the expansion.

To increase labour force efficiency at full capacity utilization, a nation must either generate more jobs for workers with low skill levels or enhance the skill mix of its workforce. It is extremely difficult to increase the number of jobs for low-skilled workers through tax incentives because many modern products require processes which cannot be performed by low-skilled workers using relatively unsophisticated machinery. Socially useful make-work projects may be needed to enhance labour force efficiency. The more appealing alternative is to upgrade the skills of the marginal members of the workforce. Traditionally, basic education, particularly the education of those likely to be marginal workers, has been the responsibility of government and has been financed by tax revenues.[9] This task can be seen as comprising two separate elements: better training of people before they reach working age (i.e. a more effective educational system) and the retraining of people whose skills have been made useless by technology. The latter is a short-run need and is more difficult because people acquire skills, general or particular, less easily as they grow older. It is also more difficult to justify widespread retraining for older workers because the skills acquired have a much shorter potential period of productivity.[10]

Now consider the labour force efficiency of the United States. The weaknesses of the US educational system are well known so that large numbers of relatively low-skilled workers are being cast adrift on the labour market in the United States. Recent technological innovations have caused the incomes curve to shift clockwise as the new technologies have substituted skilled workers for semi-skilled, blue-collar workers.[11] The steady opening up of US markets to trade with labour-surplus countries, especially through intra-firm trade by multinational corporations, will also have twisted the incomes curve clockwise by changing the mix of output in the United States (the balance on current account held constant) as more technology-intensive and skill-intensive exports are sold abroad. Recently (1991–2), this problem has been aggravated by cyclical conditions. The net result seems to be a huge increase in the number of people of working age who escape the net of the Bureau of Labour Statistics' measure of unemployment. The social implications of this trend increase in structural labour force inefficiency could be very serious as more and more despairing workers turn to outright vagrancy and, almost inevitably, crime.[12]

The potential of foreign nations to supply low-skilled, labour-intensive goods is enhanced by the ability and willingness of multinationals to invest capital in foreign labour-surplus nations and to source goods from abroad. Multinationals, possessing established marketing and distribution networks in industrialized countries, are well placed to produce goods for those markets offshore in labour surplus countries. The maquiladora in northern Mexico are an important example of this phenomenon.

It is worth distinguishing between the trade and technology effects on a global scale. Technological innovations which reduce the demand for low-skilled labour shift the global incomes curve downwards as does, with a lag, the growth of population; increased North–South trade does not affect the position of the global income curve but merely redistributes labour force inefficiency among nations. Illegal migration and pressures for illegal migration derive from rampantly unequal coefficients of labour inefficiency, as well as from quite different perceptions of subsistence income between the structurally unemployed in a poor country and in a rich country.

13.3 KINDS OF ADJUSTMENT AND THEIR COSTS

This section distinguishes between 'push' and 'pull' disturbances and then examines three characteristics of 'push' disturbances, size, severity and concentration, in terms of labour force efficiency.

13.3.1 Pull Disturbances

The reallocation of factors of production among industries is an inevitable concomitant of economic growth. Pull disturbances create their own aggregate demand and derive from expanding sectors so that resources are 'pulled' into those sectors by more favourable reqards and away from sectors fated for ultimate decline.[13] Define 'benign adjustment' as reallocation which requires no sector to contract at a rate faster than the rate at which its sector-specific capital is used up through the depreciation of physical capital and the retirement of skilled individuals. Benign adjustment is compatible with no deterioration in labour force efficiency as a result of the disturbance: interventionist policies would be needed only under quite rare circumstances.[14]

13.3.2 Push Disturbances

Push disturbances involve an initial decrease in aggregate demand as a result of some change in conditions and are best exemplified by a sharp increase in foreign capacity to serve domestic markets at competitive prices. This increased capacity can be attributed to an expansion of productive capacity in labour surplus countries (largely through foreign direct investment), to a change in the terms of trade between the industrialized countries and the developing world or to the reduction of barriers to imports from labour surplus countries.[15] Factors are displaced from import-competing sectors: social costs are imposed on the economy as the value of industry-specific attributes is eroded and as they undergo periods of unemployment while markets grope their way towards a new set of prices and outputs. These costs counteract, in part, the benefits derived from any improvement in the (double factoral) terms of trade. The crucial feature of a push disturbance is that that process requires the stimulated growth of industries, which will absorb the displaced factors. With generally applicable homogeneous factors of production, such as typify most models of international trade, push disturbances would have significant consequences for labour force efficiency only in the face of fixed-proportions production functions, i.e. right-angled isoquants. Once heterogeneity of factor of production is countenanced, particularly through the incorporation of different product-specific skills and skill levels, the likelihood that a push disturbance will seriously reduce labour force efficiency is considerably increased. Such an outcome will be positively related to the 'size', 'severity' and the 'concentration' of the (push) disturbance. The size of the push disturbances identifies the amount of reallocation that needs to be accomplished, and the severity and the concentration identify the difficulty of accomplishing the necessary reallocation.

13.3.3   Size

This is simply the proportionate change in output mix: in more familiar terms, the distance of movement across the production possibilities surface. Estimation of the size of a disturbance is made more difficult by the fact that disturbances do not come singly, but can come in relatively rapid succession so that full adjustment to the first shock will not have been accomplished before the onset of the succeeding shock. Here it is the cumulative effect of the group of shocks which is the essential measure of the strain imposed.[16] Successive shocks may not have similar origins so that an international shock may combine with one of domestic origin to cause a major push disturbance.[17]

The potential need for an active adjustment policy depends upon the qualitative difficulties, i.e. on the severity and concentration of the shock (although both are likely to be positively related to size). Disturbances can have different degrees of *severity* depending upon the skill levels used in the contracting industries and those required in the expanding industries. A shock is particularly severe when the expanding industry requires not only new skills but a higher level of skills of its new workers.[18] The need for severe upgrading of skills may involve more people than are originally displaced if each worker is capable of only a single gradation of skill improvement. Upgrading skill requirements adds the resources used in retraining to the adjustment costs and is likely to prove particularly costly given the difficulties in providing this sort of service through the public sector,[19] and given the high failure rates likely to be associated with attempts to retrain older workers. The severity of a long-lasting (sequential) disturbance is likely to increase with its duration. As the first effects of the disturbance take hold, workers with potential capacity for skill upgrading will leave the declining industries quite quickly as more promising job vacancies emerge. There is always a potential pull effect for some workers. As the process continues, the workers who are displaced will be older, have more industry-specific experience and less facility for acquiring new skills or skill levels.

The final characteristic of a shock is the *concentration* of its effects. Concentration applies only to labour markets and can be defined in terms of geography or skills and can result in labour market congestion (Parson, 1980). It is important to distinguish between macroeconomic congestion which involves labour force inefficiency and microcongestion which identifies excess labour with certain skills in excess supply in certain regions. Microcongestion will be smallest when the skills required in the expanding industry closely resemble those possessed by workers released from the declining industry and when the two industries are geographically proximate.

The magnitude of adjustment costs (and, therefore, the rationale for considering the potential value of active policy measures) is positively related to the size, severity and concentration of the change in conditions, as well as to the lack of resilience in the economy. *The greater the ex-ante degree of labour force inefficiency, the more likely are adjustment costs to be severe* and the less likely is the economy to have good qualities of structural resilience.

There remains the question of cyclical and growth factors. Manifestly all the difficulties of adjustment are magnified in a period of slow growth and above average unemployment.[20] The current recession has magnified labour force inefficiency and the prospects for the last decade of the twentieth century are not very encouraging as the US economy strives to eliminate some of the excesses of the 1980s.

13.4   LABOUR FORCE EFFICIENCY AND NAFTA

The concept of labour force efficiency can be used to address the potential problems which the successful conclusion of a North American Free Trade Area including Mexico may give rise to. Clearly, if labour force efficiency can be achieved area wide, the idea is a very positive one and the remarks made here address the problem of ensuring the minimum possible decrease in labour force efficiency in the unification process.[21] The problem is an important one because the proposed NAFTA will involve the effective merger of two industrialized countries with non-negligible but relatively small albeit growing labour force inefficiencies with a country with high labour force inefficiency (and a much higher net reproduction rate).[22]

Unification with no built-in adjustment safeguards would integrate the labour markets in the three countries relatively quickly, inducing a push disturbance of significant size, severity and concentration in the United States and Canada. Since trade is a substitute for, and complement to, migration, integration can be expected quickly to transfer (subject to the availability of transportation capacity and the lead times involved in creating new capacity in Mexico) some of the Mexican labour force inefficiency to the two northern members. Such a state of affairs could quickly arouse resentment in Canada and the United States so that the free trade agreement would be unilaterally rescinded by incoming politicians committed to such a step.[23]

There are two general policy recommendations which derive from a focus on labour force inefficiency: first, gradualism in putting the free trade area into effect for low-skill-intensive industries and heavy emphasis on improving the scope and efficiency of educational services in all countries. A reduction in the number of unskilled and low-skilled workers may not eliminate labour force inefficiency in a unified area completely because the capital stock may not support the available labour force (i.e. there would be straightforward structural unemployment), but a workforce with higher levels of skills would substantially reduce labour force inefficiency and would increase the international competitiveness of the region.

The argument for gradualism is not new (Gray, 1973). One feature of the success of the European Community has been the emphasis which placed on *gradual* elimination of impediments to trade and full membership – both originally in the Treaty of Rome and as new members have been admitted. There is no need to repeat much of that argument here[24] except to point out that the US clothing industry *and* its unions lobbied in 1989 against an increase in the minimum wage, a policy which must surely betoken a fear of a lack of alternative employment for clothing workers.[25] Labour force efficiency varies procyclically so that there is much to recommend any agreement tying the rate of unification to some measure of slack in the Canadian and US economies.

The problem of upgrading the provision of educational services is a serious one. The existing US system has been so starved of leadership and funding in important regions that it has become an object of derision – domestically and abroad. George Bush's assumption of the honorary title of 'the Education President' has been invalidated by his inability to raise more tax revenues in order to provide more public goods. Vested interests in the education sector are strong and are likely to oppose (and to do so effectively) new efficiency-enhancing measures even if they could be funded. Finally, it is important to consider the question of parental and peer-group support. Hodgkinson (1985, p. 11) gives the following description of the evolution of those who are likely to be the embodiment of labour force inefficiency:

> High-school drop-outs have a rather typical profile. They are usually from low-income or poverty settings, often from a minority group background, have very low basic academic skills, especially reading and math, have parents who are not high school graduates and who are generally uninterested in the child's progress in school, and do not provide a support system for academic progress.

Thus the educational systems must focus in on children who do not come from what Landry (1987) called 'striving families' which emphasize the upward mobility of their children at significant cost to their own material well-being and who harness community action to provide the needed support. But the prospect (in the United States) is not encouraging: the demographic trends suggest an increase in the number of children who will come from non-striving families and there has been a startling growth in the number of children born to unwed teenage mothers. These children and children from a growing number of one-parent homes generally perform far less well in school than do children from two-parent homes.[26]

13.5 CONCLUSION

This chapter has suggested that the problems of labour force inefficiency are substantial, growing and neglected both in analysis and, in the United States, in social policy.[27] In such a climate, the likelihood of a successful negotiation of a North American Free Trade Area is low. The Canadians go to the polls in 1993 and sufficiently serious economic problems perceived to derive from the Canada–United States Free Trade Agreement could raise questions as to the possible repeal of that agreement. It is certainly arguable that the benefits from free trade agreements, negotiated in times of substantial labour force inefficiency, will yield their benefits too long after their costs have aroused electorates to oppose them. In this they resemble Mr Gorbachov's venture known as perestroika (Goldman, 1988).

NOTES AND REFERENCES

1. This concept of efficiency is part of a heterodox approach to economics which argues that economists tend to develop models which focus on a single

dimension of efficiency (usually allocative efficiency) and to neglect, at significant cost to the reality of their analyses, other dimensions of efficiency and the interdependencies among them. (In addition to labour force efficiency, the approach considers allocative efficiency, social operating efficiency, social welfare efficiency, growth efficiency, cyclical efficiency and stability efficiency, but this list is by no means exhaustive.)

2. There is also the possibility that governments might, in a turbulent world of frequent disturbamces, change their institutional environments in order to increase the 'resilience' of the economy (Michalski, 1983).

3. There are obvious problems of definition which affect the construct put forward in this chapter. The age limits of the work force is a case in point as is, subsistence income. Both measures are subject to international differences in standards and subsistence income suffers from the further problem of quite substantial possible variability in the ratio of dependents to income earner. Note that international or intercultural differences in perceived levels of subsistence income could generate migration even when there are people working at less than subsistence in the country/region of inmigration.

4. It is possible that protracted absence from work could inflict mental damage and contribute to the number of such people.

5. Development economics has never had the luxury of ignoring surplus population and labour force inefficiency is a crucial feature in both the Lewis and the Ranis–Fei models of economic development. Similarly, indigence was widespread in Europe prior to industrialization (Cipolla, 1975, pp. 8–43).

6. The existence of labour force inefficiency may be self-perpetuating because sub-subsistence living reduces the quality of labour by reducing the health of workers and, through the effects of malnutrition of children, on the intellectual as well as the physical capacity of the workforce of later years. It also seems probable that the social costs of excess population are generated by labour force inefficiency in terms of crime, uprisings and revolt and/or in the costs of keeping the impoverished submissive.

7. Labour force inefficiency is compatible with a shortage of physical capital so that the marginal worker has no physical capital with which to ally him/herself and with a shortage of skilled workers (although firms will then have a direct incentive to upgrade workers).

8. Strictly the use of the incomes curve under conditions of less than full capacity utilization of the physical stock, i.e. during a cyclical downturn, raises serious questions of the conformity between current incomes and ability to survive at a subsistence level by drawing down financial reserves.

9. Porter (1990) has argued that for skilled occupations, general education should be provided by government and particular skills should be developed by the employer.

10. For a detailed consideration of the problems involved see Gray (1984) which draws heavily on Canterbery's vita theory (1979, 1980).

11. Cf. Aharoni (1991, p. 80): 'robotics and automation reduced the labour cost in car assembly from 30 percent in the 1950s to around 7 percent in the 1980s'.

12. The Bush administration, like its predecessor, argued that economic growth would reabsorb people back into the labour force, and put complete faith in a

Smithian system in which tax-financed, skill-enhancing public goods focusing on the issue of the development of a skilled labour force are not necessary.

13. This is the essence of the Schumpeterian approach to analysis recently adopted by Porter (1990).

14. The so-called 'Dutch disease' was a pull disturbance located in a natural resource sector which strengthened the Dutch guilder and put severe contractionary pressure on Dutch manufacturing and service industries.

15. Reductions to barriers would normally involve a lowering of tariffs or non-tariff barriers but could also include improved communications as market-sensitive goods with a short product life can now be produced at a greater distance from the market.

16. Some shocks reinforce their predecessors and others weaken them by countering their effects.

17. This is the premise underlying Leontief (1982) and Gray (1985) where new technologies are seen as twisting the incomes curve at the same time that increases in low-skilled, labour-intensive imports from developing countries changed the mix of output in such a way as to reinforce the twist. The adjustment costs in Canada of the Canada–United States Free Trade Agreement are likely to have been aggravated for the short term at least by the strengthening of the Canadian dollar in response to capital inflows into Canada from the United States, and by the fact that the Canadian economy had become tied more closely to that of the United States when the United States went into a deep recession.

18. In addition, significant loss of industry-specific capital (physical and human) could have macroeconomic effects by lowering the rate of saving in the economy.

19. Conglomerate firms may be more effective given their knowledge of the people involved and of their own internal needs.

20. Note that a recession refers to the direction of change of capacity utilization and the problem here is the trend level which is likely to be a function of economic growth rates.

21. Some decrease in labour force efficiency might be a cost exceeded by the benefits of the successful unification of the three economies (on the presumption that the worst effects on the structurally unemployed would be mitigated by a suitable policy of income support).

22. The incorporation of Mexico is more ambitious than the forays of the northern European countries in their expansion of the European Community to include such peripheral surplus labour countries as Greece, Spain and Portugal (Shelburne, 1991).

23. The post-Canada–US FTA job losses in Canada lowered the popularity rating of the incumbent prime minister to about 15 percent at the end of 1991. Possibly the Canadian electorate is susceptible to a *post hoc ergo propter hoc* fallacy but it could be argued that the FTA did contribute to the severity of the Canadian recession by tying the Canadian economy ever more closely to the recessionary US economy. Also the strength of the Canadian dollar contributes to the Canadian recession and is partly if not wholly due to the demand for Canadian funds on the part of US multinationals seeking to buy up Canadian firms.

24. *The Financial Times* (21 November 1991, p.4) reported: 'The textile sector could also be a sticking point. The Americans originally asked for forty years

of protection for their textile industry. According to one official present, the Mexicans and Canadians present "laughed and fell over their chairs".'

25. I am indebted to Manuel Gaetan for this observation. The clothing industry suffers from all the chronic sources of vulnerability to labour force inefficiency without NAFTA.

26. These points have been based on an unpublished paper entitled 'The Skill Capacity of the Labour Force', which develops these problems at greater depth.

27. However, Operation Head Start has survived.

Part IV
International Trade Issues

14 · Introduction

The three concluding chapters of this book deal with general issues in the area of international trade. Eckes criticizes that Washington has apparently abandoned the US's long-standing policy of cushioning temporarily US producers and workers from the injuries that may be impacted on them due to rising imports. Although some may consider the escape clause as being a protectionist anachronism, the author reminds that since the mid-1930s, similar mechanisms have helped assure continued Congressional backing for trade liberalization. The author thinks that even if a new President would be elected in 1992 (as was the case) and that even if this President were more disposed to grant escape clause relief than recent Republican presidents have been, prospective petitioners may still hesitate to file a petition until the International Trade Commission's composition changes.

E. Ray Canterbery presents a general theory of international trade and domestic employment adjustments, building upon Peter Gray's attempt to develop a 'pragmatic theory' of international trade. The author declares the purpose of his chapter as wanting to show how most trade theories can be summarized with a simplified production system that includes mark-up pricing, to integrate the author's version of Vernon's (1966) product cycle theory with the vita theory, and thirdly to suggest some broader policy implications.

The last chapter in the book, by Linda Longfellow Blodgett, refers to her empirical survey of recent shifts in global countertrade. The author points out that countertrade as a method for conducting international transactions does not only resolve the problem of the need for convertible currencies but also promotes bilateral negotiations at the expense of multilateral markets. Blodgett points out the necessity to rely heavily on examples in the absence of official countertrade statistics. Therefore, she points out that her figures are not a full record of total countertrade transactions, but that these do permit a look at relative patterns, comparing one region to another, and comparing one year to the next. The author states that the significant economic and political changes, specifically in the former Eastern European bloc, combined with liberalization programmes in many parts of the developing world, suggest that countertrade patterns will probably show significant changes as well.

15 Epitaph for the Escape Clause?

Alfred E. Eckes

15.1 INTRODUCTION

Official Washington has apparently abandoned the United States' long-standing policy of temporarily cushioning US producers and workers from the injurious impact of rising imports. For half a century – from the mid-1930s to the mid-1980s – elected officials in the United States could support tariff reductions and trade liberalization, confident that safeguards existed to protect American industries and workers against any injurious effects of surging imports. Firms and workers with trade-related complaints were advised to invoke the escape clause and petition the US International Trade Commission (ITC) for relief, not to seek special interest solutions from Congress.

Especially in the decade from 1975 to 1985, domestic firms – producing a variety of items from mushrooms and clothes pins to footwear, specialty steel and motorcycles – successfully pursued escape clause relief. Some gained a breathing space to become more competitive. In practice, this trade remedy process never functioned as well as domestic industries hoped, or perhaps as effectively as economic internationalists feared, but it did work frequently enough to divert protectionist pressures from Congress. Today, while the process remains intact, the door to escape clause relief appears to be shut fast. In the last five years no escape clause petition has succeeded and many observers believe the provision has become a dead letter.

Some may consider the escape clause (Section 201) a protectionist anachronism. But since the mid-1930s such safety valve mechanisms have helped assure continued congressional backing for trade liberalization (Eckes, 1987). Arguably, this concept remains relevant to facilitate the adjustment of trade-impacted firms to changing competitive conditions in an increasingly internationalized economy.

15.2 HISTORY

The notion that government should provide some temporary reprieve to domestic industries experiencing injury as a consequence of government trade concessions has a long history. The modern escape clause – effectively permitting the withdrawal of tariff concessions when increased imports from any foreign source caused substantial injury to domestic industries – first appeared in a 1943 bilateral reciprocal trade agreement with Mexico (Clubb, 1991; Jackson, 1986). But another version, directed only at third-country free-riders, was inserted in a number of early reciprocal trade agreements beginning with the 1935 Belgian pact. Interestingly, US officials originally fashioned the escape clause to prevent countries with low labour costs, like Japan, from gaining the principal benefits of reciprocal tariff reductions.

The version included in the Mexican agreement, was actually drafted in 1940 for inclusion in a proposed special trade agreement with Great Britain. Designed to help Britain pay for war materials, US officials proposed to open American markets to competitive woollens and cotton manufactures. But the Lend-Lease programme was adopted instead.

After World War II, congressional critics of the reciprocal trade agreements programme forced the Truman administration to include an escape clause in all trade agreements, including the General Agreement on Tariffs and Trade (Article XIX), as a condition for extending tariff-cutting authority (John Jackson, 1989). None the less, the Executive Branch remained reluctant to invoke the escape clause since the State Department was eager to enlarge the volume of US imports as part of its policy to build Cold War alliances and promote economic recovery in Western Europe and Japan.

Indeed, from 1951 to 1962 the Executive Branch exhibited reluctance to provide escape clause relief pursuant to statutory authority in the 1951 Act. In only fifteen of 112 investigations did domestic petitioners obtain some type of remedy. Even so, viewed from 1974, the Senate Finance Committee concluded that the provision had worked 'reasonably well. The criteria were fair and equitable, and relief was occasionally granted' (Senate, 1974).

However, the State Department and foreign governments remained apprehensive about the possibility of even more affirmative determinations. These would nullify concessions granted in trade negotiations and reverse the trend towards trade liberalization. Accordingly, in drafting the 1962 Trade Expansion Act, authorizing the Kennedy Round negotiations, the Executive tightened the causation requirement, so that the escape clause in effect became a dead letter during the 1960s. Indeed, from 1962 to 1969 the six-member Tariff Commission heard twenty-eight escape clause and adjustment assistance petitions, and rejected all of them (Clubb, 1991).

15.3 SECTION 201 – TRADE ACT OF 1974

Dissatisfied with lax trade law enforcement, the Nixon administration and Congress collaborated to revise laws and to revitalize the escape clause (Williams, 1971). As modified in the 1974 Trade Act, the new safeguards provision, Section 201, no longer withdrew or modified US tariff concessions. Rather Section 201 authorized only temporary relief – ranging from additional tariffs to quotas, adjustment assistance, and orderly marketing agreements – to facilitate the orderly adjustment of domestic industries to increased import competition. Industries that qualified, after proving their case to the International Trade Commission, could obtain a five-year breathing space. But first they must demonstrate that increased imports were indeed a substantial cause of serious injury, or threat thereof, to the domestic industry.

While the new law, like the older provisions, gave the International Trade Commission some flexibility to take into account 'all economic factors which it considers relevant', the 1974 statute attempted to define substantial cause as a 'cause which is important and not less than any other cause'. In essence, the law's sponsors envisaged a return to more vigorous trade remedy law administration.

Initially the 1974 law did seem to produce more affirmative determinations at the International Trade Commission, formerly the Tariff Commission (Gearhart, 1990). During the first decade of experience – from January 1975 to December 1984 – domestic industries won thirty-two of fifty four cases, for a success ratio of 59 per cent. In a significant number of cases (eighteen), Presidents then provided some relief, although not necessarily the specific remedy that the Commission majority advanced. Interestingly, the success ratio for petitioners did not vary much with different Presidents. As Table 15.1 shows, the Ford administration provided remedies in 40 per cent of the cases, the Carter administration in 31 per cent, and the Reagan administration in 30 per cent during its first term. Overall, domestic industries gained some relief in 33 per cent of the cases filed pursuant to provisions of the 1974 statute in the ten years from 1975 to 1984.

However, these statistics need cautious interpretation because individual remedies differed significantly. A tariff or quota might benefit all domestic producers and provide some general relief from imports,

Table 15.1   Section 201: escape clause cases

President	Cases filed	Commission affirmatives	President provides remedy	Percentage cases gaining some remedy
Ford	15	9	6	40%
Carter	29	18	9	31%
Reagan 1st term	10	5	3*	30%
Reagan 2nd term	7	2	1	14%

Note:
* Affirmatives include motorcycles, specialty steel, and carbon steel. In the latter case the administration provided relief in the form of restraint agreements, even as it claimed to reject the ITC solution.

while adjustment assistance provided aid only to specific victims. In particular, the Ford administration, like the prior Nixon administration, opted to pursue the adjustment assistance option. Indeed, in two such cases – footwear and flatware – the administration actually selected a remedy favoured by fewer than a majority of the ITC Commissioners. However, the Carter administration generally provided more substantial relief to politically powerful groups – specialty steel, footwear, colour televisions, fasteners and ferrochrome – although it turned down copper and flatware producers.

The single escape clause investigation with the greatest economic significance during these years involved a petition that the US automobile industry filed in 1980. Interestingly, although records in the Carter Library suggest the Carter administration had intended to provide relief to the domestic industry if the ITC rendered an affirmative determination, that situation did not arise. President Carter's own nominees voted to dismiss the case at the ITC factfinding stage. These three Commissioners (Alberger, Stern and Calhoun) – all former congressional staffers, under the age of 40 and owners of foreign-made automobiles – also turned down the President's request to expedite the administrative process and report a finding before the presidential election. Ironically, the only Republican Commissioners (Moore and Bedell) – both Nixon appointees in their mid-sixties, and drivers of American-made vehicles – voted for the US industry.

15.4   CHANGING PATTERNS

The large number of case filings (forty-four) between January 1975 and December 1980 undoubtedly reflected several circumstances. For one thing, in the aftermath of steep tariff cuts in the Kennedy Round of multilateral negotiations, the US market became more open to foreign competition than ever before. Also, Japan and the newly industrializing countries increasingly began to target the large and lucrative American market. Moreover, under the revised statute domestic industries seemed eager to test the law, and government officials seemed more disposed than previously to make affirmative determinations to domestic industries and to award import relief.

None the less, limits soon began to appear. Presidents Ford and Carter seldom provided *significant* relief to *major* industries. While the automobile industry did pursue this trade remedy, the Executive remained reluctant to concede escape clause relief to a large industry, because of the possible need to pay compensation to affected trading partners and because of the signal it would send to other industries. Also, the foreign policy agencies repeatedly expressed concerns that a presidential decision to award relief could trigger protectionist reactions in other countries against US exports (Eckes, 1992).

Indeed, the Executive had a dilemma. To satisfy Congress, and discourage quota legislation, the White House needed to demonstrate occasionally that the escape clause worked. Consequently, presidents upheld ITC recommendations to provide relief to a host of smaller industries – such as clothes pins, flatware, mushrooms, shakes and shingles, and tuna fish. Some of these seemed to lead a precarious hand-to-mouth existence, possibly using periods of escape clause relief to generate enough additional revenue to pay for the costs of filing future escape clause petitions. Others, such as the specialty steel and footwear producers, approached the government apparently confident that they were entitled to escape clause relief because they had received it in the past.

However, of the industries successfully winning relief under Section 201, only Harley-Davidson, the only US producer of motorcycles in 1983, claimed to use the period of relief to become export competitive again. Others, such as the footwear producers, had few meaningful plans for adjustment, because there was little opportunity to substitute more efficient production technology for labour-intensive production methods. Some footwear producers apparently used periods of escape clause relief to reposition their firms into specialty niches, or to develop overseas production facilities.

Why did more industries not use the 1974 escape clause to become
export competitive, as Harley-Davidson, the sole remaining US motorcycle
producer, did? In my view there are several explanations. First, under the
statute relief is costly, time-consuming and unpredictable. To present their
case, most industries choose to retain qualified, and expensive, Washington
counsel. Along with the time needed to prepare a petition, the ITC then
takes six months to conduct its factfinding investigation. In short, the
administrative process can consume a significant share of industry executives time and attention. Even if the industry persuades a majority of the
impartial six-member ITC, it must then mount a Washington-style lobbying operation to persuade the Executive Branch. At that level, a host of
intricate considerations may impact the outcome in unpredictable ways.
Perhaps the White House is concerned that a decision favourable to the
domestic industry will rattle foreign governments or upset domestic consumers of the imported product.

It has been my experience that the ITC tends to be chary about providing
escape clause relief, and officials in the Executive Branch and the White
House even more hesitant to uphold import remedies. There is a tendency
to award relief only when it is unavoidable or when the relief has minimal
trade consequences, such as in cases involving clothes pins, motorcycles,
mushrooms, and shakes and shingles.

I would suggest another pertinent explanation: the appointment to the
ITC of individuals philosophically opposed to escape clause relief. Commissioners who served in the 1970s and the early 1980s generally did not
view the decision to provide escape clause relief as a battle in the long war
between the forces of protectionism and free trade. Instead, they took the
view that Congress and the Executive had settled the fundamental trade
policy issue in writing the 1974 Trade Act. As a result, the critical issues
were more narrow: what were the facts in the case at hand? Did they satisfy
legal requirements for import remedies?

Until the end of President Reagan's first term the pattern of escape
clause administration resembled the Ford and Carter administrations. The
ITC recommended, and President Reagan concurred, in extending relief to
the clothes pin industry and in providing new import remedies for producers of motorcycles and specialty steel. While rejecting the Commission's specific remedy for carbon steel, the Reagan White House proceeded
to establish a programme of bilateral restraint agreements.

The Reagan administration's attitude began to change when the Commission sent two escape clause recommendations to the President for review in
election year 1984. Sensitive to public criticism, the administration rejected
relief for copper producers and claimed to turn down an ITC recommendation

for aid to the carbon steel industry. In 1985, the White House also dismissed a recommendation for relief to the non-rubber footwear producers. These rejections had a chilling effect on subsequent ITC proceedings.

Other evidence of a changing White House attitude appeared in the nomination of several ideologues to fill vacancies on the ITC. Indeed, beginning in mid-1984 Congress confirmed several doctrinaire individuals who believed that the escape clause was bad law because it seemed to conflict with their understanding of sound economic principles. In contrast with the generation of Commissioners who served earlier and had personal experience with the lawmaking process as congressional employees, the new Commissioners had little previous public sector experience and approached trade issues with *tabulae rasae*. Also, the new Commissioners paid little attention to former Commission practice or the legislative history, but instead interpreted the law consistent with their own personal predilections.

Table 15.2 documents the change in attitude towards escape clause enforcement at the ITC. As a group the Nixon appointees voted affirmatively for escape clause injury findings in 56.7 per cent of cases. The single Ford nominee, a Democrat with ties to the Senate Finance Committee, voted affirmatively 43 per cent. The three Carter nominees voted for domestic industries 30.8 per cent of the time. At first, the Reagan appointees conformed to this pattern. The first four appointees (Eckes, Frank, Haggart and Lodwick), all confirmed in the period 1981 to 1983, voted for the domestic industry at a 39 per cent rate.

In 1985, the ITC approach to escape clause investigations began to change. Support for use of Section 201 declined dramatically with the confirmation of three White House nominees (Liebeler, Brunsdale and Cass). As a group, these ardent deregulators, none of whom had legislative experience with Congress, supported injury findings in only 11 per cent of all votes. Indeed, in casting her only two affirmative injury votes, Commissioner Liebeler then refused to recommend specific remedies to remedy the injury she had found. Two others confirmed during this period, Commissioners Rohr and Newquist, each had strong ties to congressional Democrats, and voted more consistently with earlier appointees. They favored the domestic industry in 33 per cent of votes.

15.4 CONCLUSION

There is no indication that the present pattern of escape clause administration at the ITC or the White House will change in the months immediately ahead. Philosophically, the Bush administration was opposed to escape

Table 15.2   Voting record of commissioners grouped by administration

Commissioner aff/percentage (President/Party)	Affirmatives	Negatives	Percentage
G. Moore (R) (Nixon)	24	14	63
C. Bedell (R) (Nixon)	20	17	54
J. Parker (R) (Nixon)	17	9	65
I. Ablondi (D) (Nixon)	15	18	45
D. Minchew (D) (Ford)	13	17	43
B. Alberger (D) (Carter)	6	10	37.5
P. Stern (D) (Carter)	6 [also 2 divided votes]	15	28.6
M. Calhoun (I) (Carter)	0	2	00
A. Eckes (R) (Reagan)	7	10	41
G. Frank (R) (Reagan)	1	0	100
V. Haggart (R) (Reagan)	2	2	50
S. Lodwick (R) (Reagan)	4	10	28.6
S. Liebeler (I) (Reagan)	2	9	18
A. Brunsdale (R) (Reagan)	0	7	00
D. Rohr (D) (Reagan)	5	9	35.7
R. Cass (D) (Reagan)	0	1	00
D. Newquist (D) (Reagan)	0	1	00

Notes:
*Divided votes were excluded in several instances.
Source: Author's computations from ITC public data.

clause relief. Probably the Clinton administration will continue this free trade consensus. However, a successor Democratic administration might choose to provide more adjustment assistance to appease organized labour.

Moreover, immediate effect on the composition and philosophy of the independent ITC. As of June 1993, the ITC continued to function with six Commissioners – all appointed by Presidents Reagan and Bush. The Clinton administration has not settled on a nominee to replace Commissioner Brunsdale who continued to serve despite the expiration of her nine-year term.

Although President Clinton may be more disposed than other recent Presidents to provide escape-clause relief, prospective petitioners, remembering the 1980 automobile clause, will hesitate to bring an escape clause petition until the ITC's composition changes. Instead, domestic industries will continue to rely on countervailing and and anti-dumping law, filing so-called 'unfair trade' cases. Unlike escape clause proceedings, these are conducted according to quasi-judicial procedures, and ITC determinations face judicial review on legal criteria, not White House review on policy criteria.

16   A General Theory of
International Trade and
Domestic Employment
Adjustments

E. Ray Canterbery

16.1   INTRODUCTION

Peter Gray (1976, 1979, 1985) has attempted to develop a 'pragmatic theory' of international trade by including considerations related to specific human capital, or 'skill mix', the vita theory, the Linder thesis, and the product cycle.

Originally, the vita theory was developed to explain the personal income distribution (Canterbery, 1979). Even though the original version focused upon the labour market and a non-neoclassical theory of wages, the labour market was made the centrepiece of a later exposition (Canterbery, 1980).

Peter Gray saw the vita theory as the 'Rosetta Stone which enabled [him] to formulate all [his] misgivings about the interaction of rapid changes in trade patterns and the rate of employment in industrialized nations' (Gray, 1985, p. x). Gray relied not only upon the 1979 and 1980 papers but also upon extensive discussions. This version, summarized in section 16.3, has deliberate parallels with the Canterbery–Gray dialogue in Gray (1985). The vita approach is a part of my theory of supra-surplus capitalism (1984, 1987a, 1987b).

The purposes of this chapter are (i) to show how most trade theories can be summarized with a simplified production system that includes mark up pricing, (ii) to integrate my version of Vernon's (1966) product cycle theory with the vita theory, and (iii) to suggest some broader policy implications.

16.2   A SIMPLIFIED PRODUCTION SYSTEM

We begin with a production system in which the technical methods of production are given by a matrix of interindustry coefficients in physical units,

147

denoted by A, and by a row vector of direct labour coefficients in physical units, denoted by a_n.

The meaning of the notation is familiar to input-output theorists. Each element a_{ij} (where $a_{jj} \geq 0, j = 1, 2, ..., n-1; i = 1, 2, ..., n$) of A represents the physical quantity of the i-th commodity needed in the j-th industry for the production of one physical unit of the j-th commodity. These coefficients are decided by the optimal techniques of production, processes that are given initially for the period of production.

In compact notation

$$[A, a_n] \tag{1}$$

where A is non-singular and the transpose of which can be written as

$$[A, a_n]'. \tag{2}$$

Equation 1 is only a production possibilities matrix since we have no assurance that effective demand will be sufficient to purchase the implied outputs.

In its initial stationary state the production system produces the same physical quantities of commodities each time period of production. The inputs are physical quantities of raw materials, capital type commodities and labour time. All inputs except labour are treated as intermediate goods so that investment can only be identified as 'capital-type durable goods', including Gray's traditional or reproducible capital. These commodities (as inputs) are used up in each production period so that they have to be replaced entirely. The residual replaced is the value added in the economic system. (That is, depreciation equals investment in raw materials and capital-type goods.)

The value added in the economic system equals the value of the commodities making up its net national income (or net product). This net national income is distributed as wages, net interest and profits. In general, wages are distributed in proportion to the contributed physical quantity of labour of a particular type and quality. However, a specific money wage rate is determined in the 'labour market' for the labour type and quality required. Following the vita theory, labour *is* of different qualities and therefore the wage rates will vary by industry. Shadow wages are paid to managers and professionals.[1]

The mark up over prime costs in each industry *is* the profit rate. The firm (industry) sets the mark up and thus profit rate according to the elasticity of demand for its product (an elasticity decided primarily by the degree of closeness of substitute products) and, where applicable, by rents on those inputs fixed in supply by quantity or quality. The mark up includes then the 'returns' paid to rent-earning inputs, a 'residual' in Gray (1979, p. 90). Substitution is limited from the *consumer's* perspective when groups of commodities are considered as inputs in the consumer's production function. On the other hand, the industry has some control over demand elasticity wherever products or services can be differentiated, as is presumed in the Linder thesis.[2] The rate of profit also varies by industry but can be identical over a large number of industries of a particular class.[3]

Given $[A, a_n]'$ and the assumptions regarding money wages and profit rates, money prices can be expressed as

$$P = PA(I + \pi') + a_n W'(I + \pi), \tag{3}$$

where P denotes the row vector of prices, π' the column vector of mark ups (profit rates), and W' the column vector of wage rates. The first group of terms, $PA(I + \pi')$, reflects the cost of using commodities to produce commodities and the second, $a_n W'(I + \pi')$, reflects the variable costs of labour in production.

Wage and profit rates are decided *outside* the production system and are thus 'given' in equation 3. Therefore, we have $n-1$ equations in which to solve for $n-1$ money prices. Such money prices are then decided by a combination of the 'outside' wage and profit rates and the technical conditions of production in which various commodity inputs are intermediate goods. In the special (and highly improbable) case in which perfect competition prevails and wage rates and profit rates are uniform throughout the system, relative money prices and relative real prices of commodities would be equal. However, when the prices are expressed in money terms (as they are here), we think of them ordinarily as absolute prices.

The system must be self-consistent in terms of money prices. That is, a low price elasticity of demand in one commodity market raises the profit margin and thus prices of all commodities that use the first commodity as an input beyond what their costs would be if the input were priced at zero economic profit. This consistency is reflected in the solution of the price system which is

$$P = a_n W'(I + \pi') \{I - A(I + \pi')\}^{-1} \tag{4}$$

The inverted matrix in equation 4, $\{.\}^{-1}$, is non-negative and gives the total (direct and indirect) requirements of commodities for the production of final commodities (i.e. of consumption and new investment-type goods), taking into account their shares going to real profits in each industry. The element α_{ij} $(i, j = 1, 2, ..., n-1)$ of this inverse matrix represents the physical quantity of the i-th commodity needed in the economic system as a whole (including real profits allocations) to obtain eventually one physical unit of the j-th commodity as a final good.[4] Although money wage and profit rates come from outside the production system, equation 4 shows that money price changes are also related to the interdependencies of techniques.

For example, total production of good 1 is

$$Q_1 = \{\bar{\alpha}_{11} \ \bar{\alpha}_{12} \ ... \ \bar{\alpha}_{ij} \ ... \ _{1,n-1}\}\{\bar{y}_1 + \bar{e}_1\} \tag{5}$$

where $\bar{y}_1 + \bar{e}_1$ is a level of real final demand, again decided outside the production system, and the $\bar{\alpha}_{ij}$s denote the *traditional* direct and indirect requirements. The $\bar{y}$s represent the demands for goods produced domestically whereas the $\bar{e}$s represent the goods exported or imported (imports being *negative* exports). For the entire system,

$$Q = [I - A]^{-1} (\bar{Y} + \bar{E}) \tag{6}$$

and aggregate output is the vector

$$Q = [Q_1 \ Q_2 \ ... \ Q_{n-1}] \tag{7}$$

The money price of the j-th commodity equals the sum of the costs of the quantities of the input commodities needed in the entire economic system to produce one unit of final good. Once this price is known,

$$p_j \cdot q_j = (\bar{y}_j + \bar{e}_j) \cdot (p_j) = (y_j + e_j) \tag{8}$$

gives the gross money income or gross output of the j-th industry. In general

$$PQ = (\bar{Y} + \bar{E}) P = Y \tag{9}$$

The value added (V) in the economy is

$$V = a_n \ W'(I + \pi')\{I - A(I + \pi')\} \ Q \tag{10}$$

At any particular technology, the distribution of income depends upon wage rates and price mark ups.

We next come to the critical issues. How do labour markets and workers adjust to changes in product demand, especially when those changes are related to foreign trade? We consider the vita theory of the labour market.

16.3 THE VITA THEORY AND THE LABOUR MARKET

16.3.1 Production Labour Requirements

Let us begin with the labour requirements from the simplified production model. If labour requirements are expressed in terms of number of workers, the total employment for the stationary state is

$$a_{n1}Q_1 + a_{n2}Q_2 + \ldots a_{n,n-1}Q_{n-1} = L \tag{11}$$

where L equals total national employment at the Q levels of physical output (some of which is exported). However, this is a gross oversimplification since different qualities of labour are used in different industries (or for that matter in the *same* industry). More accurately, therefore, the a_{nj}s represent several different types of labour. Represent each labour type by $I, II, III, \ldots,$ D in which there are D labour types and

$$[a_I a_{II} a_{III} \ldots a_D] \tag{12}$$

are the types of unit labour requirements available to *each* industry, though not all industries will use all D types. The labour requirements by labour type become

$$
\begin{aligned}
L_I &= a_{I1}Q_1 + a_{I2}Q_2 + \ldots a_{I,n-1}Q_{n-1} \\
L_{II} &= a_{II1}Q_1 + a_{II2}Q_2 + \ldots a_{II,n-1}Q_{n-1} \\
&\;\; \cdot \qquad \cdot \qquad \cdot \quad \ldots \qquad \cdot \\
&\;\; \cdot \qquad \cdot \qquad \cdot \quad \ldots \qquad \cdot \\
&\;\; \cdot \qquad \cdot \qquad \cdot \quad \ldots \qquad \cdot \\
L_D &= a_{D1}Q_1 + a_{D2}Q_2 + \ldots a_{D,n-1}Q_{n-1}
\end{aligned}
\tag{13}
$$

or, compactly,

$$L = [a_{jVIV}]_{n-1XD}Q \tag{14}$$

where $[a_{jVIV}]_{n-1XD}$ is the entire matrix of labour requirements by type and Q is a column vector of output.

16.3.2 Specific Human Capital

Now, we turn more directly to the vita theory. Assume that one labour market exists for each general human capital classification. One's quantity of human capital determines *which* labour market one enters; one 'qualifies' for that market by the state of one's current vita. Determination of the vita begins at birth when one's race, sex, religion, national origin, inherent mental and physical capacity, inheritances, and family background are duly noted. The theory integrates a non-circular version of human capital and labour market theory (Canterbery, 1979, 1980).

With D labour types there are D categories of general human capital, derived from human characteristics conforming with job descriptions and meeting employer job requirements. These categories can be ranked by inherent skill requirements. For example, HCI denotes Human Capital Type 1 (the greatest quantity of human capital) and HCD the last human capital type. Each of D human capital types is potentially available in every geographically defined area. For simplicity, each industry is located in a unique geographical area so that the number of industries match the number of geographical zones.

All labour markets can be represented by a partitioned row vector,

$$HC' = [HCI_1\ HCII_1 \dots HCD_1 | HCI_2\ HCII_2 \dots HCD_2 | \qquad (15)$$
$$\dots HCI_{n-1}\ HCII_{n-1} \dots HCD_{n-1}],$$

in which D general human capital types are matched with $n-1$ labour markets in $n-1$ geographic areas for a total of $n-1{}^{*} D$ labour markets.

Now we place persons into the HC categories. Each cell of the matrix contains all persons qualified by vita to perform the tasks in question. Each person will place himself/herself in the highest cell desired and attainable. Within each cell, in turn, persons are ranked according to the comparative quality of their vitae.

One can imagine a long line of rank-ordered persons in each cell. There is a matrix of this description for each geographical area within the national labour market. A regional or geographical submarket precludes the spatial relocation of a worker in the short run. This is so even though the market for a professional such as medical doctor or university professor is defined as a national market.

Thus for each labour market we can write a column vector of vitae whose elements equal that vitae population. Assume that the largest number is s of the Dth HC type, representing the workforce population for the lowest skilled market. The i-th vitae vector for *all HC* types is:

$$V_i = \{ VI_{1i} \, VI_{2i} \ldots VI_{gi} | \, VII_{1i} \, VII_{2i} \ldots VII_{ri} | \qquad (16)$$
$$\ldots VD_{1i} \, VD_{2i} \ldots VD_{si} \}.$$

There is a national supermatrix of vitae that includes all labour markets and associated vitae (in rank order from most to least preferred employee characteristics). This ordering can best be thought of as a labour queue, but at either a local or a national level.

Within each general human capital category are a number of 'occupations' or subspecialities. Gray (1979, p. 88) has called this 'industry specific' human capital. The separation of individual tasks into occupations depends upon the elasticity of substitution in supply. Let the category of general human capital with the most occupations – probably the category of unskilled labour – have m occupations. Then there exists an n by m matrix of *specific* human capital with a large number of zero elements.

Thus, for each homogeneous labour type we can write alternatively a *column* vector of occupations, also in rank order. If the lowest skilled market, the i-th, contains m occupations, this column vector is:

$$HCO_i = \{ HCOI_{1i} \, HCOI_{2i} \ldots HCOI_{mi} | \qquad (17)$$
$$HCOII_{1i} \, HCOII_{2i} \ldots HCOII_{mi} |$$
$$\ldots HCOD_{1i} \, HCOD_{2i} \ldots HCOD_{mi} \}$$

Now, a still larger supermatrix of vitae would include all occupations and associated vitae. The occupational matrix (HCO) could be defined as a submatrix of its labour force population.

13.3.3 Excess Supplies

There is a mirror matrix for the demand for labour. Within each of its cells is the number of workers required. With firms in each region having fixed quantities of capital goods operating under a given state of technology, aggregate demand for goods and services and the categories of that demand determine the short-run amounts of labour demanded. When more labour is demanded, the producer 'opens the door' to an HC cell and invites the top-ranked workers into the shop.

The demand and supply matrices coexist at a moment in time. When they are placed in opposition, the number of workers in the cells of the supply matrix can be subtracted from the number in the matching cell in the demand matrix, generating a matrix of 'excess demand'.[5] In the presence of 'excess supply' the unemployed will be those workers lowest ranked by vitae within the cell. The probability of a perfect match is very low (except in some elusive steady state), because both matrices are in a continuous state of evolution.

16.3.4   Evolution in Demand and Supply

Demand matrix evolution is related to exogenous and to induced changes. Exogenous technological change or changes in the pattern of demand for goods alters the nature of the labour demand matrix. Also, patterns of labour and capital costs can induce changes in the labour intensity and the skill intensity of the selected capital-type goods. There is even a feedback mechanism in which changes in the personal income distribution will alter the level and mix of goods demanded.[6] Long-run evolutions in the supply matrix are mostly endogenous, as persons have time to adjust to changing patterns of excess labour demand and to anticipated future changes. However, the quality of training and education can alter the supply matrix. Over a long enough period, demographic movements and changes in the skill level of the population affect the supply matrices, and the demand matrices are transmuted by alterations in the vintages of physical capital-type goods in response to new technologies, changes in relative input costs, and changes in the mix of goods demanded.

The *birth vita* is 'added to' over one's lifespan by education, other training and experience. Since the amount of labour demanded is related to product prices and a changing technology, however, only the rare person can predict with any accuracy the derived demand for workers with vitae of his or her type. Moreover, specific labour supply conditions are a collective consequence outside personal control.

The *pre-career vita* adds to the characteristics at birth both education and 'first-time' on-the-job training. The *mature vita* (the labour market vita) also carries work experience. The individual confronts a large number of homogeneous and, thus, non-competing labour markets in which each exhibit a 'wage of central tendency'.[7]

A particular individual's wage is determined by the rate paid to occupants of the highest cell to which the individual may aspire and find employment. Thus, for the highest cell in the matrix,

$$W = W(K, k, p, m, m^*, M, R, t) \tag{18}$$

where K is human capital as described by the vita, k is non-human capital available, p is the price of the end product, m and m^* are, respectively, assessments of the ease of mobility and uncertainty surrounding the costs and benefits of relocation, M is any monopoly power in the submarket due to either a labour union's or a professional association's ability to create barriers to entry, R is a factor of discrimination and t represents experience. Both k and t can be product- or skill-specific, and the variables are then identified in terms of the relevant k or t.

For our purposes, human capital can be condensed to

$$K = K\,(G, E, k, t, s) \tag{19}$$

where G is biological inheritance, E is familial environment from the birth vita and s is the amount of formal education and training which the individual has received.

Gray (1985, p. 54) correctly perceives that the argument for commercial policy is based upon the quickness in which international disturbances occur relative to the slowness in which displaced workers can be dispersed into jobs in other industries, sectors and regions by the mechanism of the market. Alternatively put, exchange rates or tariffs can change faster than workers can be retrained. This is so whether the national labour market is suffering widespread excess supply or whether there are mismatches between the labour supply and demand matrices in the submarkets of the regional/industry matrices (e.g. Detroit).

16.4 INNOVATIONS, THE PRODUCT CYCLE AND UNDEREMPLOYMENT

According to the vita theory, unemployment and underemployment are related to innovations and demand changes whether purely domestic or (with Gray's extension) external.

A specific innovation is not equally likely in all countries but arises when several conditions are favourable: (i) a large domestic market (facilitating economies of scale), (ii) high per capita income fairly evenly distributed, (iii) a relatively high cost of labour. These conditions reduce the risk of introduction of a new product with high initial production costs.

Enter product cycle theory (Vernon, 1966). The early innovator will retain its lead for some time. Late-starting producers elsewhere, with a limited domestic market for the product, will be inclined to compete with established producers in their own market, where they have already achieved economies of scale. The innovator's head start derives from a magical combination of a large market and high per capita incomes. Facing little foreign competition, the innovator begins exporting, often finding the initial market for consumer goods among the high income groups in other countries. As incomes and labour costs rise abroad, foreign producers also become willing to buy new processes that replace labour. The exports or *e*'s become a more and more important source of sales revenue.

16.4.1   Wages and Price Competition

Eventually the demand in some foreign markets is sufficiently large to sustain a local production unit that can exploit scale economies, and the product becomes so standardized that price competition rears its ugly head. Cost considerations and thus wages begin to play a role in production location.

When labour is variable in type the price solution comparable to equation 4 is

$$P = [a_{jVIV}]_{n-1XD} \, Wa'(I + \pi)\{I - A(I + \pi')\}^{-1} \tag{20}$$

where $[a_{jVIV}]$ is the labour requirements *matrix* for all industries by labour type and Wa' is a column vector of 'labour market' wage rates. (The first π is now a *row* vector.) The wage rates are now 'labour market' wage rates and therefore more than one wage rate applies to each industry.

Let E represent the complete vector of all household goods so that in the entire system the wage rate can be expressed as the vector

$$[PE] \tag{21}$$

By substitution of *PE* for *W'* in Equation 3,

$$P = PA(I + \pi') + a_n \, PE(I + \pi) \tag{22}$$

We now have the 'standard of living' of the workers (and managers and professionals who receive a 'shadow' standard of living). At a minimum society will expect the system to maintain a demand for consumption goods equal to E and a demand for raw materials and investment-type goods sufficient to maintain E.

Assume that the lowest wage in the system, w_1, is a subsistence wage just sufficient to buy essentials, E_1, and that the overall standard of living is measured by this wage. (The rationale is that these items or close substitutes appear in *every household budget*.) Let *PE* be a price index expressed as a scaler (γ) whose initial value is $\gamma_1 = 1$. Then, by substitution of $PE = \gamma_1 = 1$ into equation 22

$$P = PA(I + \pi') + a_n \, \gamma_1(I + \pi') \tag{23}$$

and

$$P = \gamma_1 a_n (I + \pi')\{I - A(I + \pi')\}^{-1} \tag{24}$$

so that individual prices are expressed in terms of an essentials' price index as a numeraire (γ). A necessary condition of the system to have an economically meaningful solution is that det $\{I-(1-\pi)(A-\gamma_1 a_n)\} = 0$. Now, assume an exogenous increase in the prices subsumed in w_1 so that the price index doubles to 2, and $\gamma_2 = 2$. Then,

$$P = \gamma_2 a_n(I + \pi')\{I - A(I + \pi')\}^{-1} \tag{25}$$

so that – according to a rule by which all wage rates are adjusted by changes in the cost of living – a doubling in the price index results in higher prices of *all* goods that use labour in production *including the goods subsumed in w_1* so that wages are increased once again. The use of an iterative method gives a wage–price spiral as a consequence of standard of living adjustments in the wage rate. The change in relative prices would, of course, depend upon the *net* labour intensity of production in the various industries.[8]

16.4.2 Standardized Technology and Its Export

At this point another problem for the innovator emerges. Low wage countries can use standardized technology to produce the now standardized product. Producers in such countries can compete within their markets and even begin to displace the innovator, who may change from net exporter of the particular product to net importer (negative exports). The foreign facilities may be controlled by a foreign multinational firm (moving to low cost, low skilled labour markets) or by a local firm. Meanwhile, the stages of product development have gone from new to maturing to standardized product.

Consider, within the vita theory, how employment in an industry is altered over this product cycle. In the short run employment is a fixed proportion of production and the quantity of labour demanded of the i-th human capital type (HC_i) is

$$Z_i = a_i q_j$$

where q_j is the total output of product j, assumed homogeneous across the labour market.

If labour is paid its competitive value in production (as in Gray's 'eclectic theory'), the 'wage rate of central tendency' is

$$w_i = a_i^{-1}p \tag{27}$$

where p is the price of the product or service. Where wages are bargained, the labour market wage rate will be somewhere between the above wage and a premium wage in which all economic profits are paid to labour. That is, if product and labour markets are imperfect, the wage rate is bargained and is represented in the j-th labour market by

$$w_j = a_j^{-1}p + II \tag{28}$$

where II = the economic profits allocated to workers per hour of effort. In the short run, employment levels are independent of the wage rate and dependent upon output wherein labour competes by its position in the queue. National full employment occurs only when excess supplies of labour are zero across the partitioned occupation matrix. A high wage can be associated with a high unemployment rate.

16.5   ECONOMIC GROWTH AND EMPLOYMENT ADJUSTMENTS

Let us return to the complete production model. In order for economic growth to occur, technology must improve, net savings and net investment occur, or both. If the marginal propensity to consume is less than unitary, then

$$S = Y - D \tag{29}$$

where S = aggregate savings, Y = aggregate national income and D = aggregate demand. Investment in additional capital-type goods, raw materials accumulation, positive product inventories, and new technological innovation can happen.

With the possibility of net new investment,

$$Q(t) - AQ(t) = Y(t) \tag{30}$$

will no longer suffice as the definition of net national income because more than $AQ(t)$ will need to be set aside at the end of the production period. The net product of the system, $Y(t)$, is no longer devoted entirely to using the commodities produced, some is set aside to provide for the expansion of output capacity. The net product not devoted to consumption is assigned to new investment.

The simplest dynamic model has consumers' preferences, technology, the structure of prices, and the composition of consumption constant through time. Per capita consumption is constant so that the labour force and consumption grow at the same rate, g. Thus,

$$C(t) = cN(t) = cN(0)[1 + g]^t \tag{31}$$

where $C(t)$ represents consumption goods and $N(t)$ is population. Let $J(t)$ equal new investment-type goods. At a fixed technology, A,

$$J(t) = gAQ(t) \tag{32}$$

so that all physical quantities among the means of production $AQ(t)$ increase at the same rate. Thus,

$$Q(t) - AQ(t) - gAQ(t) = cN(t) \tag{33}$$

with solution

$$Q(t) = [I - (1+g)A]^{-1} cN(t), \text{ or} \tag{34}$$
$$Q(t) = [I - (1+g)A]^{-1} cN(0)[1+g]^t \tag{35}$$

and the total physical quantities in $Q(t)$ grow at the same rate, g, as do the physical quantities in $C(t)$. For the exponential growth of consumption, $C(t)$, this solution gives the total physical quantities, $Q(t)$, required – direct and indirect, including new investment – to keep the system in dynamic equilibrium.

The labour required (and assumed to be demanded) is

$$L(t) = [a_{JVIV}]_{n-1XD}Q(t) = [a_{JVIV}]_{m-1XD}[I - (1+g)A]^{-1}cN(o)[1+g]^t \tag{36}$$

so that full utilization of capacity and full employment (assuming initial full employment) further requires

$$L(t) = L^*(t) \tag{37}$$

where L^* is the workforce size, plus the presumption that *all* labour quality types grow at the same rate. Unfortunately, this dynamic equilibrium model generates improbable economic behaviour.

Even in the basic steady state model prices and the compositions of consumption and of labour requirements can change. That is, even a steady state equilibrium does not require such severe restrictions. Moreover, we know that in the long run technology mutates, requiring an alteration in the composition of labour and capital requirements. New technology that produces new consumer goods types (new industries) also changes the technology available to consumers for satisfying their needs and wants. The production coefficients in the A matrix of existing industries can change in the long run. Moreover, new industries give entirely new rows to the A matrix. With these new conditions the hypothesized wage rate and profit rate movements will cause different patterns of price variations. In contrast, for example, specify that

$$W'(t) = W'_a(0)[1+\rho]^t \tag{38}$$

where $W'_a(0) = I$ and ρ is a column vector of rates of growth in wage rates, as determined by labour market conditions, so that

$$W'(t) = [1+\rho]^t \tag{39}$$

By substitution of equation 39 into equation 20 the price system becomes

$$P(t) = [a_{JVIV}]_{n-1XD}[1+\rho]^t(I+\pi)\{I - A(I+\pi')\}^{-1} \tag{40}$$

This solution says that prices change at different rates (*even* if profit rates are constant).[9]

The constancy of the a_is is always provisional. In the mature stage of the product cycle, the ai's decrease even as the growth rates of the q_js decline. Rising wage rates lead to the substitution of capital for labour in increasingly automated factories. The amounts of labour demanded decrease, so that only the highest ranked vitae enter the employer's door. Employment declines. Since the product and the technology are standardized, more and more production is shifted abroad. Still greater 'excess supplies' of labour appear in the cells of the matrices.

In the standardized product/technology stage a balance-of-payments deficit accompanies rising unemployment and underemployment.

16.6   BEYOND THE STANDARDIZATION OF TECHNOLOGY

In J. Schumpeter's theory of capitalism, the entrepreneur is the innovator. Schumpeter begins his system in a stationary condition of Walrasian equilibrium (similar to that of section 16.2). There is no extraordinary opportunity for profits; only a circular flow of economic activity in which the system merely reproduces itself. The entrepreneur daringly raids the circular flow and diverts labour and land to investment goods. Since only the more enterprising and venturesome persons act, innovations appear in 'swarms'. In turn, the entrepreneurs create favourable conditions for other, less venturesome firms to follow.

Vernon's product cycle can be used to explain why the long wave comes to an end and Schumpeterian innovations can explain why the end ends. The older industrialized nations, those with great amounts of intra-industry trade, have had large numbers of product cycles peaking simultaneously. Most dramatically, standardization and mass production characterize the textile, steel, automotive and consumer electronics industries.

Not only is the income elasticity of demand for their products low, but export prospects among those countries producing the same goods are dim. Surely, clever manufacturers and advertising agencies can postpone mass realization of sameness, but eventually the cause becomes hopeless, especially when all opportunities for *real* as opposed to imaginary product 'improvements' have been made. Such is the nature of supra-surplus capitalism (Canterbery, 1984, 1987b).

Mensch (1979) provides data suggesting that basic innovations do occur in swarms, as Schumpeter claimed; and, importantly for the present malaise, the frequency of the most recent swarm of basic innovations peaked in 1935 (in the middle of the Great Depression!). If the average product life cycle – from basic innovation to maturity – is a half century, a large share of the 1935–centred swarm would reach maturity, or the top of their product S-curves, in 1985.

During the last half of a long-wave expansion, the unit labour requirements of the vita theory take on an unexpected realism. Once the basic process innovations are widely diffused in the economy, the industrial branch becomes remarkably rigid in its technique (fixed a_i's). True, as Vernon says, the size of plants grow large, but the same technique is simply replicated on a larger scale, at home and abroad. In the final throes of decline, ironically, the production technology finally *is* modified by *improvement* innovations (smaller a_i's); automation in the standardized product-manufacturing industries is used to replace high wage labour, at home and abroad.

A new long wave is not automatic for a particular nation. About two-thirds of the technological basic innovations that will be produced in the second half of the twentieth century will occur in the decade around 1989. The greatest surge of innovations occurred in 1985, a year comparable (on the scale of innovations) to 1825, 1886 and 1935 (ibid., p. 197). If Schumpeter and Mensch are correct, every half century or so there is a narrow window of opportunity for entrepreneurs to commercialize basic innovations, creating a temporary monopoly in the production of a new product and of new industries (new, unimagined a_i's). Thus far, however, the US, unlike Japan, has been unwilling to use positive governmental adjustment policies to speed the transition from invention to commercial application.

The integration of the product cycle and the long wave with the vita theory show the difficulties in long-term adjustments. In one view human capital augmentation policies would be added to short-term protection. Then, irrespective of the source of trade competition, multinational firms could seek US labour. In another view the US could devise policies aimed at speeding the conversion of innovations into new commercial products, processes and industries.

NOTES

1. This, of course, does not foreclose the possibility that a great number of industries may be paying identical wage rates.
2. A variation of the model would have a greater number of firms than industries so that industry structures also would influence profit rates.
3. One can abstract from monetary policy by assuming that all wage and profit distributions are made at the end of the production period. In the presence of monetary institutions, however, wages and profits can be paid in advance of production. Suffice it to assume that the money stock is sufficient to monetize the entire economic system at the given and constant money velocity.
4. The element α_{ij} should not be confused with the identical notation usually used to denote direct and indirect input requirements *unadjusted* for physical products allocated to profits.
5. Quotation marks are occasioned by the absence of neoclassical demand and supply schedules; a labour queue is *not* a schedule.
6. As we shall see, this feedback can be related to the product cycle.
7. A homogeneous non-competing labour market is defined as one bounded geographically and one in which the elasticity of substitution in production between the labour of its type and the other types within the area approaches zero. The geographic limits are set by 'reasonable' commuting distances (at current state of transportation technology) from the selected labour population centre.
8. In the more complicated version of the model, the change in relative prices also would depend upon wage changes by specific type of labour and its use by industry.

    Alternately, the model will yield a profits – price spiral that necessarily inspires a further wage inflation increment. An increase in the mark up in an industry whose output is an input in most other industries will increase the price index of essentials which gives rise to a cost of living increase for all households and a further increase in wage rates. Once again the money stock or money velocity would have to increase in order for these money wage, profit and price changes to materialize.

9. This dynamic modelling could be extended by consideration of changes (over time) in the **A** matrix coefficients as well as the introduction of new rows into **A**. Also, the theoretical structure of the system can be altered as demand requirement changes occur at different rates from growth in labour supplies by type. Moreover, it is probable that changes in the composition of consumption follows from new rows in **A** as well as from changes in prices and in the income distribution. Price dynamics are altered as consumer and producer expectations regarding future prices are included in the model.

17 Recent Shifts in Global Countertrade: An Empirical Survey

Linda Longfellow Blodgett

633F14

17.1 INTRODUCTION

Modern countertrade has its origin in Eastern Europe, where barter was revived after World War II as a way of linking centrally planned economies with the capitalist world. As a method for conducting international transactions, countertrade not only obviated the need for convertible currencies, it also promoted bilateral negotiation at the expense of multilateral markets. Since bilateral negotiation normally requires government direction, governments playing an active role in economic development were drawn to countertrade for the control that it promised. As a result, in the 1970s and 1980s, countertrade was used not only in the communist world but in many less developed countries and in some industrialized countries as well – a testimony to its broad economic appeal.

In recent years, however, the economic role of government has come under challenge in several parts of the world. Central planning has collapsed in Eastern Europe. Privatization, freer trade and liberalized regulations on foreign direct investment (FDI) are gaining ground in Latin America and in parts of Asia. Moreover, economic recession in the industrialized countries, changes in the character of the European Community, and restructuring of external trade on the part of former Soviet bloc countries have added to the uncertainty affecting many market participants. In reaction to these changes in the world economy, countertrade, a practice grounded in autarky and central planning, might be expected to change also.

The purpose of this chapter is to compare recent patterns of countertrade with patterns in the mid-1980s. Several dimensions are considered: the geographical distribution of countertrade, the types in common use, the chief motivations, and the product composition of countertrade transactions. After defining the major varieties of countertrade and discussing some of the arguments in the literature, the chapter describes the database and presents the findings in tabular form. Concluding remarks follow.

164

17.2 THE NATURE OF COUNTERTRADE

Commonly understood, countertrade is an umbrella term for deals that involve at least some element of barter. In common use are six main varieties of countertrade:

1. *Barter*: The simple exchange of goods for goods, usually on a spot basis.
2. *Bilateral clearing*: Longer term arrangements between countries that agree to conduct bilateral trade in kind. Imbalances are settled periodically by transfers of currency.
3. *Switch trading*: This method shifts the imbalances that result from bilateral clearing arrangements to third parties, who find buyers for the excess goods.
4. *Counterpurchase*: Not strictly a barter transaction, because cash is involved on both sides. What happens is that each sale, though settled in cash, is tied to a compensating purchase from the multinational company (MNC), which chooses from a list of acceptable products that the country is particularly concerned to promote. In *debt-for-goods* arrangements (a form of counterpurchase) debt repayment is made in goods, which the lending organization selects from an agreed-upon list.
5. *Buyback*: One party builds and equips a factory, then turns it over to the second party, which pays for it with currency. At the same time, the first party agrees to buy specified quantities of the goods produced in the factory.
6. *Offset agreements*: Broad-based arrangements in which one partner, usually from an industrialized country, sells an expensive item like aircraft. As a condition of the sale, the purchaser insists that the aircraft manufacturer build local manufacturing facilities, draw from local suppliers, hire local workers, and perhaps purchase unrelated local products, all to 'offset' the economic drain occasioned by the large-scale purchase.

The motivations for countertrade are diverse. Although some writers have argued that countertrade is primarily a reaction to shortages of hard currency, much current thinking regards countertrade as several different phenomena, each motivated by different objectives (e.g. Cho, 1987; Hammond, 1990; Outters-Jaeger, 1979; Rabino and Shah, 1987; Yoffie, 1985). *Barter*, for example, may be used not only when foreign exchange is lacking but when a country has an unstable currency, suffers from a poor credit rating, or does not want to set a monetary price. This may happen when a country has a high level of external debt and wishes to conceal export revenues from the scrutiny of international organizations by keeping actual value out of official trade statistics. Barter also may be attractive as a way of introducing *de facto* market pricing when a product is subject to cartel arrangements (Lecraw, 1989; Mirus and Yeung, 1986). As part of a barter deal, a product subject to a fixed cartel price can be priced in accordance with demand, while at the same time keeping the market value invisible to cartel authorities (Hennart, 1990).

Counterpurchase and buyback, on the other hand, are not true barter because they involve the exchange of money and appear to be motivated by a desire to impose reciprocity, often as part of plans for economic development. *Counterpurchase* is used primarily to penetrate foreign markets (Hennart, 1989; 1990; Lecraw, 1989). If a less developed country (LDC) can get an MNC to buy local products from a list made up by the LDC government (in return for gaining access to the local market), then the LDC has obtained access to foreign markets through the marketing channels and marketing experience of an MNC. In so doing, it has obligated the MNC to make product-specific investments in marketing (Hennart, 1990). Since counterpurchase promotes exports by forcing foreign multinationals to use them as inputs or else to dispose of the goods, counterpurchase substitutes for vertical integration between manufacturer and distributor, where home-based MNCs do not have well-developed global distribution channels and where barriers are in place against FDI (Hennart, 1989). The products that are part of counterpurchase deals tend to be differentiated manufactured and consumer goods that require marketing input (in contrast to commodities, which are more likely to be disposed of through barter).

Similarly, *buyback* serves development plans in two ways: first, it provides for the transfer of technology in the form of plant, equipment and on-site training; second, it ensures that output is exported. Thus buyback is a method of posting bond to ensure a non-opportunistic transfer of technology (Hennart, 1989, 1990; Lecraw, 1989; Mirus and Yeung, 1986). By obliging an MNC to buy the product produced in a factory that it has designed, built and furnished, buyback serves as a form of upstream vertical integration in places where technology transfer is sought and where conventional FDI is either prohibited or restricted (Hennart, 1989).

Offset carries the practice even further and provides a way for a government to impose a broad and long-lasting obligation on the seller of technology. Such deals can have a development impact on diverse sectors of the local economy, ranging from manufacturing to sectors like finance, education, and tourism (Hammond, 1990).

17.3 DATABASE

Information about countertrade is generally not available in published trade statistics. Among independent countertrade firms, however, trade publications keep track of transactions by compiling reports from correspondents placed around the world. Probably the most detailed and reliable trade publication is *Countertrade Outlook*, which comes out weekly (forty-eight issues a year) and describes a wide variety of countertrade deals. Though the collection of deals is not a record of total countertrade transactions, no bias is apparent in the distribution of transactions either by geographical region or by type of countertrade. Thus deals described in this publication may reasonably be considered a representative sample of countertrade worldwide.

The dataset was divided into two files: transactions for the year 1986 represent the mid-1980s; transactions for the years 1990 and 1991 represent the current period. For these three years, each countertrade deal was coded with respect to the following data: the participating countries, the geographical region, the country's level of economic development, the type of countertrade, the products involved, and the approximate dollar value of the transaction (when available). Several deals had to be omitted in the coding stage for lack of sufficient data. However, missing data was not a problem in general, owing to the relatively small number of variables and to the fact that these variables were crucial to any deal. Care was taken to record each deal only once, though it frequently happened that follow-up stories were included in *Countertrade Outlook*.

In all, 729 two-party countertrade deals were recorded. Because there is no way of knowing what percentage of total transactions this sample represents, this study may not assume that the frequencies reflect the size and extent of countertrade in absolute terms. The data may, however, be used to indicate relative patterns at different times and among different geographical regions. When it was desirable to characterize the activity of participants by geographical region, each transaction in effect was counted twice, to reflect the kind of transaction engaged in by each side to the deal. Thus some of the tables reflect this perspective and have larger counts than the base number of countertrade deals. The methodology was frequency analysis and crosstabulations.

Table 17.1   Global distribution of Countertrade: includes both sides of transaction, 1986 and 1990/1

Region	1986	1990/1
OECD	106.0	237.0
	21.6%	25.4%
East Europe	85.0	326.0
	17.3%	35.0%
Latin America	77.0	79.0
	15.7%	8.5%
MidEast/Africa	94.0	134.0
	19.2%	14.4%
Asia	128.0	156.0
	26.1%	16.7%
Totals	490.0	932.0
	100.0%	100.0%

17.4   FINDINGS

17.4.1   Regional Distribution of Countertrade

The regional distribution of countertrade has changed markedly since the mid-1980s (Table 17.1), primarily as a result of a substantial increase in countertrade activity by former Eastern bloc countries (EBCs). Although countertrade within the framework of the Council for Mutual Economic Assistance (COMECON) is probably not fully represented in the 1986 figures, the sizeable increase in countertrade by former Eastern bloc countries (from 17.3 per cent of all countertrade in 1986 to 35.0 per cent in 1990–91) is made up mostly of deals between Eastern European countries and countries outside the bloc. Since countertrade was developed by communist governments as a way of doing business with the capitalist world, we might expect to see decreased countertrade activity with the breakup of the Eastern bloc. That this has not happened testifies to the broader economic benefits that countertrade apparently provides.

Another notable shift has occurred in Latin America, where countertrade activity decreased from 15.7 per cent of all transactions in 1986 to 8.5 per cent in 1990–91, a change that may be attributable to liberalization programmes that have achieved some success in several Latin American countries. Asian countries also decreased their share of world countertrade (from 26.1 per cent to 16.7 per cent), as, to a lesser extent, did the Middle

Table 17.2   Countertrade partners, by economic classification, 1986 and 1990/1

Economic classification	1986	1990–1
OECD–OECD	6.0	16.0
	2.5%	3.5%
OECD–EBC	40.0	135.0
	16.8%	29.6%
OECD–LDC	45.0	67.0
	18.9%	14.7%
EBC–EBC	8.0	58.0
	3.4%	12.7%
EBC–LDC	76.0	121.0
	31.9%	26.5%
LDC–LDC	63.0	59.0
	26.5%	12.9%
Totals	238.0	456.0
	100.0%	100.0%

East/Africa (from 19.2 per cent to 14.4 per cent). Industrialized countries, members of the Organization for Economic Cooperation and Development (OECD), continued to be called upon to provide technology transfer and international marketing channels (their share was 21.6 per cent in 1986 and 25.4 per cent in 1990–91), a reflection primarily of the increased number of deals between industrialized countries and countries of the former Eastern bloc.

17.4.2   Countertrade Partners

The increased importance of transactions between OECD countries and the former Eastern bloc is demonstrated in Table 17.2. In this table, countries were sorted by primary World Bank classification: OECD, EBC and LDC. Then tabulations were made for the six possible pairings. Countertrade deals between OECD countries and the former Eastern bloc increased from 16.8 per cent to 29.6 per cent of all countertrade. At the same time, small decreases occurred in countertrade deals between OECD countries and LDCs (from 18.9 per cent to 14.7 per cent) and between former EBCs and LDCs (from 31.9 per cent to 26.5 per cent). While the increase of countertrade among East European countries is probably not in itself significant, owing to the presumed underreporting of clearing arrangements in *Countertrade Outlook* when COMECON was still in operation, it is interesting that intra-Bloc deals continue to be an important part of the region's countertrade activity. The other noteworthy change is the sharp decrease in deals between LDC partners (from 26.5 per cent to 12.9 per cent).

17.4.3   Types of Countertrade

Between the mid-1980s and 1990–1, several interesting shifts occurred in the types of countertrade employed in different parts of the world. Overall, as shown in the totals columns of Tables 17.3 and 17.4, there have been decreases of counterpurchase (from 35.5 per cent to 13.6 per cent) and of bilateral clearing (from 24.9 per cent to 15.5 per cent). In the same period, barter increased (from 26.6 per cent to 34.5 per cent) and so did buyback (from 8.5 per cent to 20.7 per cent). Smaller increases occurred in offsets, both military and civilian, and debt-for-goods agreements.

The regional breakdown of these shifts also is given in Tables 17.3 and 17.4. The main changes in OECD countries apparently have come as a result of the increased countertrade activity with the countries of Eastern Europe. Counterpurchase has decreased (from 38.0 per cent to 13.9 per cent) and buyback has increased (from 10.9 per cent to 31.1 per cent). Another interesting change was a significant increase in offset agreements (from 11.9 per cent to 28.2 per cent), which resemble buybacks in the sense that the party in the 'buyer' role is motivated by a desire for technology and economic development. In general, these changes were such that the predominant countertrade activity by OECD countries (in the 'seller' role) was counterpurchase in 1986 and buyback in 1990–91.

The main change in countertrade usage in Latin America is the very large increase in barter (from 30.0 per cent to 55.0 per cent). Corresponding decreases have occurred in counterpurchase (from 25.0 per cent to 10.0 per cent) and bilateral clearing (from 35.0 per cent to 15.0 per cent). On one hand, these changes reflect the declining importance of state planning. On the other hand, they reveal a need for short-term measures to manage the numerous economic adjustments. The figures also show the rising importance of debt-for-goods arrangements, which are currently 10.0 per cent of all Latin American countertrade. Whereas the predominant form of countertrade in 1986 was bilateral clearing, by 1990–1 barter was by far the most common countertrade activity.

The political and economic changes in Eastern Europe have affected countertrade activity, though not as one might expect. Countertrade usage has not waned, but several changes have occurred in the types of countertrade that East European countries employ. Bilateral clearing arrangements have decreased (from 32.9 per cent to 18.9 per cent), as have

Table 17.3   Types of countertrade, by region: includes both sides of transaction, 1986 (percentages)

CT type	OECD	L. Am	E. Eur	ME/Af	Asia	Total
Barter	26.0	18.0	10.0	33.0	23.0	110.0
	28.3	30.0	11.8	45.2	22.1	26.6
Counterpurchase	35.0	15.0	37.0	12.0	48.0	147.0
	38.0	25.0	43.5	16.4	46.2	35.5
Buyback	10.0	4.0	10.0	2.0	9.0	35.0
	10.9	6.7	11.8	2.7	8.7	8.5
Bilateral clearing	9.0	21.0	28.0	25.0	20.0	103.0
	9.8	35.0	32.9	34.2	19.2	24.9
Offset-military	7.0	0.0	0.0	0.0	1.0	8.0
	7.6	0.0	0.0	0.0	1.0	1.9
Offset-civilian	4.0	0.0	0.0	0.0	3.0	7.0
	4.3	0.0	0.0	0.0	2.9	1.7
Debt-for-goods	1.0	2.0	0.0	1.0	0.0	4.0
	1.1	3.3	0.0	1.4	0.0	1.0
Totals	92.0	60.0	85.0	73.0	104	414.0
	100.0	100.0	100.0	100.0	100.0	100.0

Table 17.4   Types of countertrade by region: includes both sides of transaction, 1990–1 (percentages)

CT Type	OECD	L. Am	E. Eur	ME/Af	Asia	Total
Barter	45.0	33.0	98.0	46.0	55.0	277.0
	21.5	55.0	35.6	41.1	37.7	34.5
Counterpurchase	29.0	6.0	37.0	11.0	26.0	109.0
	13.9	10.0	13.5	9.8	17.8	13.6
Buyback	65.0	1.0	72.0	10.0	18.0	166.0
	31.1	1.7	26.2	8.9	12.2	20.7
Bilateral-clearing	7.0	9.0	52.0	35.0	21.0	124.0
	3.3	15.0	18.9	31.3	14.4	15.5
Offset-military	33.0	3.0	5.0	8.0	17.0	66.0
	15.8	5.0	1.8	701.0	11.6	8.2
Offset-civilian	26.0	2.0	9.0	2.0	9.0	48.0
	12.4	3.3	3.3	1.8	6.2	6.0
Debt-for-goods	4.0	6.0	2.0	0.0	0.0	12.0
	1.9	10.0	0.7	0.0	0.0	1.5
Totals	209.0	60.0	275.0	112.0	146.0	802.0
	100.0	100.0	100.0	100.0	100.0	100.0

counterpurchase agreements (from 43.5 per cent to 13.5 per cent). During the same period, barter has increased (from 11.8 per cent to 35.6 per cent) and buyback agreements represent a much larger percentage of countertrade than before (from 11.8 per cent to 26.2 per cent). In 1986, the main form of countertrade was counterpurchase; in 1990–91, it was barter.

The dissolution of central planning in Eastern Europe probably explains the declining activity in counterpurchase and bilateral clearing arrangements, both of which require a strong role for government and a long-term state planning horizon. Problems in taming inflation and in establishing convertible currencies may have made barter attractive as a short-term measure during a time of severe economic dislocation. The popularity of buyback agreements is puzzling, because this type of arrangement usually serves as a substitute for FDI in the presence of entry restrictions on foreign companies. With the removal of many of these restrictions, as part of wide-ranging programmes of privatization and marketization, joint ventures and wholly owned subsidiaries should make buyback agreements unnecessary. The increased use of buyback, however, is consistent with a need for technology in innovation-starved industries. Also, buyback agreements do not have to be part of a government plan. Individual factories could make such arrangements not only to ensure technology transfer but also to develop external markets, which were underexploited by enterprises under communism. It may be, too, that Western businesses draw some comfort from these arrangements, because they reduce some of their risk while allowing long-term contracts with suppliers.

In contrast to the situation in Eastern Europe, countertrade usage has changed little in the Middle East and Africa. Barter continues to predominate (45.2 per cent in 1986; 41.1 per cent in 1990/91) and bilateral clearing arrangements are used extensively to provide a stable framework for trade (34.2 per cent in 1986; 31.3 per cent in 1990–1). A small decrease is observable in counterpurchase (from 16.4 per cent to 9.8 per cent), following worldwide patterns.

Asia, however, underwent important changes in countertrade activity. Much less counterpurchase is used there than in the mid-1980s (46.2 per cent in 1986; 17.8 per cent in 1990–1), a likely result of liberalization programmes and the demonstrated success of many industries in penetrating developed country markets on their own. Barter, however, has increased (from 22.1 per cent to 37.7 per cent), following the worldwide trend. Another interesting development in Asia is the sizeable increase in military offsets. The main form of countertrade in 1986 was counterpurchase; in 1990–1 it was barter.

Table 17.5 Countertrade usage worldwide, by motivation: includes both sides of transaction, 1986 (percentages)

Region	In kind	Obligations	Totals
OECD	35.0	59.0	94.0
	37.2	62.8	100.0
East Europe	38.0	47.0	85.0
	44.7	55.3	100.0
Latin America	39.0	21.0	60.0
	65.0	35.0	100.0
Mideast/Africa	58.0	17.0	75.0
	77.3	22.7	100.0
Asia	43.0	61.0	104.0
	41.3	58.7	100.0
Totals	213.0	205.0	418.0
	51.0	49.0	100.0

Table 17.6 Countertrade usage worldwide by motivation: includes both sides of transaction, 1990–1 (percentages)

Region	In kind	Obligations	Totals
OECD	56.0	181.0	237.0
	23.6	76.4	100.0
East-Europe	189.0	137.0	326.0
	58.0	42.0	100.0
Latin America	57.0	22.0	79.0
	72.2	27.8	100.0
Mideast/Africa	100.0	34.0	134.0
	74.6	25.4	100.0
Asia	83.0	73.0	456.0
	53.2	46.8	100.0
Totals	485.0	447.0	932.0
	52.0	48.0	100.0

17.4.4 Motivations for Countertrade

The recent literature on countertrade has stressed that different motivations underlie different varieties of countertrade. Hennart (1990) argued for the possibility of grouping countertrade into two categories, based on similarity of motivation. The first group, *in kind*, is characterized primarily by a desire to avoid money (barter, bilateral clearing, and switch trading). The second group, *obligations*, aims primarily to impose reciprocity on the foreign partner in the interest of promoting economic development (counterpurchase, buyback, and offset).

In Tables 17.5 and 17.6, countertrade deals are grouped into these two motivational categories to permit comparison across geographical regions and over time. In the world as a whole, there was no change between 1986 and 1990–91 in the incidence of *in kind* transactions and *obligations* transactions. *In kind* transactions were somewhat more common, with 51.0 per cent vs. 49.0 per cent in 1986 and 52.0 per cent vs. 42.0 per cent in 1990–91.

But the changes in individual regions reveal a different pattern. In Eastern Europe, *obligations* were more important in 1986 (*in kind*: 44.7 per cent vs. *obligations*: 55.3 per cent) and *in kind* deals were more important in 1990–91 (*in-kind*: 58.0 per cent vs. *obligations*: 42.0 per cent). A similar reversal occurred in Asia: 41.3 per cent vs. 58.7 per cent in 1986; 53.2 per cent vs. 46.8 per cent in 1990–91. In Latin America, the predominance of *in kind* deals increased: 65.0 per cent vs. 35.0 per cent in 1986; 72.2 per cent vs. 27.8 per cent in 1990–91.

In the Middle East and Africa, *in kind* continued to predominate and no significant change occurred: 77.3 per cent vs. 22.7 per cent in 1986; 74.6 per cent vs. 25.4 per cent in 1990–91. Only in OECD countries did *obligations* countertrade show a significant increase: 37.2 per cent vs. 62.8 per cent in 1986; 23.6 per cent vs. 76.4 per cent in 1990–91. This change reflects the increased insistence on buybacks and offsets by former Eastern bloc countries and some countries in Asia. It also, of course, reflects the fact that *in kind* deals generally are not needed, given the experience and position of OECD countries in both commodities and industrial markets. Indeed, it is remarkable that the OECD figures for *in kind* countertrade are as high as they are.

Outside the industrialized world, shifts away from obligations countertrade apparently reflect disenchantment with a strong government role in economic planning. The main shifts away from obligations countertrade occurred in Eastern Europe, Asia and Latin America. At the same time, however, *in kind* transactions apparently serve a useful function in a time of economic dislocation, when dealing in money may be a disadvantage. In Eastern Europe, inflation, monetary instability and only partial foreign exchange convertibility provide incentives to avoid the use of money. In Latin America, currency instability and high levels of external debt may explain the attractiveness of *in kind* countertrade.

Table 17.7   Product composition of countertrade deals by geographical region: includes both sides of transaction, 1986 (percentages)

Region	Com-Com	Ind-Com	Ind-Ind	Other	Totals
OECD	6.0	26.0	32.0	9.0	73.0
	8.2	35.6	43.8	12.3	100.0
East-Europe	0.0	33.0	27.0	9.0	69.0
	0.0	47.8	39.1	13.0	100.0
Latin America	5.0	39.0	15.0	9.0	68.0
	7.4	57.4	22.1	13.2	100.0
Mideast/Africa	15.0	47.0	10.0	3.0	75.0
	20.0	62.7	13.3	4.0	100.0
Asia	10.0	60.0	34.0	11.0	115.0
	8.7	52.2	29.6	9.6	100.0
Totals	36.0	205.0	118.0	41.0	400.0
	9.0	51.3	29.5	10.3	100.0

Table 17.8   Product composition of countertrade deals by geographical region: includes both sides of transaction, 1990–1 (percentages)

Region	Com-Com	Ind-Com	Ind-Ind	Other	Totals
OECD	6.0	31.0	65.0	42.0	144.0
	4.2	21.5	45.1	29.2	100.0
East Europe	27.0	94.0	87.0	90.0	298.0
	9.1	31.5	29.2	30.2	100.0
Latin America	8.0	25.0	14.0	23.0	70.0
	11.4	35.7	20.0	32.9	100.0
Mideast/Africa	12.0	61.0	18.0	29.0	120.0
	10.0	50.8	15.0	24.2	100.0
Asia	18.0	51.0	48.0	36.0	153.0
	9.0	33.4	29.6	28.0	100.0
Totals	71.0	262.0	232.0	220.0	785.0
	9.0	33.4	29.6	28.0	100.0

17.4.5   Product Composition of Countertrade

To analyze the product composition of countertrade, each countertrade deal was placed into one of four categories: (i) commodities for commodities; (ii) industrial goods (both basic industry and high technology) for commodities; (iii) industrial goods for industrial goods; (iv) and 'other'. This last category includes transactions that involve consumer goods, services and diverse collections of products. If commodities or industrial goods were a significant part of any deal, however, the transaction was put in one of the other three categories.

The geographical breakdown of product exchanges is given in Tables 17.7 and 17.8. Here we can see an important shift worldwide from transactions that pair industrial goods with commodities (from 51.3 per cent in 1986 to 33.4 per cent in 1990–91) to transactions that include more diverse items, including services and consumer goods (from 10.3 per cent in 1986 to 28.0 per cent in 1990–91). This trend was present in every geographical region.

Other changes, however, affected some regions more than others. Industrial goods–commodities exchanges declined by large percentages in Asia (from 52.2 per cent to 33.3 per cent) and in Latin America (from 57.4 per cent to 35.7 per cent). But the declines were substantial in other parts of the world, too: Middle East and Africa (from 62.7 per cent to 50.8 per cent), Eastern Europe (from 47.8 per cent to 31.5 per cent) and OECD countries (from 35.6 per cent to 21.5 per cent). This contrasts with the figures for exchanges that involve only commodities and those that involve industrial goods on both sides of the transaction, which remained the same everywhere. Only in Eastern Europe was that type of industrial exchange less common than before (39.1 per cent in 1986; 29.2 per cent in 1990–91).

Other interesting changes occurred in commodities-for-commodities trade. In Eastern Europe, such deals did not appear at all in the 1986 sample, but amounted to 9.1 per cent of the region's countertrade in 1990–91. Commodities-for-commodities deals also increased slightly in Latin America (from 7.4 per cent to 11.4 per cent) and Asia (from 8.7 per cent to 11.8 per cent), but they were a significantly smaller part of countertrade activity in the Middle East and Africa (from 20.0 per cent to 10.0 per cent). In the world as a whole, the percentage of barter did not change (at 9 per cent).

17.5   CONCLUSION

In the absence of official countertrade statistics, empirical studies of countertrade must rely heavily on examples. The comprehensiveness of the database drawn from *Countertrade Outlook* allows at least a start at systematic analysis. As a representative sample, the figures are not a full record of total countertrade transactions; but they do permit a look at relative patterns, from region to region and from one year to the next. The unprecedented economic and political changes in the former Eastern bloc, combined with liberalization programmes in many parts of the developing world, suggest that countertrade, a practice closely associated with government planning, should change as well.

This study documents regional countertrade patterns and identifies several changes that have occurred between the mid-1980s and the early 1990s. Contrary to what we might expect, Eastern Europe is still a major countertrade participant, while Latin America is less active than earlier. Most of the Eastern bloc activity is with OECD partners, but a sizeable percentage is among East European countries themselves. In all three middle-income regions – Eastern Europe, Latin America, and Asia – use of counterpurchase and bilateral clearing has decreased, while barter has increased, sometimes dramatically (as in Latin America). Surprisingly, buyback is being used more extensively, both in Eastern Europe and in Latin America.

These changes may be summarized by the observation that *obligations* transactions (which are motivated mainly by a desire to impose reciprocity on a foreign company) are down, while *in kind* transactions (which are motivated more clearly by a desire to avoid money) are up. The only exception to this pattern is in industrialized countries, which typically are the parties obliged to contribute technology and marketing know-how. As far as products go, Eastern Europe has turned increasingly to commodities-only exchanges. Worldwide, the main change has been an increase of deals involving more diverse products, including services and consumer goods.

Though a descriptive survey like this does not establish causal relationships, it can provide a starting point for empirical testing. The fact that countertrade patterns have changed along with economic and political transformations suggests the diversity of countertrade and its responsiveness to particular needs. In a general way, this provides support for arguments in the literature that the varieties of countertrade have specific, different motivations.

Bibliography

AHARONI, YAIR (1991), 'Education and Technology Transfer: Recipient Point of View', in Tamir Agmon and Mary Ann von Glinow (eds), *Technology Transfer in International Business* (London: Oxford University Press) pp. 79–102.

'The Ambush Awaiting Japan', *The Economist*, 6 July, pp. 67–8.

ANDERSON, E. and H. GATINGNON (1986), 'Modes of Foreign Entry: A Transaction Cost Analaysis and Propositions', *Journal of International Business Studies*, vol. 17, no. 3, pp. 1–26.

ANDERSON, KYM and ROD TYERS (1987), 'Japan's Agricultural Policy in International Perspective', *Journal of the Japanese and International Economies*, vol. 1, no. 2 (June) pp. 131–46.

AVISHAI, BERNARD (1991), 'A European Platform for Global Competition', *Harvard Business Review* (July–August) pp. 103–13.

BALASSA, BELA and MARCUS NOLAND (1988), *Japan in the World Economy* (Washington, DC: Institute for International Economics).

BECKERMAN, W. (1956), 'Distance in Pattern of Intra-European Trade', *Review of Economics and Statistics*, vol. 28.

BEHRMAN, JACK N. (1988), 'Restructuring and Reordering the World Economy', *The International Trade Journal*, vol. III, no. 1 (Fall) pp. 1–20.

BEHRMAN, JACK N. (1989), 'Restructuring and Reordering the World Economy', in Khosrow Fatemi (ed.), *International Trade: Existing Problems and Prospectives Solutions* (New York: Taylor & Francis) pp. 11–23.

BERGSTEN, C. FRED (1988), *America in the World Economy: A Strategy for 1990s* (Washington, DC: Institute for International Economics).

BERGSTEN, C. FRED (1990), 'From Cold War to Trade War?', *Economic Insights* (July–August) pp. 2–6.

BERGSTEN, C. FRED and WILLIAM R. CLINE (1987), *The United States–Japan Economic Problem* (Washington, DC: Institute for International Economics).

BRADFORD, COLIN I. and WILLIAM H. BRANSON (1988), 'Patterns of Trade and Structural Change', in C.I. Bradford and W.H. Branson (eds), *Trade and Structural Change in Pacific Asia* (Chicago: University of Chicago Press) pp. 3–24.

BREWER, THOMAS (1990), 'EC 1992 and the US Automotive Industry: Shifting Patterns of Trade and Investments', in Jorge Perez-Lopez *et al.* (eds), *EC 1992: Implications for US Workers* (Washington, DC: US Department of Labor).

BUCKLEY, P.J. and M. CASSON (1989), 'Multinational Enterprises in Less Developed Countries – Cultural and Economic Interactions', unpublished Working Paper, University of Reading, Department of Economics.

BURENSTAM LINDER, S. (1961), *An Essay on Trade and Transformation* (New York: John Wiley).

CALVERT, A.L. (1981), 'Mergers and Theory of Foreign Direct Investment', in A. Rugman (ed.), *New Theories of the Multinational Enterprise* (London: Croom Helm).

CALVERT, A.L. (1932), 'A Synthesis of Foreign Direct Investment Theories and Theories of the Multinational Firm', *Journal of International Business Studies*, vol. 12 (Spring–Summer) pp. 43–59.

CANTERBERY, E.R. (1979), 'A Vita Theory of Personal Income Distribution', *Southern Economic Journal*, vol. 46, no. 2 (July) pp. 12–48.

CANTERBERY, E.R. (1980), 'Welfare Economics and the Vita Theory', *Eastern Economic Journal*, vol. 6 (January) pp. 1–20.

CANTERBERY, E.R. (1984), 'Galbraith, Sraffa, Kalecki and Supra-Surplus Capitalism', *Journal of Post Keynesian Economics*, vol. 7, no. 1 (Fall) pp. 77–90.

CANTERBERY, E.R. (1987a), *The Making of Economics*, 3rd edn (Belmont, CA: Wadsworth) pp. 284–9.

CANTERBERY, E.R. (1987b), 'A Theory of Supra-Surplus Capitalism', *Eastern Economic Journal*, vol. 13, no. 4 (October–December) pp. 1–20.

CASSON, M.C. (1982), 'Transaction Costs and the Theory of the Multinational Enterprise', in A. Rugman (ed.), *New Theories of the Multinational Enterprise* (New York: St Martin's Press) pp. 24–53.

CASSON, M.C. (1985), 'The Theory of Foreign Direct Investment', in P.J. Buckley and M. Casson (eds), *Economic Theory of the Multinational Enterprise* (London: Macmillan).

CAVES, RICHARD E. (1980), 'Industrial Organization, Corporate Strategy and Structure', *Journal of Economic Literature*, vol. 18, pp. 64–92.

CAVES, RICHARD E. (1982), *Multinational Enterprise and Economic Analysis* (Cambridge: Cambridge University Press).

CHAKRAVARTHY, BALAJI S. and HOWARD V. PERLMUTTER (1985), 'Strategic Planning for a Global Business', *Columbia Journal of World Business*, vol. 20, no. 2, pp. 1–8.

CHO, K.R. (1987), 'Using Countertrade as a Competitive Management Tool', *Management International Review*, vol. 27, no. 1, pp. 50–57.

CIPOLLA, CARLO M. (1975), *Before the Industrial Revolution* (New York: W.W. Norton).

CLINE, WILLIAM R. *et al.* (1978), *Trade Negotiations in the Tokyo Round: A Quantitative Assessment* (Washington, DC: The Brookings Institution).

CLUBB, BRUCE (1991), *United States Foreign Trade Law* (Boston: Little, Brown) pp. 1,717, and 731.

COMPETITIVE COUNCIL POLICY (1992), *Building a Competitive America*, First Annual Report to the President and Congress (Washington, DC).

Congressional Quarterly Almanac (1962).

CRANDALL, R. (1987), 'Import Quotas and the Automobile Industry: The Costs of Protection', in R.E. Baldwin and J. David Richardson (eds), *International Trade and Finance Readings* (Boston: Little Brown) chapter 5.

CURZON, G. and V. CURZON (1987), 'Follies in European Trade Relations with Japan', *The World Economy*, vol. 10, no. 2, pp. 155–75.

DE MELO, JAIME and DAVID TARR (1992), *A General Equilibrium Analysis of US Foreign Trade Policy* (Cambridge MA: MIT Press).

DEANE, R.S. (1970), *Foreign Investment in New Zealand Manufacturing*, (Wellington, NZ: Sweet & Maxwell).

DINOPOULOS, E. and M.E. KREININ (1988), 'Import Quotas and VERs: A Comparative Analysis in a Three-Country Framework', *Journal of International Economics*, vol. 26, pp. 169–78.

DOBRZYNSKI, JUDITH, THANE PETERSON, and LARRY ARMSTRONG (1986), 'Fighting Back: It Can Work', *Business Week*, 26 August pp. 62–68.

DONE, KEVIN (1991), 'Crash Course', *International Management* (September) pp. 70–73.

DOZ, YVES L. (1980), 'Strategic Management in Multinational Companies', *Sloan Management Review*, vol. 21, no. 2, pp. 27–46.

DRYSDALE, PETER (1988a), *International Economic Pluralism: Economic Policy in East Asia and the Pacific* (New York: Columbia University Press).

DRYSDALE, PETER (1988b), 'Japan as a Pacific and World Economic Power', *Australian Economic Papers*, vol. 27, no. 51 (December) pp. 159–72.

DUNNING, J.H. (1988), 'The Eclectic Paradigm of International Production: A Restatement and Some Possible Extensions', *Journal of International Business Studies*, vol. 19, pp. 1–31.

ECKES, ALFRED E. (1987), 'Interface of Antitrust and Trade Laws – Conflict or Harmony? An ITC Commissioner's Perspective', *Antitrust Law Journal*, vol. 56, no. 2, pp. 417–24.

ECKES, ALFRED E. (1992), 'Trading American Interests', *Foreign Affairs*, vol. 71, no. 4, pp. 135–54.

ECONOMIST INTELLIGENCE UNIT (1991), *Europe's Motor Industry after 1992* (London: Economist Intelligence Unit).

'Export Growth Shrinks vs. Deficit', *The Fresno Bee*, May 13, 1991, page A15.

FATEMI, KHOSROW (1989), 'US Trade Imbalance and the Dollar: Is There a Correlation?', *The International Journal of Finance*, vol. I, no. 2, (Spring) pp. 32–51.

FATEMI, KHOSROW (1991), 'The Need for a New International Economic Regime', in Khosrow Fatemi (ed.), *Selected Readings in International Trade* (New York: Taylor & Francis) pp. 1–7.

FEENSTRA, R. (1984), 'Voluntary Export Restraint in US Autos, 1980–81: Quality, Employment and Welfare Effects', in R. Baldwin and A. Krueger (eds), *The Structure and Evolution of Recent US Trade Policy* (Chicago: University of Chicago Press).

FLINT, JERRY (1991), 'Will the (New) Maginot Line Hold?', *Forbes*, 8 July, pp. 58–61.

FORSGREN, M. (1989), 'Foreign Acquisitions: Internalization or Network Interdependency?', in T.S. Cavusgil (ed.), *Advances in International Marketing*, vol. 3, (Greenwich: Jai Press).

GEARHART, WILLIAM W. (1990), 'The US Escape Clause Law – Its Origin, Evolution, and Present Form', unpublished paper, USITC: Office of General Counsel, (June).

'General Alarm' (1991), *The Economist*, 21 December, p. 81–82.

GLATZ, HANNA R. (1991), 'Daimler-Benz Predicts the Shifts in the EC Auto Industry', *Journal of European Business* (July–August) pp. 18–21.

GOLDMAN, MARSHALL I., (1988) 'Gorbachov and Economic Problems in the Soviet Union', *Eastern Economic Journal*, vol. 14 (October–December) pp. 331–36.

GRAY, H. PETER (1973), 'Senile Industry Protection: A Proposal', *Southern Economic Journal* (April) pp. 569–74.

GRAY, H. PETER. (1976), *A Generalized Theory of International Trade* (London: Macmillan; New York: Holmes & Meier).

GRAY, H. PETER (1979), *International Trade, Investment, and Payments* (Boston: Houghton Mifflin Company).

GRAY, H. PETER (1984), 'Employment Arguments for Protection and the Vita Theory', *Eastern Economic Journal*, vol. 10 (January–March) pp. 1–14.

GRAY, H. PETER (1985), *Free Trade or Protection: A Pragmatic Analysis* (London: Macmillan; New York: St Martin's Press).

GREENWOOD, JOHN (1990), 'Potential for an Asian Free Trade Area', *Business Economics*, vol. 25, no. 1 (January) pp. 32–5.

GROS, D. (1992), 'A Note on EC Trade Policy after 1992: The Effects of Replacing Existing National Import Quotas by Community Quotas that are "Equally Restrictive"', *Weltwirtschaftliches Archiv*, vol. 128, no. 1, pp. 125–35.

HAMILTON, C. (1985), 'Voluntary Export Restraints and Trade Diversion', *Journal of Common Market Studies*, vol. 23, no. 4, pp. 345–55.

HAMMOND, GRANT T. (1990), *Countertrade, Offsets, and Barter in the International Political Economy* (New York: St Martin's Press).

HENDERSON, BRUCE D. (1991), 'The Origin of Strategy', in Cynthia A. Montgomery and Michael E. Porter (eds), *Strategy: Seeking and Securing Competitive Advantage* (Boston: Harvard Business School) pp. 3–9.

HENNART, JEAN-FRANCOIS, 'A Transaction Costs Theory of Equity Joint Ventures', *Strategic Management Journal*, vol. 9, pp. 361–74.

HENNART, JEAN-FRANCOIS (1989), 'The Transaction-Cost Rationale for Countertrade', *Journal of Law, Economics, and Organization*, vol. V, no. 1, pp. 127–53.

HENNART, JEAN-FRANCOIS (1990), 'Some Empirical Dimensions of Countertrade', *Journal of International Business Studies*, vol. 20, no. 1, pp. 243–70.

HISEY, K.B. and R.E. CAVES (1985), 'Diversification Strategy and Choice of Country: Diversifying Acquisitions Abroad by US Multinationals, 1978–1980', *Journal of International Business Studies*, vol. 15, pp. 51–64.

HODGKINSON, HAROLD L. (1985), *All One System: Demographics of Education – Kindergarten through Graduate School* (Washington, DC: Institute for Educational Leadership).

HOFSTEDE, G.A. (1980), *Cultures Consequences: International Differences in Work-Related Values* (Integral Ed.) (Beverly Hills, CA: Sage).

HONMA, MASAYOSHI, and YUJIRO HAYAMI (1986), 'Structure of Agricultural Protection in Industrial Countries', *Journal of International Economics*, vol. 20, no. 1/2 (February) pp. 115–29.

HÖRNELL, E., J.-E. VAHLNE and F. WIEDERSHEIM-PAUL (1973), *Export och utlandsetableringar (Export and Foreign Establishments)* (Stockholm: Almqvist & Wiksell).

HÖRNELL, E. and J.-E. VAHLNE (1973), 'Produktlinjens inverkan på val av exportkanal' (Impact of Product line Characteristics on Choice of Export Channel), in E. Hörnell, J.-E. Vahlne, and F. Wiedersheim-Paul, *Export och utlandsetableringar (Export and Foreign Establishments)* (Stockholm: Almqvist & Wiksell).

JACKSON, JOHN K. (1989), *The World Trading System* (Cambridge, MA: MIT Press) pp. 153.

JACKSON, JOHN K. and WILLIAM J. DAVEY (1986), *International Economic Relations*, 2nd edn (St Paul, MN: West) pp. 541.

JACKSON, STUART (1986), 'BW/Harris Poll: Sure, Japan Is a Problem – but not mine', *Business Week*, 26 August , pp. 68.

JOHANSON, J. and J.-E. VAHLNE (1977), 'The Internationalization Process of the Firm – A Model of Knowledge Development and Increasing Market Commitments', *Journal of Industrial Business Studies*, vol. 8 (Spring/Summer).

JOHANSON, J. and J.-E. VAHLNE (1990), 'The Mechanism of Internationalization', *The International Marketing Review*, vol. 7, no. 4, 1990, pp. 11–24.

KINDLEBERGER, C.P. (1969), *American Business Abroad: Six Lectures on Direct Investment* (New Haven, CT: Yale University Press).

KOGUT, B. (1985), 'Designing Global Strategies: Comparative and Competitive Value Added Chains', *Sloan Management Review* (Summer) pp. 15–28.

KOGUT, B. and H. SINGH (1988), 'The Effect of National Culture on the Choice of Entry Mode', *Journal of International Business Studies* (Fall) pp. 411–32.

KRAUSE, LAWRENCE (1990), 'Trade Policy in the 1990s: Good-bye Bipolarity, Hello Regions', *The World Today*, vol. 46, no. 5 (May) pp. 83–6.

KRAUSE, LAWRENCE (1991), 'Pacific Economic Regionalism and the United States', *Academic Studies Series*, Joint Korea–US Academic Symposium, vol. 1, pp. 1–17.

KRUGMAN, PAUL R. (1990), *Strategic Trade Policy and the New International Economics* (Cambridge, MA: The MIT Press).

LANDRY, BART (1987), *The New Black Middle Class* (Berkeley: University of California Press).

LEBOEUF, M. (1982), *The Productivity Challenge* (New York: McGraw-Hill).

LECRAW, DONALD J. (1989), 'The Management of Countertrade: Factors Influencing Success', *Journal of International Business Studies*, vol. 21, no. 2, pp. 41–59.

LEE, HIRO, and DAVID ROLAND-HOLST (1991), 'Bilateral Trade between the United States and Japan and the Implications of Agricultural Protection', Irvine Economics Paper no. 91-92-02, University of California, Irvine (November).

LEONTIEF, WASSILY (1982), 'The Distribution of Work and Income', *Scientific American*, vol. 245, no. 3, pp. 188–204.

LEVITT, T. (1983), *The Marketing Imagination* (New York: The Free Press).

LINCOLN, EDWARD J. (1989a), 'Japan's Role in Asia–Pacific Cooperation: Dimensions, Prospects, and Problems', *Journal of Northeast Asian Studies*, vol. 8, no. 4 (Winter) pp. 3–23.

LINCOLN, EDWARD J. (1989b), 'The Economics of US–Japan Relations in the Asia–Pacific Region', in R.A. Morse (ed.), *US–Japan Relations: An Agenda for the Future* (Lanham, MD: University Press of America).

LINCOLN, EDWARD J. (1990), *Japan's Unequal Trade* (Washington, DC: Brookings Institution).

LINDER, STAFFAN B. (1986), *The Pacific Century: Economic and Political Consequences of Asian–Pacific Dynamism* (Stanford: Stanford University Press).

LORANGE, P.P. and RICHARD F. VANCIL (1977), *Strategic Planning Systems* (Englewood Cliffs, NJ: Prentice Hall).

LORENZ, DETLEF (1989), 'Trends Towards Regionalism in the World Economy: A Contribution to a New International Economic Order?', *Intereconomics*, vol. 24, no. 2 (March), pp. 64–70.

LORENTZ, DETLEF (1991), 'Regionalisation versus Regionalism – Problems of Change in the World Economy', *Intereconomics* (January–February), pp. 3–10.

MAGNUSSON, PAUL, 'Honda: Is It an American Car?', *Business Week*, 18 November , pp. 105–12.

McGEE, J. and THOMAS H. McGEE (1986), 'Strategic Groups: Theory, Research and Taxonomy', *Strategic Management Journal*, vol. 7, no. 2, pp. 141–60.

MENSCH, G.O. (1979), *Stalemate in Technology* (Cambridge, MA: Ballinger).

MICHALET, C.-A. and M. DELAPIERRE (1976), *The Multinationalization of French Firms*, (Chicago: Academy of International Business).

MICHALSKI, WOLFGANG (1983), 'The Need for Positive Adjustment Policies in the 1980s', *Intereconomics* (January–February) pp. 42–8.

MILES, RAYMOND E. and CHARLES C. SNOW (1978), *Organizational Strategy, Structure, and Processes* (New York: McGraw-Hill, Inc).

MIRUS, ROLF and BERNARD YEUNG (1986), 'Economic Incentives for Countertrade', *Journal of International Business Studies*, vol. 17, no. 3, pp. 27–39.

MITI (1989), *The 1985 Japan–US Input–Output Table* (Tokyo: Ministry of International Trade and Industry).

MVMA (1991a) *Motor Vehicle Facts and Figures* (Detroit: Motor Vehicle Manufacturers Association).

MVMA (1991b) *World Motor Vehicle Data* (Detroit: Motor Vehicle Manufacturers Association,).

NAISBITT, I. and P.P. ABURDENE (1990) *Megatrender (Megatrends) 2000* (Stockholm: Bonniers).

NAKATANI, IWAO (1986), 'Towards the New International Economic Order – the Role of Japan in the World Economy', *Hitotsubashi Journal of Economics*, vol. 27, Special Issue, pp. 121–32.

NORDSTRÖM, K.A. (1991), *The Internationalization Process of the Firm – Searching for New Patterns and Explanations* (Stockholm: Institute of International Business) (doctoral dissertation).

North American Free Trade Agreement (1992) Washington, DC: US Special Trade Representative's Office).

O'CLEIREACAIN, S. (1990), 'Europe 1992 and Gaps in the EC's Common Commercial Policy', *Journal of Common Market Studies*, vol. 28, no. 3, pp. 201–17.

OECD (1988), *Development Cooperation* (Paris: OECD).

OHMAE, KENICHI, (1987) 'Japan's Role in the World Economy: A New Appraisal', *California Management Review*, vol. 29, no. 3 (Spring) pp. 42–58.

ORR, ROBERT M. (1990), 'Collaboration or Conflict? Foreign Aid and US–Japan Relations', *Pacific Affairs*, vol. 62, no. 4 (Winter), pp. 476–89.

OUTTERS-JAEGER, INGELITES (1979), *The Development Impact of Barter in Developing Countries* (Paris: Development Centre of the Organization for Economic Cooperation and Development).

PARK, JONG H. (1990), 'Policy Response to Countertrade and the US Trade Deficit: An Appraisal', *Business Economics*, vol. 25, no. 2 (April) pp. 38–44.

PARK, YUNG CHUL (1989), 'The Little Dragons and Structural Change in Pacific Asia', *World Economy*, vol. 12, no. 2 (June) pp. 125–61.

PARSON, D.O. (1980), 'Unemployment, the Allocation of Labor and Optimal Government Intervention', *American Economic Review*, vol. 70 (December), pp. 625–635.

PELKMANS, J. and A.L. WINTERS (1988), *Europe's Domestic Market*, Chatham House Papers no. 43 (London: Routledge).

PERLMUTTER, H.V. (1969), 'The Tortuous Evolution of the Multinational Corporation', *Columbia Journal of World Business*, (January–February).

PERRIN-PELLETIER, FRANÇOIS, (1989) 'The European Automobile Industry in the Context of 1992', *European Affairs* (Summer) pp. 85–95.

PORTER, MICHAEL E. (1990), *Competitive Advantage of the Nations* (New York: Free Press).

PORTER, M. and M.B. FULLER (1986), 'Coalitions and Global Strategy', in M.E. Porter (ed.), *Competition in Global Industries* (Boston: Harvard Business School).

'The Pride of Bavaria', *The Economist*, 4 January, 1992, pp. 59–60.

'Puny Worker-productivity Gains Called Sign of Weak Economy', *The Fresno Bee*, 6 June, 1991, p. C12.

RABINO, SAMUEL and KIRIT SHAH (1987), 'Countertrade and Penetration of LDC's Markets' *Columbia Journal of World Business*, vol. 22, no. 4, pp. 31–7.

REICH, ROBERT B. (1991), *The Work of Nations* (New York: Alfred A. Knopf).

REINERT, KENNETH A. and DAVID ROLAND-HOLST (1990), 'Parameter Estimates for US Trade Policy Analysis', Working Paper (Washington, DC: US International Trade Commission) (August).

ROOT, FRANKLIN R. (1974), 'Public Policy and Multinational Corporation', *Business Horizons* (April) pp. 67–78.

ROOT, FRANKLIN R. (1990), *International Trade and Investment*, 6th edn (Ohio: South-Western Publishing).

RUGMAN, A. (1982), 'Internationalization and Non-Equity Forms of International Involvement', in A. Rugman (ed.), *New Theories of the Multinational Enterprises* (London: Croom-Helm).

RUGMAN, ALAN M. and A. VERBEKE (1990), *Global Corporate Strategy and Trade Policy* (London: Routledge).

SCHENDEL, DAN E. and CHARLES W. HOFER (1979), *Strategic Management: A New View of Business Policy and Planning* (Boston: Little, Brown & Company).

SCHLACHTER, J. (1988), 'Asian Economics are Octopuses in Tigers' Clothing', *Los Angeles Times*, 21 February, p. 1.

SCHOTT, JEFFREY J. (1991), 'Trading Blocs and the World Trading System', *World Economy*, vol. 14, no. 1 (March) pp. 1–17.

SCOTT, W.R. (1987), *Organizations: Rational, Natural, and Open Systems*, 2nd edn (Englewood Cliffs, NJ: Prentice-Hall).

SHELBURNE, ROBERT C. (1991), 'The North American Free Trade Agreement: Comparisons with and Lessons from Southern EC Enlargement', *Economic Discussion Paper 39* (Washington, DC: Department of Labor).

SINHA, RADHA, Are EC–Japan–US Trade Relations at the Crossroads?', *Intereconomics* (September–October 1990) pp. 229–37.

SOMMARUGA, C. (1985) 'Keeping Pace with Protectionism', *Speaking of Japan* (May) pp. 13–18.

'Spirit of Agony', *The Economist*, 14 December, 1991, p. 79.

'Stalling Japan's Car Makers', *The Economist*, 3 August, 1991, p. 65.

STEVENS, C. (1987), 'Life Continues for U.S. Dollar Despite Support', *The Wall Street Journal*, 14 January, p. 25.

SWEDENBORG, B. (1979), *The Multinational Operations of Swedish Firms: An Analysis of Determinants and Effects* (Stockholm: Industrial Institute for Economic and Social Research – IUI).

SWEDENBORG, B., G. JOHANSON-CROHN and M. KINNEVALL (1988), *Den svenska industrins utlandsinvesteringar (Swedish Industry's Foreign Investments)* (Stockholm: Industrial Institute for Economic and Social Research – IUI).

TALAGA, J., R. CHANDRAN and A. PHATAK (1985), 'An Extension of the Eclectic Theory of Foreign Direct Investment', presented at the Academy of International Business Annual Meeting, New York.

TARR, D.G. and M.E. MORKRE (1984), *Aggregate Costs to the United States of Tariffs and Quotas on Imports* (Washington DC: Federal Trade Commission), Chapter 4.

TAYLOR, ALEX (1991), 'BMW and Mercedes Make Their Move', *Fortune*, 12 August, 1991, pp. 56–63.

TEMPLEMAN, JOHN (1991), 'Lining Up for the World's Biggest Demolition Derby', *Business Week*, 23 September, pp. 54–5.

TOBIN, JAMES (1991), 'On Living and Trading with Japan: United States Commercial and Macroeconomic Policies', *Business Economics*, vol. 26, no. 1 (January) pp. 5–16.

TSURUMI, Y. (1976), *The Japanese are Coming: A Multinational Spread of Japanese Firms* (Cambridge, MA: Ballinger).

TSURUMI, Y. (1982), 'Reciprocity: US–Japan Trade Dispute', *Pacific Basin Quarterly* (Summer–Spring) pp. 6–9.

TUCKER, JONATHAN, (1988) 'The International Car Industry: The Shift from Protection', *Multinational Business*, no. 4, pp. 27–36.

TULLY, SHAWN (1990a), 'Now Japan's Autos Push into Europe', *Fortune*, 29 January, pp. 96–106.

TULLY, SHAWN (1990b), 'Europe Hits the Brakes on 1992', *Fortune*, 17 December, pp. 133–40.

US DEPARTMENT OF COMMERCE (1991), *Survey of Current Business* (Washington, DC: US Department of Commerce) (May).

US INTERNATIONAL TRADE COMMISSION (USITC), (1990) 'Estimated Tariff Equivalents of US Quotas on Agricultural Imports and Analysis of Competitive Conditions in US and Foreign Markets for Sugar, Meat, Peanuts, Cotton, and Dairy Products', Publication 2276 (Washington, DC: US International Trade Commission) (April).

US SENATE, FINANCE COMMITTEE (1974), *Trade Reform Act of 1974, Report*, Publication 93-1298 (Washington, DC: US Senate) p. 119.

'US Trade Outlook', *Business America*, 18 August, 1986, pp. 2–5.

US TREASURY DEPARTMENT (1988) *Congressional Budget Office 1988 Annual Report* (Washington, DC).

VAHLNE, J.-E. and F. WIEDERSHEIM-PAUL (1973), 'Ekonomiskt avstånd – Modell och empirisk undersökning' (Economic Distance – Model and Empirical Investigation)', in E. Hörnell, J.-E. Vahlne and F. Wiedersheim-Paul, *Export och utlandsetableringar (Export and Foreign Establishments)* (Stockholm: Almqvist & Wiksell).

VERNON, R. (1966), 'International Investment and International Trade in the Product Cycle', *Quarterly Journal of Economics*, vol. 80, no. 3 (May) pp. 190–207.

Ward's Automotive Yearbook (1979, 1981, 1988, 1990, 1991) (Detroit: Ward's Communications).

WEINTRAUB, SYDNEY (1991), 'Regionalism and the GATT: The North American Initiative', *SAIS Review*, vol. 11, no. 1 (Winter–Spring) pp. 45–57.

WELCH, L.S. and R. LOUSTARINEN (1988), 'Internationalization: Evolution of a Concept', *Journal of General Management*, vol. 14, no. 2.

WILLIAMS, ALBERT (1971), *United States International Economic Policy in an Interdependent World* (Washington, DC: US Government Printing Office).

WILSON, B.D. (1980), 'The Propensity of Multinational Companies to Expand Through Acquisitions', *Journal of International Business Studies*, vol. 11, pp. 59–65.

WILSON, B.D. (1988a), 'The Surge in European Mergers and Acquisitions', *Mergers and Acquistion*, vol. 23, no. 2, p. 56.

WILSON, B.D. (1988b), 'The Technology Kicker: Merger and Acquisition Stimulus Beyond 1992,' *Mergers and Acquisitions*, vol. 23, no. 2, p. 57.

WINSTON, C. *et al.* (1987), *Blind Intersection? Policy and the Automobile Industry*, USITC Publication no. 1762.

WOLFEREN, KAREL VAN (1990), 'The Japan Problem Revisited', *Foreign Affairs*, vol. 69. no. 4, pp. 42–55.

WOMACK, JAMES P., DANIEL T. JONES and DANIEL ROOS (1990), *The Machine that Changed the World: The Story of Lean Production* (New York: Harper Collins Publishers).

WOODRUFF, DAVID, and JONATHAN B. LEVINE (1991), 'Miles Traveled, More To Go', *Business Week*, Quality Issue, 25 October, pp. 70–73.

YOFFIE, DAVID B. (1985), 'What Motivates Countertrade?', in Robert Pringle (ed.), *Countertrade in the World Economy* (New York: Group of Thirty) pp. 13–24.

YOFFIE, DAVID B. and HELEN V. MILNER (1989), 'An Alternative to Free Trade or Protectionism: Why Corporations Seek Strategic Trade Policy', *California Management Review* (Spring) pp. 111–31.

YOSHIHARA, K. (1988), 'Japanese Investment in South East Asia', Monographs of the Center for South East Asian studies, Kyoto University (Honolulu: University Press of Hawaii).

Index

Index